MW00779032

The Memoir of 1603
and The Diary of 1616–1619

...ry and Archives Canada Cataloguing in Publication

...oke, Anne Clifford Herbert, Countess of, 1590-1676

... memoir of 1603 and the diary of 1616-1619 / Anne Clifford ; edited by Katherine
...on.

...les bibliographical references and index.
...-13: 978-1-55111-339-5
...-10: 1-55111-339-2

...Pembroke, Anne Clifford Herbert, Countess of, 1590-1676.   2. Nobility—Great
...n—Diaries.   3. Great Britain—Court and courtiers—Early works to 1800.
...gland—Social life and customs—17th century—Early works to 1800.   5. Nobility—
... Britain—Biography.   I. Acheson, Katherine Osler, 1963-   II. Title.

...78.P4A3 2006   942.06092   C2006-904907-6

...dview Editions
...Broadview Editions series represents the ever-changing canon of literature in English
... inging together texts long regarded as classics with valuable lesser-known works.

...sory editor for this volume: Jennie Rubio

...dview Press is an independent, international publishing house, incorporated in 1985.
...dview believes in shared ownership, both with its employees and with the general public;
... the year 2000 Broadview shares have traded publicly on the Toronto Venture Exchange
...er the symbol BDP.

...welcome comments and suggestions regarding any aspect of our publications—please
...free to contact us at the addresses below or at broadview@broadviewpress.com.

...h America
    Office Box 1243, Peterborough, Ontario, Canada K9J 7H5
...5 California Road, Post Office Box 1015, Orchard Park, NY, USA 14127
... (705) 743-8990; Fax: (705) 743-8353;
...il: customerservice@broadviewpress.com

... Ireland, and continental Europe
...N International, Estover Road, Plymouth PL6 7PY UK
...44 (0) 1752 202300   Fax: 44 (0) 1752 202330
...il: enquiries@nbninternational.com

...tralia and New Zealand
...IREPS, University of New South Wales
...ney, NSW, 2052 Australia
...: 61 2 9664 0999; Fax: 61 2 9664 5420
...ail: info.press@unsw.edu.au

...w.broadviewpress.com

...oadview Press gratefully acknowledges the financial support of the Government of
...nada through the Book Publishing Industry Development Program for our publishing
...ivities.

...pesetting and assembly: True to Type Inc., Mississauga, Canada.

...INTED IN CANADA

broadview editions
series editor: L.W. Conolly

The Memoir of 1603
and The Diary of 1616–1

Anne Clifford

edited by
Katherine Acheson

broadview editions

©200

All rig
or by
retrie
ing, a
Stree

Libr

Peml
Th
Ache

Inclu
ISBN
ISBN

1.
Brit
4. E
Gre

DA.

Bro
The
by
Adv

Bro
Bro
sinc
unc

We
fee

No
Po
35
Te
em

UF
N
Te
en

A
U
Sy
Te
er

w

B
C
a

T
P

Contents

Acknowledgements

This edition of the diary of Anne Clifford for the years 1616, 1617, and 1619 was prepared from the manuscript in the Portland Papers, Volume XXIII, ff 80–117 by permission of the Marquess of Bath, Longleat House, Warminster, Wiltshire, for which I am grateful. *The Great Picture* of the Clifford Family is reproduced with the kind permission of the Abbot Hall Art Gallery, Kendal, Cumbria. My thanks also to Karen Hearn and to Elizabeth Chew for information about Clifford and her works.

I am grateful also to Joseph Black, Julia Gaunce, and Lynne Magnusson for their help and encouragement; to Katie Holmes for her assistance; to Germaine Warkentin, for her long service to my work and unfailing commitment to the ideals of scholarship; to Susan Acheson, for her love of Clifford, and to Andrew McMurry, for his fellowship. Some of the research for this project was supported by grants from the Social Sciences and Humanities Research Council of Canada and the Bibliographical Society of America.

Introduction

Anne Clifford (1590–1676) is now known as one of the most important female writers of the seventeenth century and one of the era's most prolific, dedicated, and artful self-documenters. What is the longest surviving autobiographical record of the early modern era records her life from conception—of which she writes "I was, through the merciful providence of God, begotten by my father, and conceived with child by my worthy mother, the first day of May in 1589 in the Lord Wharton's house in Channel Row in Westminster"—to the day before her death, when "I went not out of the house nor out of my chamber all this day" (D.J.H. Clifford 268). Throughout its length and breadth, this record represents her struggle for and ultimate enjoyment of the land and wealth to which she believed she was entitled by birth. The present volume gives the reader two of Clifford's autobiographical texts in full, and excerpts from a third in Appendix D. The two full texts are the memoir for the year 1603, the earliest surviving annual record of her life, and the diary of 1616 to 1619, written when she was a young adult, a daughter, an embattled heiress, and a wife. The excerpted text is her formal autobiography, and the selection here covers her life from the beginning to 1619, so as to overlap with the memoir and diary.

Together the memoir and diary offer us extraordinary insight into the interests, anxieties, and pleasures of a favoured girl, and later a young noblewoman, who danced in Ben Jonson's masques, heard Dr. Donne preach, socialized with Mary Sidney Herbert and Mary Wroth, and read Montaigne's *Essays* and Spenser's *The Faerie Queene* when they were hot new bestsellers. They show us her world, and the network of relations between family, friends, servants, and authority figures that composed its fabric. They bring to life her material world: she makes pancakes and jam, walks in the garden, goes sightseeing, wears appropriate—or not—clothes. Finally, they show us how intimate the relationships between reading, writing, and being are, for Anne Clifford fashioned herself in the oscillation between what she read of her world and her family's history, and what she wrote, daily, as the next chapter in that history.

The texts included in the appendices provide other versions of her identity, in her own writing and in that of others. The poem by Aemilia Lanyer, "The Description of Cooke-ham" (Appendix A), depicts her as an aristocratic girl and young woman, from the point-of-view of a female poet who desired patronage and who had received it from Clifford's mother. The dedication by Thomas Stafford to his work known as *Niobe* (Appendix B) shows her as she might be seen by a male author who was not successful in securing her or her husband's patronage; evidently, the terms of the description were offensive, as it was excised from almost all copies of the work. *The Great Picture* (Appendix C) offers an image of Clifford as she saw herself after she inherited the properties she had fought so long to obtain. The autobiography (Appendix D) gives us a version of the same vision, but in a longer time frame and in the vocabulary of verbal, rather than visual, representation. Bishop Rainbow's funeral sermon (Appendix E) depicts her as she was seen by her community when it trained its most flattering light upon her. In all, they reveal an extraordinary record of self-fashioning by this singular and distinguished woman, the Lady Anne Clifford.

The Memoir of 1603

On 24 March 1603 Queen Elizabeth I died, and the world for which she was the symbol and source of authority was thrown into disarray. Elizabeth died without an obvious heir: not only without a child, but without a sibling or other near relative to take over from her. As she lay dying, she named her cousin, King James VI of Scotland, as her successor. Given the distance of his blood claim to the throne, and with memory of the turmoil that surrounded the accession of Elizabeth herself, people feared that disorder and violence might erupt as James made his way south to London from Edinburgh to accept the English crown. An outbreak of the plague (that would kill nearly 40,000 people in London and the environs) turned risk into peril, and apprehension into justifiable fear. For those dependent on royal favour, and on the network of alliances around the throne, it was also a time of personal upheaval and shifting fortune. At the age of thirteen, Anne Clifford, only surviving child and heiress of George Clifford, Earl of Cumberland, and Margaret Russell, youngest daughter of the Earl of Bedford, was at the heart of this turbulent storm.

Clifford's memoir of this time, the first text published in this volume, is fast-paced and vivid. It is a record of actions and emotions we all recognize, of sudden movement and terrible fear, warm embrace and grateful love, peaceful moments in lives of turmoil, flashes of perception in the midst of colourful confusion.

Even though the memoir is of a time so different from ours that we would hardly understand the spoken language and certainly be confused by the customs, habits, occupations, and conditions—to say nothing of the odours, edibles, and entertainments—and even though it is the simplest of documents in a rhetorical sense, it strongly conveys the perceptions and emotions of its author, and her position in relation to the broad forces and strokes in the world around her. It was a position of vulnerability—she was a girl in a dangerous world, dependent on the good will of others and the degree to which her interests were shared by her nearest and dearest—but it was, most importantly, a position of power and privilege.

Clifford was the only child of two of the wealthiest and most powerful individuals in the country, in an age when the easiest route to social authority was to be born to it. Her father George was a favourite of the Queen, an official adventurer on the high seas, and a luminary at court. He was also profligate and adulterous, and had little involvement with Anne at the time about which the memoir was written. Her mother Margaret was, in contrast, serious, devout, and intellectual, a patron of fine poetry and religious thought and, as someone who read about alchemy and prepared and dispensed natural medicines, an early scientist. Anne was born in 1590. The couple's first son, Francis, had died in 1589, and their other boy Robert died in 1591. No more children were born to George and Margaret, as they were effectively separated soon after Robert's death. Clifford was raised, then, as a sole heiress to a great fortune and to occupy a high status position in her society.

Clifford thought of herself as taking after her mother, and because of her parents' separation and her father's death in 1605, she was certainly more influenced by Margaret and Margaret's values and priorities. Her admiration for her mother is repeated throughout her life-writings. In her biography of her mother, Clifford wrote that "she had a discerning spirit, both into the disposition of human creatures and natural causes, and into the affairs of the world.... Though she had no language but her own, yet was there few books of worth translated into English but she read them, whereby that excellent mind of hers was much enriched" (*Lives* 19). Margaret's interests in alchemy, natural medicine, theology, spirituality, and fine literature were all laudable ones for women to have and provided ample opportunity for her to exercise her "excellent mind." Less easily put forward for praise, however, was another application of that excellent mind:

Margaret was exceptionally capable at business management and investment. George, on the one hand, was at best an unfortunate and at worst a terrible businessman. He invested, and lost, much of his inherited fortune in privateering (that is, pirating) ventures. Margaret, on the other hand, was adept in financial matters. She made investments in the East India Company's first voyage in 1601 and in the Virginia Company in 1612, and she took an active interest in managing her jointure properties after her husband's death in 1605, making "investments in lead-mining in Craven and experiments in smelting iron-ore with coal" (Spence 8). Her assertive negotiation of leases and other forms of revenue from tenants on the estates helped to fund the on-going legal battles for Clifford's patrimony, and Margaret's presence in the north helped secure the claim against their rivals (Spence 33, 38). In the memoir, she presses her complaint about the fulfillment of the terms of her separation agreement with George to the King, and otherwise, with the help of her Russell relatives, manages her own and her daughter's affairs. Margaret's example to Clifford, then, was not just in her piety, or her love of fine verse and her interest in natural medicines, and other proper feminine virtues; she was more than capable in matters of business and established a model that her daughter—who would become one of the great English landowners of the century—would emulate and extend.

As an aristocratic child and heiress—and as Margaret's daughter—Clifford was raised to take on financial, moral, and social responsibility. Such responsibility was more than most women, or men, could dream of having. As an adult she would be in charge of running large households and would have had much, although not sole, responsibility for the budgeting, expenditures, and efficiency of them. The houses that she and her people occupied were not modest concerns, but more like villages in and of themselves: Knole House in Sussex, where much of the 1616 to 1619 diary was written, has hundreds of rooms, dozens of fireplaces, and had nearly a hundred full-time servants at the time. In the diary for 1617 she notes that she and her husband "had much falling out about the keeping of the house which my Lord [her husband] would have me undertake which I refused, in regard things went so ill with me" (3 August 1617) revealing the expectation that she would contribute not only as a manager, but monetarily (had her finances been stable). Her contribution would not have come from her own assets directly, but from an allowance paid to her; this would have been related to the dowry she brought into the marriage. This allowance would have been substantial, had her affairs been settled at the time. She was to become a widow at the age of 34, and would be left in charge of the financial welfare of herself and her dependents. Ultimately, as widow and heiress, she became the leader of a whole local economy: while Margaret could not have foreseen that this would happen, it was certainly her hope, and Clifford was educated to take on that role, in case the occasion should arise.

Clifford's training in "housekeeping" began early: her accounts book for August 1600 to August 1602 (Williamson 58–60), when she was ten to twelve years old, record fees paid to messengers and others who performed services for her, payments for stockings, shoes, and fabric for clothing and handkerchiefs, and disbursements to hire musicians and to purchase supplies for her education and entertainment, such as an hour glass, paper books, embroidery silk, and bunches of feathers for her hair. She was also conscious of the cost of running the household. She notes that she contributed to the housekeeping funds at North Hall in Hertfordshire (this may only mean that she was counted, along with her ten-year-old cousin Francis, as a person who shared in the cost of the housekeeping, and that a contribution was made on her behalf by her mother). Whatever the case, it is clear she was conscious of the business of maintaining a household, and that she was taught by her mother to see herself from an early age as an economic agent.

As mistress of houses such as Knole, Clifford would be in charge of establishing the tenor of other aspects of the local culture, so she was also educated to occupy a position of moral and social responsibility. She had a governess, Mrs. Anne Taylor, who is mentioned in the memoir, and who was a religious and educated woman. Her mother Margaret also hired the poet Samuel Daniel to be Clifford's tutor from the age of nine to twelve. As Spence writes, "Daniel helped develop Anne's enthusiasm for the best of English prose, poetry and history and it has been argued that he also introduced her to philosophical works in translation which, as a corpus, would have given her an education not just equaling but superior to that her male contemporaries received at university" (13). In *The Great Picture* Clifford is shown in the left hand panel at the age of 15, with the books that she associated with her youthful education, whether or not she actually read them then. These include works of geography, history, philosophy, and religion, and such familiar titles as Castiglione's *The Courtier*, Boethius' *Consolation*, St. Augustine's *City of God*,

Ovid's *Metamorphoses*, Montaigne's *Essays*, Cervantes' *Don Quixote*, Chaucer's *Works*, Sidney's *Arcadia*, and Spenser's *Works*. To us these are classic works, but to a person of the early seventeenth century, many of them were examples of contemporary literature, either recently written or translated. Clifford's reading, then, was sophisticated and contemporary, and spanned a broad terrain of learning and erudition.

In her education, some of the things Clifford learned were the skills and activities of polite society; she played the viola de gamba (depicted in *The Great Picture*), she danced, she was taught French, and she was handy with a bow and arrow. Some of her activities were considered appropriate to her gender; for instance, she embroidered as a child and as an adult "wrought much" at her needlework. Like her mother, she did not learn classical languages, which were more the province of élite boys and men. Other than that, however, her reading was not restricted to material thought to be appropriate to girls, as it included works of philosophy, history, geography, and travel, and tales of adventure and romance. Mary Ellen Lamb argues that Clifford's reading was a "means of interpellating herself into a dominant, rather than a subordinate, subject position in her culture" (32). By this Lamb means that Clifford's reading of male-authored texts intended for male readers helped her to assert herself as a person of wealth, privilege, and authority over those who would resist her claims and desires. Moreover, if she had restricted herself (or been restricted by others) to more "feminine" reading, she might have more readily accepted herself as a person of the "weaker sex," in a subordinate position to those whose power was greater than her own. This may have been the case with her later reading; it is possible that her mother was preparing her for her future of conflict.

It is more likely, however, that Clifford's childhood reading was intended by her mother to be a means to cultivate her virtue, as well as to understand and appreciate virtuous conduct in her society. All of the works listed above stress that virtue was expected and required particularly of the nobility, of both male and female; the actions of the nobility in this very hierarchical society affected the lives of many others, and their behaviour was considered exemplary. Whether or not Clifford's inheritance was disputed, she would hold a position of great power and authority because of the status of her family and the family into which she was expected to marry.

The statement that concludes the 1603 memoir echoes Clifford's awareness of the importance of reputation, or the public performance of virtue: "Now there was much talk of a masque which the Queen had at Winchester and how all the ladies about the court had gotten such ill-names that it was grown a scandalous place, and the Queen herself much fallen from her former greatness and reputation she had in the world." In the diary, and in all of her other works, Clifford shows great self-consciousness about what she calls her role "on the stage of this world," and she clearly feels, as might a modern politician or celebrity, that *doing* is not as good, and certainly not as powerful, as being *seen* to do. Elizabeth I, who was a consummate performer, might have provided a paradigm for such behaviour, and Clifford's reading (as well as her education) also emphasized the theatricality of identity in addition to the instrumental nature of virtue and power. She learned the importance of showing—not just possessing—virtue. Despite her gender, then, Clifford was educated and treated as a person who would hold and exercise authority in her society. Or put differently, she was educated and treated as a girl in her station (i.e., as an heiress within the most élite echelon of the aristocracy) according to the values and structures of the society in which she lived.

The 1603 memoir was probably written after the events it describes, but not long after. It is similar in form to the annual accounts she kept of later years, and is probably an example of what she refers to in the 1616 to 1619 diary as a "chronicle." These were works she wrote to summarize the year's events, sometime after the year had passed. The 1603 memoir was probably written when she was a young adult, perhaps soon after her marriage to Richard Sackville.

All of Clifford's writings of this sort were motivated by the desire to document the histories of her family and herself, a desire stimulated by the need to construct a picture of her lineage and rights that would help her in the legal disputes undertaken by herself and her mother, beginning in 1605. The 1603 memoir depicts her position, the interests that sprung from it and from her training, and the events and interactions important to her and to her kin and social group. The first sentence of the memoir reflects the status of her family, her hopes for favour in the future, and how those hopes had changed upon the death of the old Queen:

> In Christmas I used to go much to the Court, and sometimes did I lie in my aunt of Warwick's chamber on a pallet, to whom I was much bound for her continual care and love of me: in so

much as if Queen Elizabeth had lived, she intended to have preferred me to be of the Privy Chamber, for at that time there was as much hope and expectation of me both for my person and my fortunes as of any other young lady whatsoever.

Throughout the memoir she observes the jostling for power, the ambitions and disappointments ("every man expecting mountains and finding molehills"), and the ascendancy of some families and individuals (the Cecils, for example, and the Howards; also the Scottish people who came south with the new King and Queen). She makes note of changes to the structure of her immediate circle and the aristocracy in general, such as when "innumerable" knights are created, and when the Earls of Essex and Southampton, imprisoned for their participation in a plot to overthrow Elizabeth, are restored to their lands and titles. She is free and blunt with her judgements on the new state of affairs: "we all saw a great change between the fashion of the court as it is now, and of that in the Queen's, for we were all lousy by sitting in Sir Thomas Erskine's chamber." Clifford pays particular attention to the female aristocrats who collected around the new King and Queen. She notes, for example, the new Queen's favourites, such as the Countess of Bedford, who "was then so great a woman with the Queen as every body much respected her," and the fickleness of that favour: "Now was my Lady Rich grown great with the Queen insomuch as my Lady of Bedford was something out with her and when she came to Hampton Court was entertained but even indifferently, and yet continued to be of the bedchamber." She is concerned for the status of her aunts and her mother in the new court, for they have business to conduct, lawsuits to bring to successful conclusion. And her own position is literally not as high as she would like it to be:

> When the corpse of Queen Elizabeth had continued at White-hall as long as the Council had thought fit, it was carried from thence with great solemnity to Westminster, the Lords and Ladies going on foot to attend it, my mother and my aunt of Warwick being mourners, but I was not allowed to be one, because I was not high enough, which did much trouble me then, but yet I stood in the church at Westminster to see the solemnity performed.

Despite these concerns, the memoir is also a record of child-hood and its adventures, pleasures, and conflicts. For instance, there is the time she rode ahead with Mr Menerell, who the next day "as he went abroad fell down suddenly and died," perhaps of the plague. For riding ahead she was punished by her mother, who, "in her anger commanded that I should lie in a chamber alone, which I could not endure, but my cousin Frances got the key of my chamber and lay with me which was the first time I loved her so very well." This cousin Frances Bourchier was the boon companion of her youth, and in the time recorded by the memoir "was the first beginning of the greatness between us." In the course of the memoir, Clifford eats too much ("breakfasts, and pear pies and such things") and blames the onset of her episodic illness, the "green sickness" (anemia, understood to be related to the physiological changes undergone by adolescent girls) on this surfeit. She wears her hair-coloured (that is, a rich, reddish brown) velvet gown every day while at North Hall, and she learns to sing and play on the bass viol of the obviously irresistible Jack Jenkins. She and the other children are "merry," just as the poor Queen falls "from her former greatness and reputation," even in the eyes of this sharp-witted thirteen-year-old girl.

The Diary of 1616-1619

Between the time recorded in the 1603 memoir and the events of the 1616 diary, much happened in Clifford's life. Her father died in 1605, leaving her as his only lineal heir and descendant. By his will, however, he left all of his estates to his brother, with stipulation to provide his daughter with a very generous "portion" or dowry (£10,000 unconditionally, and £15,000 if she agreed not to contest the will). In her autobiography, Clifford writes that her father made this will, rather than leave her the lands, "for the love he bore to his brother, and the advancement of the heirs male of his house" (Lives, 36), and for the "preservation of his name and house" (11). According to Clifford's biographers, George made his will this way so as to provide the best defence against creditors, and the best hope of recovering the financial health of the estates. Spence says, rightly, that the estates were not cleared of debt until more than sixty years after George's death, and argues that the task would have been beyond Clifford and her mother, not because of their lack of ability, but because the creditors and others would have been less likely to extend their generosity to an underage girl and her female guardian. And as Spence and Williamson point out, whatever George's motive in making his will, it all worked out better for Clifford in the end than she could possibly have dreamed; ultimately, she inherited the property, but in the meantime had enjoyed her huge dowry, and additional monies for compensation for yielding up the estates to her uncle. What is undeniable, however, is that Clifford's sense of injury and entitlement was the grain of sand around which the layers of her personality were built over the years, and that she never perceived the advantage to her of accepting the settlement rather than persisting in the suits.

In her decades of legal struggle, Clifford was fighting for two related things. One was the titles that belonged to the baronies of Clifford, Westmorland, and Vescy, and which had been in her family for over 300 years. Baronies were the oldest titles in the English peerage. They were not the highest titles in the aristocratic pantheon (earls, marquesses, and dukes were higher) but they were the basis for higher titles (an earldom was not awarded without a preceding barony) and they were a keystone of the political structure of the aristocracy. Barons were those liegemen of the king summoned to Parliament as early as the twelfth century. They were military deputies, landholders on whom the monarch depended for support and defence. The titles represented a reciprocal recognition: in return for military readiness and action, oligarchic representation was allowed. These titles were always attached, then, to land, rather than to just immediate favour, and therefore represented to Clifford and many of her peers the root of authority and good governance in their realm.

With regard to the titles, Clifford and her mother advanced their claims on two fronts. One way to become a baron was to have been summoned as a feudal lord to the Parliament by the king; one of Clifford's ancestors, Robert de Clifford, had enjoyed such summons as early as 1299. Clifford and her mother claimed that this sort of baronial right theoretically allowed for the inheritance by a female of the titles. The basis for the title was the provision of military service and protection for the king, in return for which the king shared power with the barons. Obviously, being unable to actively engage in military campaigns didn't disallow a male heir from baronial privilege; his military duty would be fulfilled by someone else whom he paid, and there was no reason why a woman could not take the same approach. It had been the occasional practice to allow for female inheritance of baronies, or inheritance through the female line, for centuries; but the law was not settled in one way or another, and in cases throughout the sixteenth century the matter was decided on the whim of the monarch and the influence of the parties involved, rather than on principle. The first known example of the recognition of the female right to inherit in this way was in 1542; this, however, was not a court case, and it concerned a woman of royal blood, Elizabeth Tailboys. In 1591 William Cecil was permitted to inherit the barony of Roos through his mother, at the behest of the Queen and in deference to his family. The first court case that granted this right was that of Margaret, the wife of Samson Lennard, to succeed her brother Gregory in the Barony of Dacre; it was decided in 1597. The law was not finally settled in this regard until 1674, at which time it became the right of women in the position Clifford was in to inherit and hold baronial titles (see Doubleday, "Earldoms").

The other way to establish a credible claim to a baronial title was to occupy the lands associated with a feudal lordship, which established a right by tenure. This was more than just a squatter's right—it involved the history of the family and the inheritance of the land, and the loyalty and obeisance of the tenants of the land. Clifford and her mother made the argument about tenure for several reasons: first, the law regarding barony by writ was still unsettled; second, some of the honours and lands to which she laid claim had been owned by her family prior to the first parliamentary writ of summons; finally, some of the lands and honours that she claimed had been passed, prior to the writ, by female inheritance. As Spence points out, the case brought by Clifford's lawyers avoided the question of whether or not this was a *human* right or a matter of *equity*: "man in his sex be more excellent than woman, yet in quality we see often women excel men" (quoted in Spence 41). Hence, argued the lawyers, men had been allowed to inherit through and by the women who were their daughters or their mothers, exceptional women whose quality was attested to by their affinity with their men.

Some of the lands in question in the suits had come to the Clifford family through Isabella de Veteripont, who married Roger de Clifford the Younger in 1269—prior to the first writ of summons, that is. Tenure did not in itself constitute the possession of an inheritable right but, as the oldest basis for the title of baron, it was held to contribute to that right (particularly in cases when it was qualified by a writ at some later date). The perceived significance of tenure can be seen in the diary, in the actions of both Clifford and her uncle Francis—particularly on the death of her mother—when the physical possession of the estates is contested between them. Similarly, as Clifford writes in the autobiography, in 1607 "by reason of those great suits in law my mother and I were in a manner forced for our own good to go together from London down into Westmorland." The allegiance of the local tenants and authorities bolstered claims of right by tenure; on the same trip, Clifford says "my mother and I would have gone into the Castle of Skipton to have seen it, but were not permitted so to do, the doors thereof being shut against us by my uncle of Cumberland's officers in an uncivil and disdainful manner." Despite their efforts, in terms of the titles, Clifford and her mother were unsuccessful in their claims in her lifetime. In 1690, her grandson Thomas Tufton, 6th Earl of Thanet, petitioned to be recognized as Baron Clifford through his descent from her; he was successful, and so Clifford was posthumously awarded the title she had sought for so long.

The land was a more complicated matter. To begin with, the estates themselves were extensive and each one was complex. The main income unit of holdings such as the Cliffords' was the manor house, of which there were dozens included in their possessions. Each manor house included some or all of a host of potential income earners, such as arable land, parks, chases, mills, houses, cottages, tenements, coal, lead, and tin mines, various forms of rents, inns, moors, mosses, peat lands, forfeited or lost goods, and fees which were paid for various reasons to authorities (in lieu of military service, for hunting and fishing privileges, and in court, for example). The estates that comprised the disputed inheritance had come into the family at different times, and through different means—one set, for instance, as dowry, another as royal grant, another by acquisition. They spread over hundreds of square miles, and provided the structure for the communities that inhabited them and the adjoining properties. To possess them was not just to hold the basis for extraordinary wealth; it was to own the means to govern the local people, landscape, and culture.

George's father, Clifford's grandfather, had made a will entailing the properties on heirs male (that is, restricting their inheritance to males in the blood-line, and preventing them from being sold or used as collateral or in any way which threatened their alienation from the estate). The entail restricted the ways in which the properties could be used—aside from precluding sale or use as collateral, they had to be kept intact as an inheritance. George wanted to break the entail, giving him more room to manoeuvre financially (Spence 42). The process by which an entail or other obligation, such as a jointure agreement, was broken was called a "fine." "Recovery" signified the means by which the person who owned the entailed property was sued by the other for wrongfully keeping him out of possession; the first person then acknowledged the claim, and conveyed the property. This is the process by which Clifford's lands in Westmorland and Skipton were eventually conveyed to her uncle, described in her diary in April of 1617. In the case of George's will, the transfer would have been from George Clifford as heir (under entail) to George Clifford as owner (out of the entail). But this process does not work unless the title to the estate is clear and absolute: a person who "owns" a house that has a mortgage on it cannot give it away to satisfy a debt or claim, because the mortgage-holder's interests would legally prevent that from happening. In the case of the Clifford estates, there was no mortgage, but the crown held reversion rights in the land. In general what this meant was that the crown could regain control over lands for which there was no heir, and award their use and revenue to another. The reversion rights also meant that the lands could not be alienated by the fine and recovery process, but would have to be re-granted through the crown and outright title given before the entail could be broken. George's lawyers had neglected to seek this re-grant, and the will could not be valid for lands in which the reversionary rights were held by the crown. For these lands, eventually determined to be those in Westmorland and pertaining to Skipton Castle, Anne, and not her uncle or her cousin, was the proper heir: if both the entail and the breaking of the entail could not apply to these lands, then the normal order of succession would apply and that would give priority to the most immediate heir of the blood, whatever the sex of that heir.

Making even this determination took many years and much litigation. For Clifford and her mother, the first step in fighting the will was to go to court. To enable this, Margaret applied for the wardship of her daughter, which would make her responsible for tending to Clifford's financial needs, arranging her marriage, and representing her in legal matters. All heirs of lands in which the Crown had reversion rights were wards of the Crown. The Crown auctioned off (or distributed as a form of favour) the wardships of these youngsters, and the successful bidder (or recipient) would hold custody of the lands and have authority over decisions such as marriage until the heir came of age. A ward whose estates were lucrative or who had elevated expectations in the marriage market was clearly "worth" more than one whose prospects were not so good. Once the price was agreed and the fee paid, the purchaser of the "wardship" then managed the child's estates until he or she came of age. As Clifford notes in the "Life of Me," (Appendix D) her uncle Francis applied for her wardship, in an effort to gain control over Clifford's affairs and quash any potential claim by her against him. By obtaining the wardship, Margaret retained control of Clifford's interests, and was able to initiate legal action in the interests of her daughter as she did, in the Court of Wards, in 1606.

The Court was sympathetic to Clifford's claims against her father's will and ordered an examination of the question of the ownership of the disputed lands in 1609, which was completed in 1612. The findings of the examination were sent on to the Court of Common Pleas in 1613, and the case to determine title to the lands on the basis of the findings began in 1615. The Court's decision, which Clifford refers to in the diary as the "Judges' Award," divided the right to the lands between Clifford and her uncle Francis, but Francis was to retain the use of all of them and pay Clifford a "composition" or compensation. This settlement was to include payment of the dowry promised by her father, and the amounts were £20,000 if she agreed to the disposition of the properties outlined by the Judges, and £17,000 if she refused to guarantee that she would not persist in her legal action. Also, the further inheritance of the lands in question was restricted to Francis' male heirs—meaning that in the event there were no surviving males of his line, the inheritance would revert to the "heirs general" (of whom Clifford had priority over, say, female descendants of Francis). This was a condition much desired by Clifford, and it was this part of the Judges' Award and subsequent agreement that brought about her inheritance in the longer run. Her ultimate inheritance (in 1643) was also eased, ironically, by the fact that James I did give her uncle Francis clear title over the lands of his inheritance, thus giving up the reversion rights which had hampered George's intentions and removing the residual authority of the Crown over their disposition. Whether or not Clifford agreed to forego future legal action, the settlement required the consent of all parties, including Margaret's and her own.

At the opening of the 1616 diary, the Judges' Award has been issued, but the agreement had not been signed. Complicating matters at this point was Clifford's marriage. In 1609 she married Richard Sackville, as his father lay dying; two days later he was the third Earl of Dorset. The marriage was hastily arranged and performed without banns: as Sackville was only nineteen and therefore underage, he would have become a ward of the Crown if he had not been married upon his father's death. The alliance had been under discussion for nearly two years, however, and was evidently selected above other possibilities for her. The marriage was primarily dynastic: Sackville was a match for her socially, but they had little else in common. He gambled, drank, and was routinely unfaithful; he spent much more money than he should have, and made much less than he needed to. According to Lawrence Stone, between 1614 and 1623 Sackville spent £17,000 that he obtained from the settlement and Clifford's dowry, £80,000 raised from the sale of land, and £6,000 per year in income from his estates, an average of nearly £16,000 a year (in modern terms, this would be roughly £1.5 million). His accounts for October 1621 to September 1622, a typical year, show that he was given £3,100 in spending money by the steward at Dorset House (his house in London), aside from expenses for fuel, wine, food, boardwages, garden maintenance, horses, etc., and not including expenses incurred when in residence elsewhere. His extravagance is shown in the diary by the sums he wins and loses at cocking and footraces, and his cash-flow problems are shown in his spurts of parsimony, and in his dealings regarding the prospective settlement of Clifford's suits.

Sackville and Clifford seem to have had a relatively passionate relationship for an arranged, dynastic marriage of the period. They had intense conflict over the lawsuits and the settlement, to which I will return below; they had protracted struggles over money problems, which are also expressed in the diary (for instance on 5 April 1617 she wrote, "my Lord went up to my closet and saw how little money I had left, contrary to all that they had told him"); she resented the favour shown Mathew Caldicot, who Sackville uses as an intermediary, and who was also probably Sackville's lover. But a vein of great affection runs through their dealings with each other and their correspondence. A letter of 6 October 1617 begins with a message for their daughter Margaret: "first sweet heart you must remember me to the little lady with the hot foot how dreamed her Lord father was stolen away with bulbuggars, and cried so sweetly with her little warm tears," and continues, "[I] commend my love to your self whom in all things I love and hold a sober woman, your land only excepted which transports you beyond your self and makes you devoid of all reason." Similarly, Clifford tends to see his recalcitrant and uncooperative attitude about her lawsuits as an aberrant streak in his personality, an exception to an otherwise much loved soul. On 20 December 1615 she wrote to her mother that "my Lord to her [Margaret] is a very kind, loving and dear father, and in everything will I commend him, saving in this business of my land, wherein I think some malign spirit works for in this he is as violent as is possible, so I must either do it the next term or else break all friendship and love with him." A few months later, on 26 April 1616, she writes again to her mother, defending Sackville, charging her mother has been too "bitter against him": "I am in the greatest strait that any poor creature was," she writes, "but Madam, whatsoever you think of my Lord yet I have found him, do find him, and I think shall find him, the best and most worthiest man that ever breathed." In modern terms, their relationship is not one to envy or emulate. But, as we tend to think of arranged marriages, especially ones in which the parties do not have common interests, as emotionally moderate, even cold, the degree of passion between them is remarkable.

The bone of their contention was, of course, the legal matters, and it remained so during the period covered by the diary. Sackville always sought to maximize his profits from the suits, whether by pressing them, or by agreeing to settlement. By and large he favoured settlement, once the price was satisfactory to him. His cash-flow problems—caused by his own profligacy, but exacerbated by the fact that while the suits remained unsettled, he did not and would not receive the very large dowry promised with Clifford—directed him towards this solution. But the death of Clifford's mother in May of 1616 changed the picture for him and shifted his interests towards persisting in the suits rather than settling. Why did Margaret's death change things? Because while she was alive, the lands in question were used by her, and supported her, according to the terms of her jointure. A jointure (also called "thirds" in the diary) was the property settled on the widow for use during her lifetime and after the death of her husband. It was, by custom and in common law, equal to a third of the value of the estates of the husband, and normally about equal in value to the dowry or "portion" provided on the bride's behalf. It was usually settled legally—that is, the lands and other sources of income which it included were assigned to the bride's agent—as part of the arrangements for the marriage; the continuing struggle in the diary to have Clifford's own jointure settled reflects the facts that her dowry hadn't been paid, and Sackville did not want to tie up income-providing properties. While Margaret was alive, even if Clifford was considered the rightful owner of the lands, Sackville could not profit from them as he would have wished to (they could not be sold or borrowed against).

After her death, however, they could belong outright to him, through his wife.

The consequence of Margaret's death, then, was to drive the two parties, Earl Francis Clifford on the one hand, and Sackville and Clifford on the other, to further adjudication, given that they could not agree on the settlement proposed by the Judges' Award. The next and final option was to go to the King, as the highest judicial power in the land. The King's Award, issued on 14 March 1617, was consistent with the earlier findings of the Court of Common Pleas—that although Clifford's claim to the lands in Westmorland and Skipton was valid, it was nevertheless the most suitable arrangement for them to be in Francis' possession. To this end he should pay Clifford compensation. This decision was legally binding, and did not require Clifford's consent, although the King wanted her agreement. By the terms of the Award, Clifford and Sackville were to receive £20,000—the last £3,000 of which was contingent on Clifford accepting the Award. The ownership of the lands would be transferred to Francis through the fine and recovery process. The line of inheritance was stipulated: if there were no male heirs, Clifford, or her heirs, would inherit. Sackville had to put up £25,000 worth of land as insurance against Anne suing again, unless she would agree formally to those terms—which she would not. "Upon the 16th [of April, 1617] my Lord and I had much talk about these businesses, he urging me still to go to London and to sign and seal but I told him that my promise was so far passed to my mother and to all the world that I would never do it whatsoever became of me and mine. Yet still I strived as much as I could to settle a good opinion in him towards me."

Clifford's refusal to abandon future legal action meant that even though the King's Award was binding, it was not easily enforced. The tenants questioned its validity, and therefore the security of their leases. For everyone except Clifford, the insecurity was costly: Sackville was short £3,000, and had to assure properties against the chance that Clifford might restart legal proceedings; Francis and his son Henry held estates that were lessened in value by the uncertainty around their ownership; the tenants were insecure in their leases and allegiances. Eventually things did settle, but Clifford never did accept the Award and agree to its terms. The imposition of the Award was completed by 1619, as is recorded in the diary: on 24 June, for example, she records the final payment of her "portion" or dowry. The smaller bits of business in 1619 document the winding up of her mother's affairs and the relinquishing of her immediate claim over the properties; for instance, on 15 December she and Sackville signed letters authorizing Ralph Conniston to receive residual debts on behalf of Margaret's estate. On that day she and Sackville "had a great falling out, he saying that if ever my Land came to me, I should assure it as he would have me"—by which he meant that if she ever inherited by the terms of her father's will, he demanded that she should assign the titles of the properties to him or to his agents and for his purposes. Her spirit is still resistant, but Sackville is the only one left to fight against, as the Award inhibits her from pursuing further legal action.

Like the memoir, the diary survives because of the legal conflicts that Clifford wanted to document for the future uses of her family members and herself. Much more is recorded, however, and it is her feelings, thoughts, readings, relationships, and day-to-day activities that interest us now. She records visits to and from a range of people, including family retainers, numerous relatives, social figures and preachers, divines, and lawyers. She makes note of gifts, household activities such as "dressing the house" in August of 1616, and her solitary and domestic entertainments such as needlepoint work, reading, and playing cards. She mentions her clothing, and on one occasion that she strung "the pearls and diamonds my mother left me into a necklace." She records the events in the growth and life of her daughter, (a new tooth, a "grudging" of the fever, her first whalebone bodice). Many of the entries concern the ups and downs of her marriage with Sackville, largely over the property disputes, but also over his relationship with Mathew Caldicot and, to a lesser degree, Lady Penniston, his mistress.

Of especial note in the diary is the record of her social life. As Spence points out in his chapter on her marriage to Sackville, what Clifford would later characterize as a profoundly isolated life was intensely social, as busy in sections as the whirlwind affair of the memoir. The fabric of this social life, and the connections within it that Clifford forges and maintains, tell us much about her life, and much about the lives of aristocratic women in that time and place. The first thing that we notice about the society depicted in the diary is that it is small, and essentially tribal in its structure. The genealogical connections between the members of the society are made apparent here by the footnotes, which reveal relations between people whose names do not indicate their kinship. Clifford is related to many of the people with whom she socializes, and these connections would have been known and clear to the members of the society: for instance, all of her acquaintances would have known of her relation to the Howard family, and of her identity as a "Russell" woman, due to her mother's lineage. We see in the diary that Clifford works hard to strengthen and exploit favourable family connections in order to buttress the chances of success in her lawsuits, focusing in particular on those relatives who could go either way, given their attachment to Sackville or Francis Clifford.

A society organized around lineage and consanguinity is most often patriarchal (although not necessarily so), and usually rigidly so—property and power pass through the male line, and women are by and large valued for their relations to men, as daughters, wives, and mothers. Women in such societies do not usually own or control property (unless they are widows), nor do they contribute to governance or participate to any significant degree in the public sphere. Nonetheless, it is evident that Clifford perceived that she and other women in her society possessed authority that could be used to affect outcomes in the workings of their world and that they joined their authority when necessary and possible. We have looked briefly at how Clifford's education contributed to this attitude and the capabilities that were needed to back it up. In the diary we also see women of the highest status in this society, acting with what appears to be a certain degree of independence from social convention and approbation; it is clear that they can use their positions to take liberties with the dominant ideology and evade or thwart its constraints. These are not proto-feminists—they do not seek access to resources or power for *women* as a group. Neither, however, are they dupes and puppets for their male masters, as Clifford's own life and actions make clear. They are women who worked both individually and in groups to enhance their positions in their immediate world, and to exercise power normally denied their sex.

At the beginning of the 1616 diary, for example, Clifford circulates among the wealthy widows in town, making sure to solicit the support of every faction she can think of. On 4 January, for instance, she sees Lady Effingham at Lady Lumley's. Lady Effingham was a favourite of Queen Anne; Queen Anne was the fulcrum of power for the female aristocracy in the present. Lady Lumley was a member of Elizabeth's inner circle, and so can be seen as representing the old guard, and residual loyalty—we remember from the 1603 memoir the importance of Clifford's "Aunt of Warwick" to Queen Elizabeth. She then goes on to see

Lady Shrewsbury, the wife of the wealthiest man in England (other than the king), and daughter of Bess of Hardwick. Clifford visits with two of their daughters within days of this, and they and their kin are mentioned throughout the rest of the diary. This family were representative of new kinds of wealth and an emergent influence in the aristocracy. In these visits, then, we see Clifford engaged in a kind of social politicking, attempting to work to her advantage the structures of influence and power in her society. She well knew that such structures are ones in which women—although excluded from the main—could operate in the rich and eddying back channels to real effect, for their own benefit, and not just for that of their spouses and children.

The women with whom Clifford circulates have some money of their own, which allows them to help each other and themselves. She mentions sending money to her sister-in-law Lady Compton, and how her other sister-in-law, Lady Beauchamp "grew great with my Lord of Hertford and so got the upper hand" in the matter of the disposition of family property. These women were also often cultured, sometimes writers and often patrons of other writers. Among the writers were Mary Wroth; Elizabeth Grey, Countess of Kent; Elizabeth Knyvett, Countess of Lincoln; and Mary Sidney Herbert, dowager Countess of Pembroke. Among those who were noted patrons of literary work are Bridget Morison, Lady Sussex; Alice, Countess of Derby; Clifford's mother; and Clifford herself. When Clifford attends a performance (a play or a masque) it is notably in the company of other women. In part this is a feature of the gender-segregated society in which she lived, but it is also a sign of the independence of women's cultural experience and valuation, which contributes to their own work and patronage. Indeed, we can see that a society that so strictly segregates the sexes creates the conditions in which women can comprise a sub-culture with its own support networks, priorities, and even values. It is not clear from this slice of the historical record that the advent of what Lawrence Stone famously called the "affective marriage"—one based on feeling, love, mutual interest, and sexual fidelity—marked an improvement in the social conditions of women, as it moved them away from their female peers and family members.

Finally, the women in Clifford's circles—whom we usually think of as constrained by marriage, and sexually oppressed, if not repressed—quite often enjoyed irregular sexual relationships. For instance, Elizabeth Howard, Lady Knollys, mentioned in June 1616, was reputed to have had a long-standing affair with the man who would be her second husband, Edward Vaux, which began long before her first husband died. Mary Wroth's affair with William Herbert, Earl of Pembroke, was well known. Lady Gray, mentioned in February 1616, is said to have lived out of wedlock with the historian John Selden; she is also purported to have been the mistress of Sir Edward Herbert, a judge. Lettice Knollys, mentioned as Lady Paget in August 1617, had a notorious history as an adulteress. And several of the great scandals mentioned in the diary involved women with apparently independent inclinations in these matters. Frances Howard, Lady Carr (later Lady Somerset) is quite well known in history, and the story of her adulterous attachment to Robert Carr and the associated murder of Thomas Overbury are recounted in the annotations to the diary. Another of the great scandals of the time is also mentioned in the diary. Frances, daughter of Sir Edward Coke and Elizabeth Cecil, Lady Hatton, was forced to marry John Villiers, but left him soon after and fell in love with Sir Robert Howard. She and Robert had a son in 1624 and were arrested for adultery. Several of the women in the diary are separated from their husbands at some point, including both Clifford and her mother. For instance, Lady Norris (mentioned in August 1617), who was Bridget de Vere, was at this time separated from her husband, Francis Norris, and in the diary Clifford's sister-in-law Compton and her husband "were now on terms of parting.... It was agreed that she should have a 100 lb a year and he to take the children from her" (February 1617). Clearly, then, the lives and authority of aristocratic women were not identical to those of women in other classes; while in some respects their behaviour was more closely scrutinized, they had freedoms attendant upon their status and wealth, and often made use of these freedoms.

After 1619

Clifford had three sons who died at birth or in infancy when she was married to Sackville, the daughter Margaret (born in 1614) mentioned in the diary, and a second daughter, Isabella, born in 1622, both of whom survived to adulthood. Richard Sackville died suddenly, of an illness, in 1624. Clifford was stricken with smallpox shortly after Sackville's death, and resolved never to marry again. In 1630, however, she married Philip Herbert, then Earl of Pembroke, who appears in the diary as "my Lord of Montgomery." Clifford described Herbert as "of a very quick apprehension, a sharp understanding, very crafty withal, and of a discerning spirit, but extremely choleric by nature" (1916, 55). With Herbert's help, she registered claims in 1632 and 1637; but these were no more successful than previous claims had been. Herbert and Clifford lived together for a time at Wilton House in Wiltshire, during the period of the renovations designed by Inigo Jones. Clifford was forty when they married, but she and Pembroke had two sons: they were born prematurely and died, making in all five sons for her that did not live beyond a few weeks. She and Pembroke were separated after four and a half years of marriage, and during their separation she lived primarily at Wilton House, while Pembroke lived at his lodgings in Whitehall. When the Civil Wars between the Parliamentary and Royalist forces began in 1642, she and Isabella moved to Baynard's Castle in London, her Pembroke jointure house. She stayed there—in her own chamber—for nearly seven years, until the wars ended with Parliamentary victory and the execution of King Charles I. A staunch supporter of the Royalist cause, Clifford's fortunes were protected during the wars by her husband's loyalty to Parliament; although the northern Clifford castles were extensively damaged, she was also protected informally from sequestration (i.e., having her property taken from her) by Parliament after the war ended in 1649. It was to those northern castles that she retired after the wars, delivered by time, and through (she thought) the good graces of her provident god. It was then that the life she had longed for since the age of fifteen began, and she put behind her the two marriages and the struggles of those times: "the marble pillars of Knole in Kent and Wilton in Wiltshire," she wrote in her autobiography, "were to me oftentimes but the gay arbours of anguish."

In 1641 her uncle Francis died, and in 1643 his son Henry also died without male heir. By the terms of her father's will Clifford inherited the family estates she had first claimed 37 years before. When the wars ended she moved north and began to restore and renovate the castles, damaged by the wars and by decades of neglect, and to manage her estates: "I employed myself," she writes in the autobiography, "in building and reparation at Skipton, at Barden Tower, and in causing the bounds to be ridden, and my courts kept in my several manors in Craven, and in these kind of country affairs about my estate, which I found extreme[ly] disorder[ed]" (Lives, 56). What she thought of as "the contentments and innocent pleasures of a country life" (Lives, 59) included commissioning the restoration of the castles and local churches and renovations of her homes to include bake-houses, apiaries, and stables, founding an almshouse for widows in Appleby and revitalizing another founded by her mother, reorganizing the leasing system on her estates to introduce higher rents through negotiations with (and sometimes ruthless legal action against) her tenants, and designing and commissioning funerary monuments for her father, mother, and self. She went on progresses between her castles along rude and rough tracks and cart roads, taking with her servants and retainers, friends and neighbours, her bedding and hangings and selected pieces of furniture. She participated in local justice and politics, involved herself in the schools and social life, and gave to charity. Clifford's daughters had married (Margaret to John Tufton, Earl of Thanet, and Isabella to James Compton, Earl of Northampton) and between them produced seventeen children, of whom twelve survived to adulthood; the twelve surviving grandchildren in turn had nineteen children before Clifford's death. She records dozens of visits from and gestures of support to these children. She had commissioned *The Great Picture* in 1646 (see Appendix C) and continued to have copies of the head and shoulders' portion of the right hand portrait of her made as gifts for the next thirty years; dated the years of their composition, the series of them (from the 1650s to the 1670s) presents a startling image of an ageless matriarch, soberly dressed, steadfastly oriented to the worlds both within and without herself.

Clifford also continued, during these years, to read and to write. The books she owned from this period, as shown in *The Great Picture*, include works on mortality, religious works including sermons by Donne and John King and George Sandys' *Paraphrase upon the Psalms*, Henry Wotton's *The Element of Architecture*, and literary works by Ben Jonson, George Herbert, and Fulke Greville. Of her reading in these later years we have the following record, in a letter to her secretary John Selden from 1649, in which an allusion to Spenser's *The Faerie Queene* is embedded in a reference to Chaucer: "If I had not excellent Chaucer's book here to comfort me I were in a pitiful case, having so many troubles as I have, but when I read in that I scorn and make light of them all, and a little part of his divine spirit infuses itself in me." Clifford also spent the last 27 years of her life organizing, writing, and re-writing the documents of her life and family. With the help of several secretaries, she assembled and composed the documents she and her mother had gathered over the years into *The Great Books of the Clifford Family* (an excerpt of which is included in Appendix D), which includes her autobiography and annual accounts for the years 1650 to 1675. She continued as well the habit of keeping a diary, until the day before her death. Many of the entries in the diary of her later life record her reading in the earlier accounts, showing how her versions of her younger selves were absorbed into her present, and how her writing and reading reinforced the development of her sense of self, purpose, and meaning.

Critical History and Further Reading

Clifford's biography and her writings have been of interest to select audiences since her death. From the eighteenth until the early twentieth centuries, her life and work received considerable attention from historians of her family and region and of the nobility, and memoirists of notable women. Historical and biographical interest in Clifford persists and recent important publications in this vein include D.J.H. Clifford's editions of the diaries, including the ones from her later life, and Spence's invaluable biography. The first literary critic to make note of Clifford, with reference to the Sackville-West edition of the 1603 memoir and the 1616 to 1619 diary, was Virginia Woolf. In her essay "Donne after three centuries," Woolf used Clifford to mark the birth of the English common reader:

> though active and practical and little educated ... [she] felt, we can gather from the bald statements of her diary, a duty towards literature and to the makers of it as her mother, the patroness of the poet Daniel, had before her. A great heiress, infected with all the passion of her age for lands and houses, busied with all the cares of wealth and property, she still read good English books as naturally as she ate good beef and mutton. (40)

Clifford's work did not attract much attention, however, from those who followed up on Woolf's call to imagine the lives and discover the writings of Shakespeare's sister, the feminist critics of early modern writing and of women's autobiography of the 1970s and 1980s. This may be because although Clifford's work is concerned with managing the opportunities and constraints of her gendered identity, it is not characterized by expressions of gendered insecurity. It also endorses patriarchal class privilege as a means for exceptional women to obtain and exercise power.

Later feminist criticism, by Mary Ellen Lamb, Helen Wilcox, Barbara K. Lewalski, Katharine Hodgkin, Mihiko Suzuki, and myself, have grappled more readily with the conflation in Clifford's work of the discourses of aristocratic privilege and gender difference. For instance, Clifford commonly depicts herself, in writing and in painting, as having the best features and capabilities of both her father and her mother; the opening of the "Autobiography," included here in Appendix D, and *The Great Picture* (Appendix C), both emphasize her possession of feminine virtue and male authority. While Clifford's self-representation is more assertive than most, this combination is typical of women writers of the period, such as Mary Sidney, Elizabeth Cary, and Mary Wroth. For these women, the discourse of resistance to patriarchy as we know it (or as it would become available in the later seventeenth century) was not available; and if it had been available, it would have been of little use. Their strategy—and for each it was effective—was to draw upon the prototype of the "exceptional woman": this is a woman who is permitted a position of authority in patriarchal culture by virtue of the structure of that culture. She has been attributed by her culture a greater power than most other people, and she self-consciously uses that position to improve the lives of those around her through her virtuous action. Clifford was exceptional even in this group: as Amy Louise Erickson's work discusses, and Spence has thoroughly documented, Clifford was not just wealthy *for a woman*, or more independent *than most women*: on both counts she was extraordinary, in comparison to men as well. Lewalski characterizes Clifford's writings as "not overt rebellion against patriarchy but a subversive re-writing in which [she] laid stubborn claim to a place of power within it" (151). Bishop Rainbow's sermon (Appendix E) shows, however, that the subversion was very public, and we should recognize that of the women writers we know from her era, Clifford stands out as signally unapologetic for the fact of her writing, and indubitably and even aggressively bold in her depiction of herself as the one who has been trusted to deliver certain truths to her people.

The most recent scholarship on Clifford's works has focused on her patronage of painters and sculptors and on her architectural commissions. Elizabeth Chew's work on Clifford's rebuilding of her estates (principally six Norman castles in various states of disrepair) and the projects she initiated (an almshouse, reparations to local churches, sundry public buildings, commemorative monuments, and funerary sculpture) shows the extent to which Clifford was self-consciously designing a world in which she figured as the pivotal point, politically, materially, and ideologically. The 2003 exhibition of *The Great Picture* at the Tate Britain Gallery in London produced a volume of essays on Clifford's art and architectural patronage which will be edited by Lynn Hulse and published soon by the Yorkshire Archeological Society. Spence's excellent biography has rightly characterized Clifford as a prominent courtier, a landowner of significance, an intellectual of some proportions, and one of the leading antiquaries and family historians of her era. These will draw more attention to the vast and various body of her work, which has much more to teach us. And so Clifford's intention to be remembered by future generations will be fulfilled, even beyond her wildest imaginings.

Anne Clifford: A Brief Chronology

1590 Anne Clifford is born on 30 January, the second surviving child of George Clifford, third Earl of Cumberland and his wife Margaret Russell.

1591 On 24 May, Clifford's brother Robert dies, leaving Anne the only surviving child. George and Margaret being separated, there is no expectation of more children. George designates his brother Francis as his heir.

1603 In March Queen Elizabeth I dies, and King James ascends the English throne.

1605 George Clifford dies on 30 October. His brother Francis inherits all his estates, including those Clifford and her mother believe to be rightfully and inalienably hers. The will provides for a dowry of £15,000 to be paid to Clifford's husband by Francis upon her marriage. This settlement is deferred due to the lawsuits over the estates pursued by Margaret and Clifford.

1606 Margaret initiates claims on behalf of Clifford for the baronial titles and lands left by George's will to Francis. These suits, and various attempts to settle them, last until January 1619.

1609 Clifford marries Richard Sackville, Lord Buckhurst, two days before his father's death, after which he becomes the third Earl of Dorset.

1614 Clifford's daughter Margaret is born on 2 July.

1616 Margaret Clifford dies in May, at her jointure property in the north.

1617 The King's Award is issued on 14 March. It acknowledges the validity of Clifford's claim but upholds her father's decision to will the properties to Francis. It proposes a financial settlement of the claims that will be higher if Clifford agrees to the terms of the Award. She does not, which angers Sackville, who is eager to complete the financial transactions to his greatest benefit.

1622 In August, Henry, the last surviving son of Clifford's cousin Henry, dies, making it very likely that Clifford will eventually inherit under the terms of her father's will. Clifford's daughter Isabella is born on 6 October.

1624 Richard Sackville dies at the age of 34. Margaret and Clifford contract smallpox. Richard is succeeded by his brother Edward, to whom Clifford refers throughout the

Life of Me as her enemy. Sackville's death leaves Clifford with a generous jointure comprised of a variety of different income-earning properties.

1625   James I dies, and Charles I takes the throne.

1630   On 3 June, Clifford marries Philip Herbert, third Earl of Pembroke, in the Russell family (her mother's) church at Cheyneys.

1634   Clifford and Herbert separate and Clifford lives at Baynard's Castle, near London, where she remains until the conclusion of the Civil Wars.

1641   The outbreak of the English Civil Wars.

1643   Henry, Clifford's cousin, dies in December. As he has no male heir, Clifford then inherits the Westmorland and Skipton estates, for which she and her mother had fought. Because of the wars, however, she remains at Baynard's Castle.

1649   Clifford leaves Baynard's Castle for her northern estates, where she would live for the remainder of her life.

1650   Philip Herbert dies, leaving another rich jointure to Clifford.

1676   Clifford dies on 22 March, at Brougham, and is buried in Appleby.

A Note on the Text

There is no surviving original version of the memoir or of the diary, either in Clifford's hand or in that of one of her secretaries; neither is there a copy from her lifetime. Williamson suggests that the original was destroyed because it was too embarrassing (366–67), and Bishop Edward Rainbow, in the funeral sermon included in this volume, refers to the "censures others may pass on this exactness of diary as too minute and trivial a diligence." He states on the same page that "I confess, I have been informed, that after some reviews, these [the diaries] were laid aside." It seems the diaries were not destroyed by Clifford herself, but by her descendants. While she may not have wished them to survive in her formal documentation of her life, it is clear that she retained them in her possession, and made use of them in her daily life. Throughout the diary of her final year, for instance, she seems to be going over the diaries of previous years. For example she notes on 20 January 1676:

> I remembered how this day was 59 years I went with my first Lord [Sackville] to the Court at Whitehall, where in the inner withdrawing chamber King James desired and urged me to submit to the Award which he would make concerning my lands of inheritance, but I absolutely denied to do so, wherein I was guided by a great Providence of God for the good of me and mine. And that day also had my first and then only child a dangerous fit of her long ague in Knole house in Kent, where she then lay. (D.J.H. Clifford, 240)

It is fortunate for the modern reader that posthumous copies of the diary and memoir have survived.

In the preparation of this edition, two sources were used. The source of the 1616 to 1619 diary is the manuscript known as the Portland manuscript, which is the best available source, and the likely source of the other surviving text. To prove this, I examined the two manuscripts, and found that one was made on paper that was clearly dated "1825" and "1826." The other one was not dated, but when I compared them, letter-by-letter, I found that the later one was an imperfect, but direct, copy of the earlier one. I was able to date the earlier one (the Portland manuscript) by comparing the handwriting it is in to other handwritten works in the same collection. By matching the handwriting of the Portland manuscript to other examples by Margaret Cavendish Harley Bentinck (1715–85), the Duchess of Portland, granddaughter of Robert Harley, the first Earl of Oxford, and the daughter of Edward Harley, second Earl, I was also able to identify its scribe. The papers in the collection containing the Portland manuscript belong to the Marquess of Bath and are part of the great collection at Longleat House in Wiltshire. This part of the collection is made up of the remains of the famous Harleain manuscript collection that were left after the bulk of the collection was sold to the nation in 1753. According to Spence, Robert Harley visited Appleby Castle in 1725 and inspected some of Clifford's documents (250). He then commissioned the 1737 abridgement of *The Great Books of the Clifford Family* which was included in the Harley collection sold in 1753, published in 1916. There are other Clifford papers in the Portland collection, which include the following: another scribal copy of the autobiography; the 1603 memoir; copies of numerous letters from Anne; and the autobiographical letter written by Margaret Clifford to her spiritual advisor, Dr. John Layfield. All except the autobiography are in the hand of Margaret Bentinck. Evidently, then, the great manuscript collector, Robert Harley, had a significant interest in Clifford, and his grand-daughter maintained that interest. She too was an embattled heiress, unjustly dispossessed of her rightful inheritance: perhaps she sympathized with Clifford!

The other surviving copy of the 1616 to 1619 diary, which also includes the 1603 memoir, is known as the Knole manuscript presently in the Kent County Records Office. The scribes of the Knole manuscript were probably Elizabeth Sackville and her sister Mary, based on comparison with other samples of their handwriting in the same collection. It is likely that they made their copy of the diary at the time that their estate was being divided—another instance of women challenged by inheritance disputes finding comfort, or at least a bond, in Clifford's work.

While both the Knole and Portland manuscripts include the 1603 memoir, there is another version that merits mention here. That is the version presented in the fourth edition of William Seward's *Anecdotes of some distinguished persons chiefly of the present and two preceding centuries*, published in 1804. Clearly this is dated after the Portland manuscript was made (Margaret Bentinck died in 1785). However, there are features of the Seward text and of the results of its comparison with the Portland manuscript that suggest that it was made either from a source closer to the original than Portland, or from the same source but with greater concern for accuracy. It is unlikely, first, that the Seward copy was made from the Portland manuscript, as there are numerous small contractions and omissions in Portland of features found in the Seward edition—for example, "my" in front of "Lord," "did run a course at the field" instead of "did run at the field," "who was one of the King's bedchamber" instead of "who was of the King's bedchamber," and "Frances" rather than "Francis" in reference to her female cousin. It is also impossible that Portland was made from, and only from, Seward. The Portland manuscript has three mentions of the "green sickness": Seward has omitted all three references, marking their absence with rows of asterisks. The two versions are, however, apparently closely affiliated. They share an odd internal reference: "as appears in the marginal note in the 9th leaf" is inserted in a sentence that otherwise reads "From Lancelevel we went ... to Mr Dulon's, where we continued about a week and had great entertainment." This reference does not make sense in either text and appears to have been copied from a manuscript source; in the Portland manuscript it is struck out, as if the scribe noticed belatedly that the reference was irrelevant. Finally, we should note that the spelling in Seward has many more characteristic features of early modern English spelling than does Portland, such as "ie" instead of "y," doubled terminal consonants (e.g., "mett"), colons to mark abbreviations, "en" rather than "n" endings (in "growen," for example), shifted vowels ("hir," "bin") and use or lack of terminal "e" (in "Queene," or "delicat"). This suggests either that Seward's source was closer to the original composition than the Portland source, or, if they had the same source, that the Seward transcription is less modernized and perhaps therefore more accurate than the Portland.

The sum of the evidence indicates that the source for both texts was probably a single manuscript (unless multiple copies recorded the internal reference, which is certainly possible), but that Seward's copy was more accurate with regard to the spelling and the inclusion of small words and some names. Seward does not record the source of his texts, noting only that he has collected his stories about famous people from other authors such as Holinshed and earlier biographers, so that they may be "perused with great pleasure by those who love ancient times, ancient manners, and ancient virtues" (I. 25). For the purposes of this edition, Seward's text has been used as the basis, with the additions from the Portland of the mentions of the "green sickness," apparently deliberately excised from the Seward text. This is the first modern edition of the memoir to use Seward's text as a base.

For this edition, the spelling of both the documents has been modernized, as has the punctuation. Additions (or removal) of articles, conjunctions, and the occasional small word (e.g., in the entry for 15 September 1617, the manuscript reads "was sad to how ill things" which has been emended to "sad to *see*") necessary to grammatical sense have been made silently. All people that could be identified are noted, and the index will help readers find the first annotated mention of a name.

The Memoir of 1603

I was at Queen Elizabeth's death 13 years old and two months and this day Mr Richard Sackville was 14 years, he being then at Dorset House with his grandfather and that great family. At the death of this worthy Queen my mother and I lay at Austin Friars in the same chamber where afterwards I was married.

The first time that King sent to the Lords in England he gave command that the Earls of Northumberland[1] and Cumberland,[2] the Lord Thomas Howard[3] and the Lord Mountjoy[4] should be added to the Council.[5]

---

1 Henry Percy, 9th Earl of Northumberland (1564–1632).
2 Clifford's father, George, 3rd Earl of Cumberland (1558–1605). He was an important courtier to Queen Elizabeth.
3 Thomas Howard (1561–1626), created 1st Earl of Suffolk below. He would be Lord Chamberlain from 1603 to 1614, and Lord Treasurer from 1614–18. He and his wife Catherine Knyvett (1583?–1633) were later tried and convicted of embezzlement; in her entry in *The Diary* for 20 November 1619, Clifford notes they were sent to the Tower and released on 30 December.
4 Charles Blount (1563–1606), 8th Baron Mountjoy and later 1st Earl of Devonshire. At James' accession, he returned from Ireland, where he had been a successful commander and viceroy in the campaign. Penelope Devereux, Lady Rich, had been his mistress since 1590; they had six children. They were welcomed into the new court, but later fell out of favour because of Lady Rich's divorce.
5 Privy Council; probably the most powerful single organization in the country. Its members were appointed by the crown, and they supported the exercise of sovereign power outside of parliament.

1603

In Christmas I used to go much to the Court, and sometimes did
I lie in my aunt of Warwick's[1] chamber on a pallet, to whom I was
much bound for her continual care and love of me: in so much as
if Queen Elizabeth had lived, she intended to have preferred me
to be of the Privy Chamber, for at that time there was as much
hope and expectation of me both for my person and my fortunes
as of any other young lady whatsoever. A little after the Queen
removed to Richmond she began to grow sickly. My Lady[2] used
to go often thither and carried me with her in the coach, and using
to wait in the coffer chamber, and many times came home very
late. About the 21st or 22nd of March my aunt of Warwick sent my
mother word about six of the clock at night, she living then at
Clerkenwell, that she should remove to Austin Friars[3] her house,
for fear of some commotion, though God in his mercy did deliver
us from it. Upon the 24th Mr Flocknell, my aunt of Warwick's
man, brought us word from his Lady that the Queen died about
two [or] three of the clock in the morning. This message was delivered to my mother and me in the same chamber where afterwards
I was married. About ten o' the clock King James was proclaimed
in Cheapside by all the Council with great joy and triumph, which
triumph I went to see and hear. This peaceable coming in of the
King was unexpected of all sorts of people.[4]

---

1 Anne Russell (1548–1604), eldest daughter of Francis Russell, 2nd Earl
  of Bedford, and Margaret St. John; widow of Ambrose Dudley
  (1528?–90), 21st Earl of Warwick, to whom she was third wife. She was
  learned and witty, and a member of the inner circle of Queen Elizabeth's court. She is depicted in *The Great Picture*, in the central panel
  (see Appendix C, 215).
    Clifford's mother had been pursuing her suit for payment of spousal and
  child support from her husband through her sister, whose intimacy with
  Queen Elizabeth should have brought good results for Margaret. The
  death of the Queen was untimely and unfortunate for Margaret and Anne.
2 Margaret Russell, Clifford's mother; see Introduction, 11-12.
3 I.e., her house in the former monastery of the Hermits of Saint Augustine, founded in 1253, and taken over by the Crown in the mid sixteenth century. It is located in the heart of the old City of London.
4 Elizabeth I had no obvious successor and did not name one until she was
  on her deathbed. Remembering the violence that followed her brother
  Edward's death (which led first to the nine-day reign of Lady Jane Grey,
  and then to her sister Mary's troubled queenship), and fearful of foreign
  or Catholic attempts to seize the throne, the English people were appre-
  hensive about the transition from Elizabeth's rule to that of James.

Queen Elizabeth's funeral was on the 28th day of April being Thursday.

Within two or three days we returned to Clerkenwell again. A little after this Queen Elizabeth's corpse came by night in a barge from Richmond to Whitehall, my mother and a great company of Ladies attending it, where it continued a good while standing in the drawing chamber, where it was watched all night by several Lords and Ladies, my mother sitting up with it two or three nights, but my Lady would not give me leave to watch by reason I was held too young. At this time we used to go very much to Whitehall and walked much in the garden which was much frequented with Lords and Ladies, being all full of several hopes, every man expecting mountains and finding molehills, excepting Sir Robert Cecil[5] and the house of the Howards, who hated my mother and did not much love my aunt of Warwick. About this time my Lord of Southampton[6] was enlarged of his imprisonment out of the Tower. When the corpse of Queen Elizabeth had continued at Whitehall as long as the Council had thought fit, it was carried from thence with great solemnity to Westminster, the Lords and Ladies going on foot to attend it, my mother and my aunt of Warwick being mourners, but I was not allowed to be one, because I was not high enough, which did much trouble me then, but yet I stood in the church at Westminster to see the solemnity performed.

A little after this my Lady and a great deal of other company as Mrs Elizabeth Bridges, my Lady Newton and her daughter [and] my Lady Finch went down with my aunt of Warwick to North Hall, and from thence we all went to Theobalds[7] to see the King, who used my mother and my aunt very graciously, but we all saw a great change between the fashion of the court as it is

---

5 Robert Cecil (1563–1612), later 1st Earl of Salisbury. His father was key advisor to Elizabeth I; Robert succeeded him as her chief minister, and continued under James. He was the most successful politician of his era, and had a hand in every important policy and government action during his time in power, from suppression of Catholicism to financial management to international relations.

6 Henry Wriothesley (1573–1624), 3rd Earl of Southampton. Courtier, patron of poets, probably the young man of Shakespeare's sonnets; imprisoned as a conspirator in the Earl of Essex's plot (1601) to depose Queen Elizabeth.

7 Built by William Cecil to entertain the Queen, it is the paradigm of the Elizabethan "prodigy house." In 1607 Robert Cecil exchanged it with James I for Hatfield House.

A dispute between George, Earl of Cumberland and the Lord Burleigh about carrying the sword before the King at York adjudged in favour of said Earl.

now, and of that in the Queen's, for we were all lousy by sitting in Sir Thomas Erskine's[8] chamber.

As the King came out of Scotland, when he lay at York, there was a strife between my father and my Lord Burleigh,[9] who was then President,[10] who should carry the sword, but it was adjudged on my father's side, because it was his office by inheritance, and so is lineally descended on me. From Theobalds the King went to Charterhouse, where my Lord Thomas Howard was created Earl of Suffolk and my Lord Mountjoy Earl of Devonshire and [he] restored my Lord[s] of Southampton and Essex[11] who stood attainted. Likewise he created many Barons, amongst which my uncle Russell[12] was made Lord Russell of Thornaugh, and for Knights they were innumerable.

All this spring I had my health very well, not having so much as a taste of the green sickness.[13] My father used to come sometimes to us at Clerkenwell,[14] but not often, for he at this time as it were wholly left my mother, yet the house was kept still at his charge.

About this time my Aunt of Bath and her Lord[15] came to London and brought with them my Lord Fitzwarren[16] and my cousin Frances Bourchier[17] whom I met at Bagshot, where I lay all

---

8 Thomas Erskine (1566-1639), a schoolfellow of the King's and a favourite throughout the King's life.

9 Robert Cecil; see 45n5.

10 Of the Council of the North, formed in 1530 to maintain order in the northern border regions.

11 Robert Devereux (1591-1646), 3rd Earl of Essex. His title, like that of Southampton, had been under attainder (withdrawn by royal prerogative) since 1601, when his father was executed for plotting to overthrow the Queen.

12 William Russell (1558?-1613), Margaret's brother and nearest her in age. A veteran of campaigns in the Low Countries and in Ireland, he withdrew from the Jacobean court soon after this date, returning only for the funeral of Prince Henry. He helped to support, financially and morally, Margaret and Anne.

13 See A Note on the Text, 39. "Green sickness" was a term used for anemia, common in adolescent girls.

14 In the suburbs of London.

15 William Bourchier (1557–1623), 3rd Earl of Bath, and Elizabeth Russell (d. 1605), Margaret's sister.

16 Richard Bourchier, second son of William Bourchier and Elizabeth Russell.

17 Frances Bourchier (1586?–1612), Richard's sister. She died (unmarried) at the age of 26, and Clifford erected a monument to her (Williamson 70).

night with my cousin Frances Bourchier and Mrs Mary Cary,[18] which was the first beginning of the greatness between us. About five miles from London there met them my mother, my Lord of Bedford and his Lady,[19] my uncle Russell and much other company, so that we were in number about 300, which did all accompany them to Bath House, where they continued most of that summer, whither I went daily and visited them and grew more inward with my cousin Frances and Mrs Cary. About this time my aunt of Warwick went to meet the Queen, having Mrs Bridges with her and my cousin Anne Vavasour.[20] My mother and I should have gone with them, but that her horses, which she borrowed of Mr Elmers,[21] and old Mr Hickly, were not ready; yet I went the same night and overtook my aunt at Tyttenhanger, my Lady Blount's house, where my mother came the next day to me about noon, my aunt being gone before. Then my mother and I went on our journey to overtake her, and killed three horses that day with extreme of heat and came to Wrest, my Lord of Kent's, where we found the doors shut and none in the house but one servant who only had the keys of the hall, so that we were enforced to lie in the hall all night, till towards morning at which time came a man and let us into the higher rooms, where we slept three or four hours. This morning we hasted away betimes and came that night to Rockingham Castle where we overtook my aunt of Warwick and her company, where we continued a day or two with old Sir Edward Watson and his Lady, then we went to my Lady Needum's who once served my aunt of Warwick, and from thence to a sister of hers whose name I have forgotten. Thither came my Lady of Bedford, who was then so great a woman with the Queen as every body much respected her, she having attended the Queen from out of Scotland. The next day we

---

18 Probably Mary Cary, daughter of George Cary and Catherine Russell; another relative.
19 Edward Russell and Lucy Harington.
20 Anne Vavasour (c. 1565–?), daughter of Henry Vavasour and Margaret Knyvett. She was lady of the bedchamber to Queen Elizabeth, and had an illegitimate child in 1581 fathered by Edward de Vere, 17th Earl of Oxford. This affair caused years of violent skirmish and verbal denunciation between de Vere and his followers, and the Knyvett family. She is also thought to have had a child with Sir Henry Lee (1532–1611), the Queen's Champion. There is a painting of her (c. 1605) in the collection of the Armourers and Brasiers of the City of London. This editor does not know how she is related to Clifford.
21 Alice Elmers, a relative, was Margaret's caregiver or nurse until she was eight years old (Spence 3).

The Queen and the Prince[6] came to Althorp the 25th of June being Saturday but as I remember my aunt of Warwick, my mother and I came not thither till the next day. 30th Sunday was kept with great solemnity, there being an infinite number of Lords and Ladies. Here we saw my cousin Clifford first, then we saw the Queen's favour to my Lady Hatton[7] and my Lady Cecil,[8] for she showed no favour to the elderly Ladies but to my Lady Rich[9] and such-like company.

---

6 Prince Henry Frederick Stuart (1594–1612).

7 Elizabeth Cecil, daughter of Thomas Cecil, 1st Earl of Exeter, and Lady Dorothy Neville, married first (as his second wife), Sir William Hatton (d. 1597), and in 1598, Sir Edward Coke (1552–1634). This is an example of a woman continuing to be known by the title of her first husband, as her second marriage would give her a lesser title.

8 Elizabeth Drury (1578–1654), daughter of Sir William Drury of Hawstead and Elizabeth Stafford, second wife of William Cecil (1566–1640), later 2nd Earl of Exeter (1623), and sister-in-law to Lady Hatton above.

9 Penelope Devereux (1562–1607), daughter of Walter Devereux, 1st Earl of Essex, and Lettice Knollys; married first to Robert Rich, later 1st Earl of Warwick, but divorced from him in 1605, for reason of her long-term adultery with Charles Blount. Even as an adulteress, living openly with her lover, Devereux was given precedence and privilege at court, but as a divorcee, she was exiled and forbidden to remarry. She and Mountjoy were married privately by Archbishop William Laud, but this did not legitimize their children, nor did it ease their return to court. She is perhaps most famous now as "Stella" of Philip Sidney's sonnets.

went to M[r] Griffin of Dingley's, which was the first time I ever saw the Queen and Prince Henry, where she kissed us all and used us kindly. Thither came my Lady of Suffolk, my young Lady Derby[22] and my Lady Walsingham,[23] which three ladies were the great favourites of Sir Robert Cecil. That night we went along with the Queen's train, there being an infinite number of coaches, and as I take it my aunt and my mother and I lay at Sir Richard Knightley's, where my Lady Elizabeth Knightley made exceedingly much of us. The same night my mother and I and my cousin Anne Vavasour rid on horseback through Coventry and went to a Gentleman's House where the Lady Elizabeth[24] her Grace lay, which was the first time I ever saw her, my Lady Kildare and the Lady Harington[25] being her governesses. The same night we returned to Sir Richard Knightley's. The next day, as I take it, we went along with the Queen to Althorpe, my Lord Spencer's[26] House, where my mother and I saw my cousin Henry Clifford[27] my uncle's son, which was the first time we ever saw him. From thence the 29th being Monday the Queen went to Hatton Fermers, where the King met her, where

---

22 Elizabeth de Vere (before 1584–1626). William Stanley, 6th Earl of Derby, her husband, was the son of Clifford's paternal aunt, Margaret, so he and Clifford are first cousins.

23 Etheldreda (Audrey) Shelton, wife of Sir Thomas Walsingham (1561–1630). She accompanied the new Queen from Scotland to London, and she and her husband were subsequently appointed keepers of the Queen's wardrobe.

24 Princess Elizabeth (1596–1662), eldest daughter of James and Anne. She later married Frederick V, Elector Palatine of the Rhine and for a few months King of Bohemia. She and her husband lived much of their lives in exile because of wars in his homeland. Clifford corresponded with her, as an affectionate friend, until Elizabeth's death.

25 Elizabeth Kelway (1551–?), daughter of Robert Kelway, wife of John Harington, created Lord Harington of Exton during these festivities. They were English, but of Scots ancestry, and affiliated themselves with the King upon his accession. They were charged with the education of the Princess Elizabeth, and she lived with them from several years beginning in October of this year. Their daughter, Lucy, Countess of Bedford, mentioned below.

26 Sir Robert Spencer (1570–1627), soon to be 1st Baron Spencer of Wormleighton, son of Sir John Spencer and Mary Catlin. He was a member of parliament and held other local offices. He was made a Knight of the Garter by 1601. He entertained the Queen and Prince Henry for two days on this journey. The performances included Ben Jonson's masque of "The Satyr."

27 Henry Clifford (1592-1643), son of Francis Clifford and Grisold Hughes; Clifford's Uncle's heir.

At Windsor there was such infinite number of Ladies sworn of the Queen's Privy Chamber as made the place of no esteem or credit. Once I spoke to my Lady of Bedford[10] to be one, but had the good fortune to miss it.

At Hampton Court my mother, my self and the other Ladies dined in the presence[11] as they used in Queen Elizabeth's time, but that custom lasted not long.

---

10 Lucy Harington (1581–1627), daughter of Sir John Harington and Elizabeth Kelway; wife of Edward Russell (1572–1627), 3rd Earl of Bedford. Edward was first cousin to Clifford. Lucy was a waiting woman to Queen Anne, a patron of Jonson, Daniel, and others, and probably a poet herself. She had money under her own control, and in 1608 bought Twickenham Park from Francis Bacon; she moved with her husband to another house in 1617, where they died within days of each other. Her portrait was painted several times, and Donne and Jonson wrote poems to her.

11 Presence-chamber, in which the sovereign receives guests. The presence-chamber was not part of the private apartments of the sovereign, and was not "intimate"—but it was the most privileged of the spaces in which there were gatherings of this sort. Shakespeare's *Henry V* opens in the King's presence-chamber. Hampton Court is in Surrey, not far from London; it was an important centre of courtly life for Henry VIII, and became that again for James I, in part because James enjoyed the hunting there.

there were an infinite company of Lords and Ladies and other people that the county could scarce lodge them. From thence the Court removed and was banqueted with great royalty by my father at Grafton where the King and Queen were entertained with speeches and delicate presents, at which time my Lord and the Alexanders[28] did run a course at the field, where he hurt Henry Alexander very dangerously. Where the court lay this night I am uncertain. At this time of the King's being at Grafton, my mother was there, but not held as mistress of the House, by reason of the difference between my Lord and her, which was grown to a great height. The night after my aunt of Warwick, my mother and I, as I take it, lay at Doctor Challoner's, (where my aunt of Bath and my uncle Russell met us, which house my grandfather of Bedford used to lie much at) being in Amersham. The next day the Queen went to a gentleman's house (whose name I cannot remember) where there met her many great Ladies to kiss her hands; as the Marquess of Winchester,[29] my Lady of Northumberland, my Lady of Southampton, etc. From thence the court removed to Windsor where the feast of St George was solemnized, though it should have been done before. There I stood with my Lady Elizabeth's Grace in the shrine in the Great Hall at Windsor to see the King and all the Knights sit at dinner. Thither came the Archduke's ambassador,[30] who was received by the King and Queen in the Great Hall where there was such an infinite company of Lords and Ladies and so great a court as I think I shall never see the like. From Windsor the court removed to Hampton Court, where my mother and I lay at Hampton Court in one of the round Towers, round about which

---

28 The family of William Alexander (1567–1640), later first Earl of Stirling, and his wife, Janet Erskine (before 1585–1649). He was tutor to Prince Henry, and after Henry's death in 1612 a member of the household of Prince Charles. He was also a published poet, composer, and playwright. In 1621 he was granted a charter for Nova Scotia, but his colonization efforts failed. He was bankrupt when he died.

29 William Paulet (d. 1628), 4th Marquess of Winchester, married (in 1587) to Lucy Cecil (d. 1614), daughter of Thomas Cecil, first Earl of Exeter, and Dorothy Neville. Again, we see the Cecil family at the centre of the court.

30 Of Austria; a representative from the Habsburg rulers.

About this time my Lady of Hertford[12] began to grow great with the Queen and the Queen wore her picture.

My cousin Frances Bourchier stood to see the coronation though she had no robes and went not amongst the company.

---

12 Frances Howard (1578–1639), daughter of Thomas Howard, 1st Viscount Howard of Bindon, and Mabel Burton. She and Edward Seymour, 1st Earl of Hertford (1539–1621), were secretly married in 1600, and they were imprisoned in consequence. (He was the son of the attainted Duke of Somerset, and widower of Lady Catherine Grey; those with such close ties to the monarchy required royal assent for their marriages, and this was not given for the Howard-Seymour union. His son William ran into much the same set of problems with his marriage to Arabella Stuart in 1610.) She later married Lodovic Stuart, Duke of Lennox. She was an accomplished poet.

were tents, where they died two or three in a day of the plague. There I fell extremely sick of a fever so as my mother was in some doubt it might turn to the plague but within two or three days I grew reasonable well, and was sent away to my cousin Stidall's at Norbury, Mrs Carniston going with me, for Mrs Taylor[31] was newly put away from me, her husband dying of the plague shortly after. A little afore this time my mother and my aunt of Bath and my cousin Frances went to North Hall, my mother being extreme angry with me for riding before with Mr Menerell, where my mother in her anger commanded that I should lie in a chamber alone, which I could not endure, but my cousin Frances got the key of my chamber and lay with me which was the first time I loved her so very well. The next day Mr Menerell as he went abroad fell down suddenly and died, so as most thought it was of the plague, which was then very rife; it put us all in great fear and amazement for my aunt had then a suit to follow in court and my mother to attend the King about the business between my father and her.[32] My aunt of Warwick sent us medicine from a little house near Hampton Court where she then lay with Sir Moyle Finch and his Lady. Now was the Master of Orkney[33] and the Lord Tillibarne much in love with Mrs Cary and came thither to see us with George Murray in their company who was one of the King's bedchamber. Within nine or ten days we were allowed to come to the court again, which was before I went to my cousin Stidall's. Upon the 25th of July the King and Queen were crowned at Westminster, my father and my mother both attending them in their robes, my aunt of Bath and my Uncle Russell, which solemn sight my mother would not let me see because the plague was so hot in London; therefore I continued at Norbury where my cousin did feed me with breakfasts, and pear pies and such things, as shortly after I fell into the green sickness.

After the coronation, the court returned to Hampton court, where my mother fetched me from Norbury, and so we lay at a

---

31 Mrs. Anne Taylor, her governess; in *The Great Picture*, her husband is identified as Mr. William Taylor, and it is said she had "diverse" children who all died before her, without issue.

32 Margaret's goal is to persuade the King to enforce the agreement she has with George for financial support. According to Spence, George had agreed to pay £1,000 a year, but "with empty coffers and huge debts he could hardly support himself let alone his family" (17), and they had been living on much less.

33 Henry Stewart (b. before 1589), son of Robert Stewart, 1st Earl of Orkney, and Janet Kennedy. He, like James I, was a grandson of James V of Scotland.

Between Lance-level and Mr Dulon's we lay at one Sir Edmund Fetti-place's called Besilesee where we had great entertainment. Then we lay a night or two at Wandage at Gregory Webbs', a tenant of my Lord of Bath's and from his house to Mr Dulon's.

little house near Hampton Court about a fortnight and my aunt of Bath lay in Huggin's lodgings, where my cousin Frances and I and Mary Cary did use to walk much about the gardens and house when the King and Queen were gone.

About this time my cousin Anne Vavasour was married to Sir Richard Warburton. From Hampton Court, my mother, my aunt of Bath, my self and all our company went to Lance-level, Lord Francis Palmer his house, where we continued as long as the court lay at Basingstoke and I went often to the Queen and my Lady Arabella.[34] Now was my Lady Rich grown great with the Queen insomuch as my Lady of Bedford was something out with her and when she came to Hampton Court was entertained but even indifferently, and yet continued to be of the bedchamber. One day the Queen went from Basingstoke and dined at Sir Henry Wallop's where my Lady, my aunt and I had lain two or three nights before, and did help to entertain her. As we rid from my Lady Wallop's to Lance-level, riding late by reason of our stay at Basingstoke, we saw a strange comet in the night like a canopy in the air, which was a thing observed all over England. From Lance-level we went to M[r] Dulon's where we continued about a week and had great entertainment and at that time kept a fast by reason of the plague which was then generally observed all over England. From M[r] Dulon's we went to Barton to one M[rs] Dormer's where M[rs] Humphrie her mother and she entertained us with great kindness. From thence we went often to the court at Woodstock where my aunt of Bath followed her suit to the King, and my mother wrote letters to the King, and her means was by my Lord Fenton and to the Queen by my Lady of Bedford. My father at this time followed his suit to the King about the border lands, so that sometimes my mother and he did meet by chance, where their countenance did show the dislike they had of one another, yet he would speak to me in a slight fashion, and give me his blessing. While we lay here we rid through Oxford once or twice, but whither we went I remember not. There we saw the Spanish Ambassador who was then new come into England about the peace.

---

34 Arabella Stuart (1575–1615), the ill-fated daughter of Charles Stuart, 5th Earl of Lennox, and Elizabeth Cavendish. She was imprisoned after marrying William Seymour, 2nd Duke of Somerset, in 1610 in a secret ceremony. Both Arabella and William had credible claims to the throne. William is the brother of Lord Beauchamp mentioned in the diary, who was married to Sackville's sister Anne.

Not long before Michaelmas my self, my cousin Frances Bourchier, Mrs Goodwin and Mrs Hawkridge waiting on us went in to my mother's coach from Barton to Cookham, where my uncle Russell, his wife and son[13] then lay. From thence the next day we went to Nonsuch where Prince Henry and her Grace lay where I stayed about a week and left my cousin Frances there who was proposed to continue with her Grace, but I came back by Cookham and came to Barton before my Aunt of Bath came in to the country.

---

13 William Russell, Elizabeth Long, and their son Francis Russell (1593-1641), referred to as "my cousin Russell" in the later diary.

While we lay at Barton I kept so ill a diet with Mrs Mary Cary and Mrs Harrison in eating fruit so as I fell shortly after into the green sickness. From this place my aunt of Bath having little hope of her suit took her leave of my mother and returned into the West Country. While they lay at Barton my mother and my aunt paid for the charge of the house equally. Some week or fortnight after my aunt was gone, which was about Michaelmas, my Lady went from Barton to Green's Norton and lay one night at my cousin Thomas Sellinger's where we saw old Mr Hicklin, where he and his daughter preferred William Pond to serve my Lady. To this place we came about ten o' the clock in the night and I was so weary as I could not tell whether I should sleep or eat first. The next day we went to North Hall where we found my aunt of Warwick something ill and melancholy. She herself had not been there passing a month but lay at Sir Moyle Finch's in Kent by reason of the great plague, which was then much about North Hall. Not long after Michaelmas my uncle Russell, my aunt Russell his wife, their son, my Lord of Bedford, my mother and I gave all allowance to Mr Chambers my aunt's steward, in which sort the House was kept during our being there. I used to wear my hair coloured velvet gown every day, and learned to sing and play on the bass viol of Jack Jenkins, my aunt's boy. Before Christmas my cousin Frances was sent for from Nonsuch to North Hall by reason that her Grace was to go from thence to be brought up with Lady Harington in the country. All this time we were merry at North Hall, my cousin Frances Bourchier, my cousin Francis Russell and I did use to walk much in the garden and were great with each other. At this time I fell directly in to the green sickness. Now there was much talk of a masque which the Queen had at Winchester and how all the ladies about the court had gotten such ill-names that it was grown a scandalous place, and the Queen herself much fallen from her former greatness and reputation she had in the world.

The Diary of 1616–1619

The first day Sir George Villiers[1] was made Master of the Horse, and my Lord of Worcester[2] Lord Privy Seal.

Upon the 5th, being Twelfth Eve, my Lord played at Dice in the Court and won nine hundred twenty shilling pieces[3] and gave me but twenty.

---

1 George Villiers (1592–1628) was introduced to King James in 1614 and began his rapid ascent in favour, a part of which is charted in *The Diary*, as he rises from knight to earl in two years. Of this time, Clifford wrote to her mother that "we have a changing world here, and I hope for the better, for my worthy Lady Shrewsbury is come out of the Tower and has her full liberty, my Lord of Pembroke is Lord Chamberlain, Sir George Villiers is Master of the Horse...." The Master of the Horse was nominally in charge of everything to do with the stables and kennels of the sovereign, but was more importantly a member of the Privy Council and one of the highest ranking officers of the King's household.

2 Edward Somerset (1553–1628), 4th Earl of Worcester. He had previously been Master of the Horse.

3 Equal to £900.

1616

January

Upon New Year's Day I kept my Chamber all the day, my Lady Rich[1] and my sister Sackville[2] dining with me, but my Lord[3] and all the company at Dorset House[4] went to see the masque at the Court.[5]

Upon the 3rd died my Lady Thomas Howard's[6] son.

Upon the 4th I went to see my Lady of Effingham[7] at my Lady Lumley's[8] and went to sup at my Lady Shrewsbury's[9] where there was a great company and a play after supper.

Upon the 6th, being Twelfth Day,[10] I supped with my Lady of

---

1 Frances, daughter of Sir William Hatton and Elizabeth Gawdy; raised by Hatton's second wife Elizabeth Cecil (Lady Hatton of the 1603 memoir) and wife of Sir Robert Rich, later 2nd Earl of Warwick. She should not be confused with her step-sister Frances Hatton (1603–45), subject of a kidnapping attempt involving Edward Sackville and John Villiers; or, after December 1616, with her stepmother-in-law, Frances Wray, who was also known as Lady Rich and is mentioned below. This is a good example of how the changes in women's names due to marriage complicate the task of recognizing or appreciating their histories.

2 Mary Curzon (1586–1645), daughter and heiress of George Curzon; wife of Edward Sackville, Clifford's brother-in-law.

3 Clifford refers to her husband as "my Lord" throughout the diary.

4 Their London home.

5 "The Golden Age Restored," by Ben Jonson.

6 Elizabeth (d. 1672), daughter and co-heir of William Cecil, married to Thomas Howard, who was first cousin to Sackville. She is the daughter of "Lady Cecil" of the 1603 memoir.

7 Anne, daughter of John, Lord St. John, and widow of William, Lord Howard of Effingham; related to Clifford through the St. John family. She was a favourite of Queen Anne's; it is Clifford's hope that she can offer help with the politicking around the agreement.

8 Elizabeth (d. 1618), daughter of John, Lord Darcy of Chiche, second wife of John (1534–1609), 7th Baron Lumley. He was an influential peer under Elizabeth, and an antiquarian, painter, and book collector.

9 Mary (1556–1632), daughter of William Cavendish and Elizabeth (Bess) Hardwick, wife of Gilbert Talbot, 7th Earl of Shrewsbury. Talbot was the wealthiest man in England other than the King. Their daughter is "Lady Arundel" of the next entry.

10 The last day of the traditional Christmas holiday; the Feast of the Epiphany, and the occasion for much revelry. Shakespeare's play *Twelfth Night, or What you Will* is written in the spirit of this festivity, and probably for the celebration of that day.

This twelfth day at night my Lady of Arundel made a great supper to the Florentine Embassador, where I was and carried my sister Sackville along with me so she sat with me in the box to see the masque. This night the Queen wore a gown with a long train which my Lady Bedford bore up.

Upon the 14th my Lord supped at the Globe.

Arundel[11] and sat with her in her Ladyship's box to see the masque which was the second time it was presented before the King and Queen.

Upon the 8th I went to see Lady Raleigh[12] at the Tower.

Upon the 21st, being Sunday, my Lord and I went to Church at Sevenoaks[13] to grace the Bishop of St. David's prayers.

February 1616

All the time I stayed in the Country[14] I was sometimes merry and sometimes sad, as I heard news from London.[15]

Upon Thursday the 8th of February I came to London, my Lord Bishop of S[t] David's[16] riding with me in the coach and Mary Neville.[17] This time I was sent up for by my Lord about the Composition with my Uncle of Cumberland.[18]

Upon Monday the 12th, my Lord Roos was married to M[rs] Anne Lake,[19] the Secretary's daughter.

---

11 Alethea (1584–1654), daughter of Gilbert Talbot and Mary Cavendish above; wife of Thomas Howard (1586–1646), 21st Earl of Arundel. She and her husband were the most important private art collectors of the century in England. Portraits of her by Daniel Mytens, Anthony van Dyck, and Peter Paul Rubens survive.

12 Elizabeth Throckmorton (1565–1647), wife of Sir Walter Raleigh. She and her husband were first imprisoned as punishment for their secret marriage. She was party to the conspiracy in 1603 to put Arabella Stuart on the throne; she was not imprisoned, but lived with her husband in the Tower from 1608 until his execution in 1618. According to Kathy Lynn Emerson, "she had his head embalmed and kept it with her in a red leather bag until her death."

13 The town near Knole House.

14 At Knole House.

15 I.e., news about her lawsuits, and Sackville's attempts to persuade her to agree to the proposed settlement.

16 Richard Milbourne, who was consecrated in July 1615.

17 A daughter of Mary Sackville (d. before 1616), Richard's aunt, and Henry Neville, later 7th Lord Abergavenny; she was goddaughter to Richard. It was customary for the nobility and gentry to have their children live with other parts of the extended family or community.

18 Francis Clifford (1559–1641), 4th Earl of Cumberland, son of Henry Clifford, 2nd Earl, and Anne Dacres; brother of George Clifford, and Clifford's opponent in the lawsuits over her patrimony.

19 William Cecil, Baron Ros or Roos (d. 1618), son of William Cecil and Elizabeth Manners, and Anne Lake, daughter of Thomas Lake, Secretary of State, and Mary Ryder. The course of this marriage is referred to

Upon Thursday the 15th my Lord and I went to see my young Lady Arundel and in the afternoon my Lady Willough-by[20] came to see me. My Lady Gray[21] brought my Lady

---

again. Briefly, the couple soon separated, but there was a dispute over the disposition of property; Anne's brother assaulted Roos; Anne and her mother threatened to charge Lord Roos with an incestuous rela-tion with Frances Brydges, the Countess of Exeter and the wife of Lord Roos' grandfather, Thomas Cecil. Roos took refuge in Italy and died in Naples in 1618. Anne Lake continued her actions against the Countess, forging letters about the incest, and alleging that the Count-ess had tried to poison Anne and her father. Late in 1618 Lady Exeter charged four members of the Lake family with defamation in the Star Chamber. They were found guilty, sentenced to prison, and fined more than £20,000. Anne confessed her guilt in 1619 and was then released from prison.

20 This is another example of the challenge of sorting out women in the historical record. There are three women to whom this title could refer at this time. First, there is Mary (1554–1624), daughter of John de Vere, 16th Earl of Oxford (1512–62), and Margery Golding; widow of Peregrine Bertie, 12th Baron Willoughby d'Eresby (1555–1601); this is the least likely case, as Clifford would normally call a dowager baroness "Old Lady Willoughby." Second, it could be Mary de Vere's daughter-in-law, Elizabeth (1586?–1654), daughter of Edward, Lord Monatgue and wife of Robert Bertie, 13th Baron Willoughby d'Eresby and later first Earl of Lindsey. Third, it could be Frances, daughter of John Manners, 4th Earl of Rutland (d. 1588) and Elizabeth Charleton; wife of William Willoughby, 3rd Baron of Parham (d. 1617) and aunt of Lord Roos, mentioned in the previous paragraph. The context favours the third choice, but the second is possible as the individual referred to as Lord Willoughby in the entry for the 21st of February below is Robert Bertie.

21 Elizabeth Talbot (1582–1651), sister of Lady Arundel above, wife of Henry Grey or Gray, later 7th Earl of Kent. Two works published in several editions after her death are attributed to her. One is medical, entitled *A choice manual of rare and select secrets in physick and chyrurgery collected and practised by the Right Honourable, the Countesse of Kent, late deceased*, and the other is called *A true gentlewoman's delight wherein is contained all manner of cookery: together with preserving, conserving, drying, and candying*.

Carr[22] to play at glecko[23] with me when I lost fifteen pounds to them, they two and my Lady Grantham[24] and Sir George Manners[25] supping here with me.

Upon the 16th my Lady Grantham and M[rs] Newton came to see me. My Lady Grantham told me the Archbishop of Canterbury[26] would come to me the next day and she persuaded me very earnestly to agree to this business which I took as a great argument of her love. Also my Cousin Russell[27] came to see me the same day and chid me and told me of all my faults and errors in this business and he made me weep bitterly, then I spoke a prayer and went to see my Lady Wotton[28] at Whitehall where we walked five or six turns but spoke nothing of this business though her heart and mine were both full of it.

---

22 Frances Howard (1590–1632), daughter of Thomas Howard, 1st Earl of Suffolk, and Katherine Knyvett, married to Robert Carr, later Earl of Somerset. She is mentioned again in March and May as Lady Somerset. She was spectacularly divorced from her first husband, Robert Devereux, 3rd Earl of Essex. There was an examination in court of her person to assure virginity, thus supporting the claim that the marriage was unconsummated; later it was alleged that she used magic, with the help of the astrologer Simon Forman, the sinister Mrs. Anne Taylor, and a little doll made of wax, to make Essex impotent. She married the King's favourite, Robert Carr, in 1611. Frances and Carr (created Earl of Somerset in 1613) were convicted in May 1616 of the murder of Sir Thomas Overbury, a court figure who had cast suspicion on the claims made in the divorce proceedings. They were said to have murdered him by gifts of poisoned delicacies while he was held in the Tower on minor, trumped-up charges. Lady Somerset was pardoned and released soon after this date, but her husband lived out his life in the Tower.

23 A three-person card game now known as "gleek."

24 This is probably the wife of Sir Thomas Grantham of Lincoln, knighted by James in 1603. No other information is known about her.

25 George Manners, 3rd son of John Manners, 4th Earl of Rutland (d. 1588), and Elizabeth Charleton; brother of the third choice for "Lady Willoughby" above.

26 George Abbot (1562–1633). At Oxford he was private chaplain to Thomas Sackville (Richard's grandfather), who helped him with his further career. He was made Archbishop of Canterbury in 1611. He is here acting in his office as Archbishop, but his loyalty to the Sackville family would and could not be set aside in the matter.

27 Francis Russell (1593–1641), mentioned in 1603 when he was a child.

28 Margaret (1581–1659), daughter of William, 3rd Baron Wharton, and George Clifford's sister Frances, second wife of Sir Edward Wotton; Clifford's first cousin.

After it was concluded I should go into the north to my mother then my Uncle Cumberland and my Cousin Clifford came down into the Gallery, for they had all this while been in some other chamber with lawyers and others of their party.

From hence I went to the Abbey at Westminster where I saw the Queen of Scots her tomb and all the other tombs and came home by water where I took an extreme cold.

Upon the 17th, being Saturday, my Lord Archbishop of Canterbury, my Lord William Howard,[29] my Lord Roos, my Cousin Russell, my Brother Sackville[30] and a great company of men of note were all in the gallery at Dorset House where the Archbishop of Canterbury took me aside and talked with me privately one hour and a half and persuaded me both by divine and human means to set my hand to these agreements but my answer to his Lordship was that I would do nothing till my Lady[31] and I had conferred together. Much persuasion was used by him and all the company, sometimes terrifying me and sometimes flattering me, but at length it was concluded that I should have leave to go to my Mother and send an answer by the 22nd of March next whether I will agree to this business or not and to this prayer my Lord of Canterbury and the rest of the Lords have set their hands.

Next day was a marvellous day to me through the mercy of God for it was generally thought that I must either have sealed to the agreement or else to have parted with my Lord.

Upon the 19th I sent Tobias and Thomas Beddings to most of the Ladies in the town of my acquaintance to let them know of my journey into the North.

---

29 William Howard (1563–1640), Sackville's uncle; his wife was a relative of Clifford's. His home was Naworth, near Brougham, one of the disputed Clifford castles, where Margaret is now living. Clifford trusted him, and tried many times to mitigate the anger between him and her mother. He helped Sackville and Clifford to secure Margaret's effects upon her death. Ultimately, he sided with Sackville in the suits, or rather with the combination of Sackville and Francis and Henry Clifford.

30 Edward Sackville (1591–1652), younger brother of Richard. Educated at Oxford, he held many important posts, including Governor of Bermuda, Privy Counsellor under Charles I, and Lord Chamberlain for Henrietta Marie. He inherited the earldom when Richard died in 1624, and with it the many debts his brother had accumulated. His interest is firmly with Richard in the matter, as the cash settlement would help bolster the wealth of his family.

31 Margaret is presently living at Brougham castle in Westmorland, one of her jointure properties and part of the disputed inheritance. In a letter of 1615 Clifford wrote to her, sending "wishes of all comforts and happinesses your heart can desire, that those castles of Appleby and Brougham that in themselves be so melancholy may yet be places of joy and contentment to you."

At this meeting my Lord's footman Acteon[4] won the race from the northern man, and my Lord won both at [blank] and stayed there a fortnight with my Lord of Essex and my Lord Willoughby. Before they came to London they heard that three of Lord Abergavenny's sons[5] were drowned between Gravesend and London and about this time the marriage between Sir Robert Sidney[6] and my Lady Dorothy Percy[7] was openly known.

---

4 Acteon Curvett, Chief Footman.
5 Sons of Edward Neville (d. 1621), 6th Baron Abergavenny, and Rachel Lennard (d. 1613), and brothers of Henry Neville who was married to Sackville's sister Mary.
6 Robert Sidney (1595–1677), later 2nd Earl of Leicester, son of Robert Sidney (1563–1626) and Barbara Gamage (1562–1621).
7 Dorothy (b. 1598), daughter of Dorothy Devereux (1564–1619) and Henry Percy (1564–1632), 9th Earl of Northumberland.

Upon the 20th came my Lord Russell and my Cousin Gorge.[32] In all this time of my troubles my Cousin Russell was exceeding careful and kind to me.

Upon the 21st my Lord and I began our journey northward. The same day my Lord Willoughby came and broke his fast with my Lord. We had two coaches in our company with four horses apiece and about six and twenty horsemen, I having no women to attend me but Willoughby and Judith, Thomas Glemham[33] going with my Lord.

Upon the 26th we went from Lichfield to Croxall, and about a mile from Croxall my Lord and I parted, he returning to Lichfield and I going on to Derby. I came to my lodging with a heavy heart considering how things stood between my Lord and I. I had in my company ten persons and thirteen horses.

March 1616

Upon the 1st we went from the parson's house over the dangerous moors being eight miles, and afterwards the ways being so dangerous that the horses were fain to be taken out of the coach and the coach to be lifted down the hills. This day Rivers' horse fell from a bridge into the River. We came to Manchester about ten o'clock at night. Upon the 20th in the morning my Lord William Howard with his son my Cousin William Howard and Mr John Dudley[34]

---

32 Sir Edward Gorge, son of Sir Thomas Gorge(s) (d. 1610) and Helena von Snakenborg (1549–1635). According to Nichols, the family claimed affiliation with the Russells, Earls of Bedford, which is confirmed by Clifford's reference here.

33 Possibly one of the children of Anne Sackville, Sackville's aunt, and Sir Henry Glemham of Suffolk. If so, he was knighted in 1617. He is referred to in the diary as late as 21 June 1619 as simply "Tom Glemham," but "Sir Thomas Glemham" is also recorded, although this reference is in a marginal note for 21 June 1618, and the marginal notes appear to have been added after the time at which the main entries were made.

34 Again, while this name is not significant in terms of history, it is interesting in that almost all of the people that Clifford deals with in these proceedings are related to her in one way or another: the aristocracy, in other words, is extremely tribal, which works both for and against her, and of which she is very conscious. This is probably one of the illegitimate children of Edward Sutton, Lord Dudley (d. 1643), and Elizabeth, daughter of William Tomlinson. He is later referred to as Clifford's cousin; the family did have a distant connection to the Cliffords, and by marriage to the Sackvilles. He is probably then also the brother of Mary, referred to below as "Lady Hume," and "Mrs Mary Dudley."

This Lent I kept very strictly and did eat nothing that had butter in it.

Upon the 24th my Lady Somerset was sent from Blackfriars by water as prisoner to the Tower.

As I came away I heard that John Digby[8] who was late Embassador in Spain was made Vice Chamberlain to the King and swore one of the Privy Council.

---

8 John Digby (1580–1654), later 1st Earl of Bristol, son of Sir George Digby and Abigail Hevingham; a diplomat and statesman. He had recently returned from failed negotiations for the marriage of Prince Charles and the Spanish princess, the Infanta Maria; he went again in 1617 on the same task.

came hither to take the answer of my mother and my self, which was a direct denial to stand to the Judges' Award.[35] The same day came Sir Timothy Whittington hither who did do all he could to mitigate the anger between my Lord William Howard and my mother, so as at the last we parted all good friends and it was agreed upon that my men and horses should stay, and we should go up to London together after Easter.

Upon the 22nd my Lady and I went in a Coach together to Whinfield and rid about the Park and saw all the woods.

Upon the 27th my Cousin William Howard sent me a dapple grey nag for my own saddle.

Upon the 31st, being Easter Day, I received with my Lady in the chapel at Brougham.

April 1616

Upon the first came my Cousin Charles Howard and Mr John Dudley, with letters to shew that it was my Lord's pleasure that the men and horses should come away without me and after much falling out betwixt my Lady and them all my folks went away, there being a paper drawn to show that their going was by my Lord's direction and contrary to my will.[36] At night I sent two messengers to my folks to entreat them to stay. For some two nights my mother and I lay together and had much talk about this business.

Upon the 2nd I went after my folks in my Lady's coach, she bringing me a quarter of a mile in the way where she and I had a heavy and grievous parting.[37] Most part of the way I did rid on horseback behind Mr Hodgson.

---

35 The judges were the Attorney General (Francis Bacon), the Solicitor General (Sir Henry Yelverton), the Lord Chief Justice of the Common Pleas (Sir Henry Hobart), and the Lord Chief Justice of the King's Bench (Sir Henry Montagu). See introduction, 22.

36 In his anger at her refusal to sign the agreement, Sackville is trying to effect the threatened separation by ordering his servants back to his side. The "paper" was drawn up to show that Clifford was not sending his men back of her own accord, which might make it look like she had left him and open her to charges of desertion. It reads in part, "now my desire is that all the world shall know that this stay of mine proceeds only from my husband's command, contrary to my consent or agreement." On reflection, she thinks this is insufficient, sends after her retinue, and follows them.

37 In 1654 Clifford erected a monument in this place, called the Countess' Pillar.

Not long after this my cousin Sir Oliver St Johns[9] was made Lord Deputy of Ireland in the place of Sir Arthur Chichester.[10]

Upon the 17th my mother sickened as she came from prayers being taken with a cold chillness in the manner of an ague,[11] which afterwards turned to great heats and pains in her side so as when she was opened it was plainly perceived to be an impostume.[12]

---

9 Sir Oliver St. Johns (1559–1630), later Viscount Grandison and Baron Tregoz, a career soldier who served as Lord Deputy of Ireland until 1622. He is Clifford's great-uncle on her mother's side.

10 Sir Arthur Chichester (1563–1625), Baron of Belfast. He was made Lord Treasurer of Ireland after stepping down as Lord Deputy.

11 An acute or violent fever, especially malarial, marked by successive fits. As later with the Child's illness, it can refer to the shivering stage of the sequence (cold, hot, sweating).

12 A swelling, cyst, or tumour; possibly an infection.

Upon the 10th we went from Ware to Tottenham where my Lord's coach with his men and horses met me and came to London to Lesser Dorset House.

Upon the 11th I came from London to Knole where I had but a cold welcome from my Lord. My Lady Margaret[38] met me at the outermost gate and my Lord came to me in the drawing chamber.

Upon the 12th I told my Lord how I had left those writings which the Judges and my Lord would have me sign and seal behind with my mother.

Upon the 13th my Lord and Thomas Glemham went up to London.

Upon the 17th came Tom Woodgate[39] from London but brought no news of my going up which I daily look for.

Upon the 18th Basket[40] came hither and brought me a letter from my Lord to let me know this was the last time of asking me whether I would set my hand to this award of the Judges.

Upon the 19th, being Friday, I returned my answer to my Lord that I would not stand to this Award of the Judges what misery soever it brought me to. This morning the Bishop of St David's and my little child were brought to speak to me.

About this time I used to rise early in the morning and go to the standing in the garden and taking my prayer book with me and beseech God to be merciful towards me and to help me in this as He hath always done.

---

38 Clifford's daughter, born 2 July 1614 at Dorset House. She is usually referred to as the "Child," although after her fifth birthday she is called "my Lady Margaret" more often. There is a van Dyck portrait of her with her husband Thomas Tufton; as a child, she was painted by Paul van Somer (see 22 July 1619).

39 Listed in the catalogue of the Knole servants printed in Sackville-West's edition of the diaries and memoir as "Yeoman of the great chamber." A yeoman was a servant of higher rank, between a "sergeant" and a "groom."

40 Peter Basket is listed in the Knole catalogue as "Gentleman of the Horse."

About this time I heard my sister Beauchamp[13] was with child.

My Lady Margaret lay in the great house at Dorset House for now my Lord and his whole company were removed from the little house where I lay when I was first married.

About this time died my Lord of Shrewsbury[14] at his house in Broad Street.

Upon the 10th early in the morning I writ a very earnest letter to my Lord to beseech him that I might not go to the little house which was appointed for me, but that I might go to Horsely and sojourn there with my child and to the same effect I wrote to my sister Beauchamp.

13 Anne Sackville, Richard's sister, wife of Edward Seymour, Lord Beauchamp (1587–1618).
14 Gilbert Talbot (1552–1616), 7th Earl of Shrewsbury.

May 1616

Upon the 1ˢᵗ Rivers came from London in the afternoon, and brought me word that I should neither live at Knole nor Bollbroke.[41]

Upon the 3ʳᵈ came Basket down from London and brought me a letter from my Lord by which I might see that it was his pleasure that the Child should go the next day to London which at the first was somewhat grievous to me but when I considered that it would both make my Lord more angry with me and be worse for the Child, I resolved to let her go after I had sent for Mʳ Legge and talked with him about that and other matters and wept bitterly.

Upon the 4ᵗʰ being Saturday between ten and eleven o'clock the Child went into the litter to go to London, Mʳˢ Bathurst and her two maids with Mʳ Legge and a good company of the servants going with her. In the afternoon came a man called Hilton born in Craven from my Lady Willoughby to see me which I took as a great argument of her love being in the midst of all my misery.

Upon the 8ᵗʰ I dispatched a letter to my mother.

Upon the 9ᵗʰ I received a letter from Mʳ Bellasis how extreme ill my mother had been and in the afternoon came Humphrey Golding's son with letters that my mother was exceeding ill, and as they thought in some danger of death so as I sent Rivers presently to London with letters to be sent to her and certain cordials and conserves. At night was brought me a letter from my Lord to let me know that his determination was the Child should go live at Horsely and not come hither anymore, so this was a grievous and sorrowful day to me.

Upon the 10ᵗʰ Rivers came from London and brought me word from Lord William that she was not in such danger as I feared.

---

41 Sackville does not carry through with her eviction, but he does take the child away, and his use of Mathew Caldicot (see the 11th, below) as an intermediary during these weeks was designed to provoke her further. Bollbroke was Clifford's chief jointure-property—that is, part of what was assigned for her use and support in the event of her husband's death before her. Her jointure was not legally settled at this time, because her dowry had not been paid, and was not finalized until just before Richard's death. The jointure properties were not just for her sustenance; when he died, Richard left provision for his daughters' dowries, which was to come from properties in which Anne had been given a life-interest as part of her jointure (Spence 83).

The same day came the Stewards from London whom I expected would have given warning to many of the servants to go away because the audit was newly come up.[42]

Upon the 11th being Sunday before M[r] Legge[43] went away I talked with him an hour or two about all the business and matters between me and my Lord, so as I gave him better satisfaction and made him conceive a better opinion of me than ever he did. A little before dinner came Mathew[44] down from London, my Lord sending me by him the wedding ring that my Lord Treasurer and my Old Lady[45] were married withal, and a message that my Lord would be here the next week, and that the Child would not as yet go down to Horsely, and I sent my Lord the wedding ring that my Lord and I was married with. The same day came M[r] Marsh[46] from London and persuaded me much to consent to this agreement.

The 12th at night Grosvenor[47] came hither and told me how my Lord had won two hundred pounds at cocking, and that my Lord of Essex and my Lord Willoughby who were on my Lord's side won a great deal, and how there were some unkind words passed between my Lord and his side and Sir William Herbert[48] and his side. This day my Lady Grantham sent me a letter about these businesses between my Uncle Cumberland and me and I returned her an answer.

---

42 Clifford expects the examination of Sackville's accounts will result in economies.

43 Edward Legge is Steward at Knole. As such he is in charge of the household expenditures and with managing the servants and the household materials in that respect.

44 Mathew Caldicott is listed in the catalogue of the household at Knole as "my Lord's favourite"; Sackville's closest personal servant, a friend, confidante, and possibly lover. Clifford often blames him for her turbulent relations with Sackville.

45 Thomas Sackville (1536–1608), 1st Earl of Dorset, Lord Treasurer under Elizabeth and reappointed for life by James, poet and playwright, and his wife Cecily Baker (d. 1615). They were Sackville's grandparents.

46 Marsh is Clifford's personal servant, listed in the Knole catalogue as "Attendant on my Lady." His duties include reading to her and writing for her.

47 Grosvenor is listed in the Knole catalogue as "Gentleman Usher," which is a deputy to the Steward, and in charge of the private chambers of the principals of the household.

48 Possibly Sir William Herbert (1572?–1655), later Lord Powis, son and heir of Edward Herbert, the second son of William Herbert, 1st Earl of Pembroke, and Mary Stanley.

My Lord was at London when my mother died, but he went to Lewes before he heard the news of her death.

Upon the 20th went my child with Mary Neville and Mrs Bathurst to West Horsely from London. Mary Hitchin went with her for still she lay in bed with Lady Margaret.

All this time my Lord was at London where he had infinite and great resort coming to him. He went much abroad to cocking, to bowling alleys, to plays and horse races and was commended by all the world. I stayed in the country having many times a sorrowful and heavy heart, and being condemned by most folks because I would not consent to the agreements, so as I may truly say I am like an owl in the desert.[49]

Upon the 13th, being Monday, my Lady's footman Thomas Petty brought me letters out of Westmorland by which I perceived how very sick and full of grievous pain my dear mother was so as she was not able to write herself to me, and most of her people about her feared she would hardly recover [from] this sickness. At night I went out and prayed to God my only helper that she might not die in this pitiful case.

The 14th Richard Jones came from London to see me and brought a letter with him from Mathew the effect whereof was to persuade me to yield to my Lord's desire in this business at this time or else I was undone for ever.

Upon the 15th my Lord and my cousin Cecily Neville came down from London, my Lord lying in Leicester chamber and I in my own.

Upon the 17th my Lord and I after supper had talk about these businesses, Mathew being in the room, where we all fell out, and so we parted for that night.

Upon the 18th being Saturday in the morning my Lord and I having much talk about these businesses we agreed that M[r] Marsh should go presently down to my mother and that by him I should write a letter to persuade her to give over her jointure presently to my Lord and that he would give her yearly as much as it was worth.[50] This day my Lord went from Knole to London.

---

49 Psalm 102:6: "My heart is smitten, and withered like grass; so that I forget to eat my bread. By reason of the voice of my groaning my bones cleave to my skin. I am like a pelican of the wilderness: I am like an owl of the desert. I watch, and am as a sparrow alone upon the house top. Mine enemies reproach me all the day; and they that are mad against me are sworn against me."

50 Because these properties are among the disputed ones, having possession of them would help Sackville come to a beneficial deal with Francis Clifford. Inhabiting the lands, establishing relations with the tenants, securing the loyalty of local officials and neighbouring gentry—these are all factors in not only conducting the business of estates, but in buttressing their ownership.

Upon the 24th, being Friday, between the hours of six and seven at night died my dear mother at Brougham in the same chamber where my father was born, thirteen years and two months after the death of Queen Elizabeth and ten years and four months after the death of my father, I being then 26 years old and four months and the child two years old wanting a month.

At this great meeting at Lewes, my Lord Compton,[15] my Lord Mordaunt,[16] Tom Neville,[17] Jo. Herbert and all that crew with Walter Raleigh,[18] Jack Lewice and a multitude of such company were there. There was bowling, bull-baiting, cards and dice with such sports to entertain the time.

---

15 William (1568–1630), 2nd Lord Compton, later first Earl of Nottingham.
16 John (d. 1642), 5th Baron Mordaunt and later 1st Earl of Peterborough.
17 Thomas Neville (d. 1628), only son of Henry Neville and the late Mary Sackville. He married Frances Mordaunt, daughter of Lord Mordaunt.
18 Walter Raleigh (1593–1618), son of Sir Walter Raleigh and Elizabeth Throckmorton. He was tutored by Ben Jonson. He was killed in battle on his father's last voyage to Guiana.

Upon the 20th, being Monday, I dispatched Mr Marsh with letters to my mother about the business aforesaid. I sent them unsealed because [so that] my Lord might see them.

My brother Compton[51] and his wife kept house at West Horsely and my brother Beauchamp[52] and my sister his wife sojourned with them, so as the Child was with both her aunts.

Upon the 22nd Mr Davies[53] came down from London and brought me word that my mother was very well recovered of her dangerous sickness. By him I writ a letter to my Lord that Mr Amherst and Mr Davies might confer together about my jointure, to free it from the payment of debts and all other encumbrances.

Upon the 24th my Lady Somerset was arraigned and condemned at Westminster Hall where she confessed her fault and asked the King's mercy and was much pitied of all the beholders.

Upon the 25th my Lord of Somerset was arraigned and condemned in the same place and stood much upon his innocency.

Upon the 27th, being Monday, my Lord came down to Buckhurst. My Lord Vaux[54] and his Uncle Sir Henry Neville[55] and diverse others came with him, but the Lords that promised to go with him stayed behind agreeing to meet him the next day at Lewes.

Upon the 28th my Lady Selby[56] came hither to see me and told me that she had heard some folks say that I have done well in not consenting to the Composition.

---

51 Sir Henry Compton and Cecily Sackville, Richard's sister.
52 Edward Seymour (1587–1618), Lord Beauchamp, son of Edward
   Seymour (1561–1612) and Honora Rogers. Sackville's brother-in-law.
53 John Davies and Richard Amherst were Clifford's lawyers.
54 Edward Vaux (1591–1662), 4th Baron of Harrowden, son of George
   Vaux, 3rd Baron, and Elizabeth Roper (granddaughter of Thomas
   More). He was raised a Catholic by his mother, who was one of the suspects in the Gunpowder Plot. He spent much time on the continent to
   evade persecution. In 1632 he married Elizabeth Howard, mentioned
   below as "Lady Knollys." They were reputed to have had a longstanding
   affair prior to her husband's death.
55 The limited number of names in the aristocratic pool can also make the
   identification of men difficult. This is Sir Henry Neville (d. 1629), son
   of Sir Henry (1564–1615) and Anne Killigrew. He is not the same
   Henry Neville, later Lord Abergavenny, who is widower of Sackville's
   sister Mary and the father of the Neville children mentioned in the
   diary.
56 Presumably the wife of Sir William, mentioned below. He was knighted
   in 1603. Their home was in Hearne, Kent, and they were neighbours to
   Clifford at Knole.

And on the 30th at night or the 31st my Lord was told the news of my mother's death, he being then at Lewes with all this company.

Upon the 29th Kendall came and brought me the heavy news of my mother's death, which I held as the greatest and most lamentable cross that could befall me. Also he brought her will along with him, wherein she appointed her body should be buried in the parish church of Anwick, which was a double grief to me when I considered her body should be carried away, and not be interred at Skipton, so I took that as a sign that I should be disinherited of the inheritance of my forefathers.[57] The same night I sent Hammon[58] away with the will to my Lord who was then at Lewes.

Upon the 30th the Bishop of St David's came to me in the morning to comfort me in these my afflictions, and in the afternoon I sent for Sir William Selby to speak to him about the conveyance of my dear mother's body into Northumberland and about the building of a little chapel wherein I intended she should be buried.

Upon the 31st came Mr Amherst from my Lord to me and brought me word that my Lord would be here on Saturday. The same day Mr Jones brought me a letter from Mr Woolrich[59] wherein it seemed that it was my mother's pleasure her body should be conveyed to what place I appointed and which was some contentment to my aggrieved soul.

June 1616

Upon the 1st being Saturday my Lord left all the company at Buckhurst and came hither about seven o'clock in the morning and so went to bed and slept till twelve, when I made Rivers write my letter to Sir Christopher Pickering,[60] Mr Woolrich, Mr

---

57 Margaret has asked to be buried with her brother Francis rather than on Clifford lands. As Clifford notes on 31 May, however, a codicil to Margaret's will gave her, Clifford, the choice of where to bury her mother's body. Margaret was buried at Appleby, and Clifford commissioned one of the finest funerary monuments of the era for the church there. Margaret may have wished to put her connection with the Clifford family firmly in the earthly realm by returning her remains to her birth family, but Clifford wanted her mother to be signified as part of her own birth family.

58 This may be Thomas Harman, listed in the Knole catalogue as seated with members of the "Kitchen and Scullery."

59 Mr. Woolrich appears to be a lawyer, as is Mr. Jones.

60 Of Yorkshire; knighted in 1607. He is a family friend who had been helping to look after Brougham.

About this time came my Lady Cavendish,[19] Sir Robert Yately and Mr Watson to see me and comfort me after the loss of my mother, and persuaded me much to consent to the agreement.

---

19 Christina or Christian (1595–1675), daughter of Edward, 1st Lord Bruce of Kinloss, and his wife Magdalene; wife of William Cavendish (1591?–1628), later 2nd Earl of Devonshire; the King assisted in this marriage by providing the bride with £10,000 as a dowry. William Herbert wrote a volume of verse in praise of Christina and Lady Rich (mentioned above), published with a dedication to Christina by Donne.

Dombvill and Ralph Conniston[61] wherein I told them that my Lord had determined to keep possession for my right, and to desire that the body might be wrapped in lead[62] till they heard from me. About four of the clock my Lord went to London.

Upon the 4th Mr Marsh and Rivers came down from London and gave me to understand how my Lord by the knowledge and consent of Lord William Howard and the advice of his learned Council[63] had sent a letter down into Westmorland to my Lady's servants and tenants to keep possession for him and me, which was a thing I little expected but gave me much contentment for I thought my Lord of Cumberland had taken possession of her jointure quietly.[64]

Upon the 8th, being Saturday, Rivers and Mr Burridge were sent down into Westmorland with letters from the Council for the restoring of the possession of Appleby Castle as it was at my Lady's decease.

At this time my Lord desired to have me pass my right of the lands in Westmorland to him and my Child and to this end he brought my Lord William Howard to persuade me, and then my Lord told me I should go presently to Knole and so I was sent away upon half an hour's warning leaving my cousin Cecily Neville and Willoughby behind me at London and so went down

---

61 A servant of Margaret's, and one of the executors of her will. He is probably related to Wat Conniston, referred to in the diary several times and listed in the Knole catalogue as attendant to Clifford.

62 Lead was used to preserve the body.

63 The Council of the North, which had the administrative and judicial functions of the Privy Council in the north of England. Howard was not a member of the Council at this time, but he was Commissioner of the Borders, and therefore had influence. Although Howard was distrusted by Margaret, Sackville seems to have persuaded him to act in support of Clifford's claim in this instance.

64 Francis knew of Margaret's death before Clifford did, and he acted quickly to try to secure the estates for himself, as heir to his brother. Sackville quickly retaliated, as he now had hope of realizing the value of the lands. The skirmishes that follow are the upshots of the unclear title—the tenants do not know to whom they should commit themselves, and are under conflicting orders to complete or neglect their usual tasks. It is important to remember that these estates are not simply large homes, but full communities, of which the lord of the manor is head; with competing contenders for the leadership, violence and disorder is inevitable.

This summer the King of Spain's eldest daughter called Anna Maria came into France and was married to the French King and the French King's eldest sister went into Spain and was married to the King of Spain's eldest son.[20]

About this time I went into the Tiltyard to see my Lady Knollys[21] where I saw my Lady Somerset's little child[22] being the first time I ever saw it.

---

20 The marriages of Anna Maria of Austria (daughter of Philip III of Spain) to Louis XII, and of Elizabeth (daughter of Henry IV of France) to Philip (son of Philip III and later Philip IV) were intended to confirm peace between the two nations.

21 Elizabeth (1586–1658), daughter of Thomas Howard, Earl of Suffolk, and Catherine Knyvet; wife of William Knollys (1547–1632), later Earl of Banbury (and reputed mistress of Edward Vaux, mentioned above).

22 Anne (9 December 1615–84), born in the Tower. In 1637 she married Clifford's cousin, William Russell, 5th Earl and first Duke of Bedford. She was painted by van Dyck.

alone with Katherine Buxton[65] about eight o'clock at night so as it was twelve before we came to Knole.[66]

Upon the 15th came the Steward to Knole with whom I had much talk. At this time I wrought very hard and made an end of one of my cushions of Irish stitch work.

Upon the 17th came down Dr Layfield,[67] Ralph Conniston and Basket, Dr Layfield bringing with him the conveyance which Mr Walter had drawn and persuaded me to go up and set my hand to it, which I refused, because my Lord had sent me down so suddenly two days before.

Upon the 19th my Lord came down for me and Doctor Layfield with him, when my Lord persuaded me to consent to his business, and assured me how good and kind a husband he would be to me.

Upon the 20th my Lord and I, Doctor Layfield and Katherine Buxton went up to London and the same day as I take it I passed (by fine before my Lord Hobart) the inheritance of Westmorland to my Lord if I had no heirs of my own body.

Upon the 21st, being Friday, my Lord wrote his letters to my Lord William Howard and gave directions to Mr Marsh to go with them and that the possession of Brougham castle should be very carefully looked to. The same day he went down to Horsely to see the Child at his sister's.

Upon Sunday the 23rd my Lord and I went in the morning to St Bride's church and heard a sermon.

Upon the 24th my Lord and my Lord [blank] and my cousin Cecily Neville went by barge to Greenwich and waited on the King and Queen to chapel and dined at my Lady Bedford's where I met my Lady Hume[68] my old acquaintance. After dinner

---

65 Her father is later identified as Sir Edward Buxton; her name may be "Burton."

66 Sackville's abrupt and aggressive behaviour is attributable to the swiftly changing circumstances in the northern situation, and their distance from it. He wants Clifford to give to him her claim to the northern lands, so that then he can act as their owner, albeit a disputed one.

67 John Layfield (d. 1617), Doctor of Divinity. One of the translators of the King James Version of the Bible; probably chaplain and attendant to George Clifford on his journey to the West Indies in 1598; one of the executors of Margaret's will. Margaret addressed her spiritual autobiography, in letter-form, to him (1591).

68 Mary, illegitmate daughter of Edward Sutton, Lord Dudley, and Mary Tomlinson; second wife of Alexander Home or Hume, 6th Lord Home and 1st Earl of Home. She is later referred to as "Mrs Mary Dudley."

About this time Acteon my Lord's footman lost his race to my Lord Salisbury's[23] Irish footman and my Lord lost 200 twenty shilling pieces by betting on his side.

---

23 William Cecil (1591–1688), 2nd Earl of Salisbury, son of Robert (1563?–1612), 1st Earl, and Elizabeth Brooke (1565–97).

we went up to the gallery where the Queen used me exceeding well.

Upon the 28th came Kendall with letters from my Lord William so as my Lord determined I should go presently into the north.

Upon the 30th, being Sunday, presently after dinner my Lady Robert Rich, my cousin Cecily Neville and I went down by barge to Greenwich where in the gallery there passed some unkind words between my Lady Knollys and me; I took my leave of the Queen and all my friends there. About this time it was agreed between my Lord and me that Mrs Bathurst should go away from the Child and that Willoughby should have the charge of her till I should appoint it otherwise. He gave me his faithful promise that he would come after me into the north as soon as he could, and that the Child should come out of hand so that my Lord and I were never greater friends than at this time.

July 1616

Upon the 1st my Lord Hobart[69] came to Dorset House where I acknowledged a fine to him of a great part of my thirds in my Lord's land but my Lord gave me his faithful word and promise that in Michaelmas term next he would make me a jointure of the full thirds of his living.[70]

About one o'clock I set forward on my journey. My Lord brought me down to the coach side where we had a loving and kind parting.

Upon the 11th Ralph brought me word that it[71] could not be buried at Appleby so I sent Rivers away presently who got their consents.[72] About five o'clock came my cousin William Howard and about five or six of his [men]. About eight we set forward, the body going in my Lady's own coach with my four horses and my

---

69 Sir Henry Hobart (d. 1625), Attorney General from 1606 to 1613, currently Chief Justice of the Court of Common Pleas.

70 "Thirds" is another term for jointure: the reason for this is that a jointure was usually about a third of the value of the husband's estate, and usually about equal to the property brought to the marriage by the wife. Here Clifford has given back the jointure lands settled on her. This will enable Sackville to use them in his dealings.

71 I.e., her mother's body.

72 Appleby Castle was part of the Clifford inheritance, but the town of Appleby was a separately chartered borough; perhaps its permission was needed to bury the body there.

About this time my Lady Exeter[24] was brought to bed of a daughter and my Lady Montgomery[25] of a son being her first son.

---

24 Frances (1580–1632) Brydges, 2nd wife of Thomas Cecil, Earl of
   Exeter. See above 65-67n19, where she is involved with the Roos-Lake
   scandal. This daughter, Georgi-Anna, lived only until 1621.
25 Susan de Vere (1587–1629), daughter of Edward, 17th Earl of Oxford,
   and Anne Cecil; she is the sister of Lady Derby below, and the wife of
   Philip Herbert, Earl of Montgomery and later Earl of Pembroke, who
   would be Clifford's second husband.

self following it in my own coach with two horses and most of the men and women on horseback, so as there was about 40 in the company and we came to Appleby about half an hour after eleven o'clock and about 12 the body was put into the grave. About three o'clock in the morning we came home where I showed my cousin Howard my letter that I writ to my Lord.

Upon the 17th I rid into Whinfield Park and there I willed the tenants that were carrying off hay at Gillian's Bower that they should keep the money in their own hands till it were known who had a right to it.[73]

Upon the 25th I signed a warrant for the killing of a stag in Stainsmore being the first warrant I ever had signed of that kind.[74]

Upon the 29th I sent my folks into the Park to make hay when they being interrupted by my Uncle Cumberland's people, two of my uncle's people were hurt by M[r] Kidd the one in the leg, the other in the foot, whereupon complaint was presently made to the judges at Carlisle and a warrant sent forth for the apprehending of all my folks that were in the field at that time to put in surety to appear at Kendal at the assizes.[75]

August 1616

Upon the 1st day came Baron Bromley[76] and Judge Nicolls[77] to see me as they came from Carlisle and ended the matter about the hurting of my Uncle Cumberland's men and have released my folks that were bound to appear at the assizes.

Upon the 4th my cousin John Dudley supped here and told me that I had given very good satisfaction to the Judges and all the company that was with them.

Upon the 11th came M[r] Marsh and brought a letter of the King's hand to it, that I should not be molested in Brougham

---

73 Here, and in the next passage, Clifford is acting as landlord to the tenants of the estates to which she has laid claim. The entry for 29 July shows that her uncle is trying to assert himself in the same way.

74 This document authorizes the bearer to commit an act otherwise forbidden.

75 That is, they had to deposit a sum of money that would be refunded to them when they made their court appearance; like bail.

76 Sir Edward Bromley, a judge.

77 Sir Augustine Nicolls, a judge on the Northern assize circuit. He died two days after this entry.

Upon Saturday and Sunday my Lord showed me his will whereby he gave all his land to the child saving three thousand five hundred pound a year to my brother Sackville and fifteen hundred pounds a year which is appointed for the payment of his debts, and my jointure excepted, which was a matter I little expected.

Castle and withall how all things went well and that my Lord would be here very shortly.

Upon the 22^(nd) I met my Lord at Appleby towns-end where he came with a great company of horse, Lord William Howard, he and I riding in the coach together and so we came that night to Brougham.[78] There came with him Thomas Glemham, Coventry, Grosvenor, Grey Duck[79] etc., etc. The same night Prudence, Bess, Penelope[80] and some of the men came hither but the stuff was not yet come so as they were fain to lie three or four in a bed.

Upon the 24^(th) in the afternoon I dressed the chamber where my Lady died and set up the green velvet bed where the same night we went to lie there.

Upon the 26^(th) came my cousin Clifford to Appleby, but with far less train than my Lord.

Upon the 27^(th) our folks being all at [Penrith] there passed some ill words between Mathew, one of the keepers, and William Dunn whereupon they fell to blows and Grosvenor, Grey Duck, Thomas Todd and Edwards'[81] swords made a great uproar in the town and three or four were hurt and the man who went to ring the bell fell from a ladder and was sore hurt.[82]

Upon the 28^(th) we made an end of dressing the house in the forenoon and in the afternoon I wrought Irish stitch and my Lord sat and read by me.

---

78 As Clifford points out in her autobiography, this is the only time that Sackville visited her estates.

79 Coventry and Grey Dick or Duck are servants of Sackville's.

80 Prudence Butcher of the Laundry Maids' table; Bess "of the Laundry" and Penelope Tutty, Maid to Lady Margaret, the "Child."

81 Thomas Todd is unidentified; this is the only mention of him in the diary. Edwards is most likely Griffin Edwards, Groom of my Lady's Horse, although the Knole catalogue lists John Edwards as Clerk of the Kitchen and Mr. Edwards as Secretary.

82 This is another instance of the continuing disagreement between Clifford and her uncle: matters were not settled. As Spence writes, earlier in the month a commission of eight local justices had been struck to determine the rightful ownership of the property; not surprisingly, given the difficulty of the case, they had not agreed, but split 5–3 (55). This difficult situation would continue through the fall.

Upon the 18th, being Friday, died my Lady Margaret's old beagle.

Upon the 4th Prince Charles was created Prince of Wales in the Great Hall at Whitehall where he had been created Duke of York about 13 years before.

There was barriers and running at the ring but it was not half so great pomp as was at the creation of Prince Henry.[26] Not long after this Lord Chancellor was created Viscount Brackley[27] and my Lord Knollys Viscount Wallingford,[28] my Lord Coke[29] was displaced and Montagu[30] was made Lord Chief Justice in his place.

---

26 Prince Henry was created Prince of Wales in 1610.

27 Sir Thomas Egerton (1540?–1617), Baron Ellesmere and Viscount Brackley, illegitimate son of Sir Richard Egerton and Alice Sparke; Lord Keeper under Elizabeth.

28 William Knollys (1547–1632), later 1st Earl of Banbury, son of Sir Francis Knollys and Catherine Carey; public servant under Elizabeth and James.

29 Sir Edward Coke (1552–1634), judge and legal writer; he was suspended from legal office 30 June 1616, accused of embezzlement.

30 Sir Henry Montagu (1563–1642), later Earl of Manchester; judge and statesman, here created Chief Justice of the King's Bench.

September 1616[83]

October 1616

Upon the 11th Mrs Samford went to London by whom I sent a very earnest letter to my Lord that I might come up to London.

The 17th was the first day that I put on my black silk grogram gown.

Upon the 22nd came Rivers down to Brougham and brought me word that I could not go to London all this winter.

Upon the 31st I rid into Whinfield in the afternoon. This month I spent in working[84] and reading. Mr Dumbell read a great part of the History of the Netherlands.[85]

November 1616

Upon the 1st I rose betimes in the morning and went up to the pagan tower[86] to my prayers and saw the sun rise.

Upon the 4th I sat in the drawing chamber all the day at my work.

Upon the 9th I sat at my work and heard Rivers and Marsh read Montaigne's Essays,[87] which book they have read almost this fortnight.

Upon the 12th I made an end of the long cushion of Irish stitch

---

83 There are no entries for September in the manuscripts of the diary, although there is this heading. For several days Clifford and Sackville visited with William Howard at Naworth Castle, and on 19 and 20 September their case was pleaded in York before Edmund, Lord Sheffield, President of the Council of the North (a copy of the claim survives in the Hothfield Papers). Again, however, there was no decision, and the matter was headed for determination by the King in the new year, as we see in the entry for January 1617.

84 I.e., on needlework.

85 Identified by Suzuki as *A Tragical History of the Troubles and Civil Wars of the Low Countries, 1559–1581*, translated by Thomas Stock and published in 1583.

86 Probably the Norman keep (or tower) of the castle, which was thought to have been built by Romans. Similar structures at Appleby and Brough are called "Caesar's Tower" and the "Roman Tower."

87 Michel de Montaigne, *The essayes or morall, politike and militarie discourses* (English translation by John Florio, published 1603). These essays and George Sandys' *Relation of a journey* (1615) (which she reports reading in January of 1617) provided Clifford with good examples of plain style, which is characterized by lack of ornament and ostentation in vocabu-

Upon the 23rd Baker, Hookfield, Harry the Caterer, Will [?] and Tom Fool[31] went from hence toward London.

Upon the 24th Basket set out from London to Brougham Castle to fetch me up.

---

31 None of these names are listed in the Knole catalogue. They are probably servants of Margaret Clifford.

which my cousin Cecily Neville began when she went with me to the Bath, it being my chief help to pass away the time to work.

Upon the 19th William Dunn came down from London with letters from my Lord, whereby I perceived there had passed a challenge between him and my cousin Clifford which my Lord sent him by my cousin Cheyny. The Lords of the Council sent for them both and the King made them friends, giving my Lord marvelous good words and willed him to send for me, because he meant to make an agreement himself between us. This going up to London of mine I little expected at this time. By him I also heard that my sister Sackville[88] was dead.

Upon the 20th I spent most of the day in playing at tables.[89] All this time since my Lord went away I wore my black taffeta nightgown and a yellow taffeta waistcoat and used to rise betimes in the morning and walk upon the leads and afterwards to hear reading.

Upon the 22nd I did string the pearls and diamonds my mother left me into a necklace.

Upon the 23rd I went to Mr Blinke's house in Cumberland where I stayed an hour or two and heard music and saw all the house and gardens.

Upon the 26th Thomas Hilton came hither and told me of some quarrels that would be between some gentlemen that took my Lord's part and my cousin Clifford which did much trouble me.

Upon the 29th I bought of Mr Cliborne who came to see me a cloak and a saveguard[90] of cloth laced with black lace to keep me warm in my journey.

December 1616

Upon the 4th came Basket with all the horses to carry me to London but he left the coach behind him at Roos.

---

lary, syntax, and obvious rhetorical structure. Her choice of book here emphasizes how contemporary and modern much of her reading was, and how closely she was aligned with the literary culture of the day: Florio was brother-in-law to her childhood tutor, Samuel Daniel, and Sandys was her father's godson.

88 Sackville had four sisters; this one is not named in any of the sources used by the editor.

89 Backgammon.

90 Outer skirt worn for warmth and to protect clothing when riding.

Upon the 12th William Dunn overtook us at Wentbridge, having found the diamond ring at Roos which I was very glad of.

The 15th day was M[r] John Tufton[32] just eight years old being he what was after married to my first child in the church at S[t] Bartholomew's.

The child was brought down to me in the gallery which was the first time I had seen her after my mother died.

---

32 John, Lord Tufton (1608–1676), son and heir of Nicholas Tufton (1578–1631), 1st Earl of Thanet, and Frances Cecil (1581–1631). He married Margaret Sackville in 1629. This example is evidence that the marginal notes were written later than the main text of the diary, possibly many years after.

Upon the 9th I set out from Brougham Castle towards London. About three o'clock in the afternoon we came to Roos. All this day I rode on horseback on Rivers his mare 29 miles that day.

Upon the 11th I went to York. Three of Lord Sheffield's daughters[91] and Mrs Mathews[92] the Bishop's wife came to see me this night. Mrs Mathews lay with me. About this time died Mr Marshall my Lord's Auditor and Surveyor and left me a purse of ten Angels as a remembrance of his love.

Upon the 18th I alighted at Islington where my Lord was, who came in my Lady Withypole's[93] coach which he had borrowed. My Lady Effingham the widow, my sister Beauchamp and a great many more came to meet me so that we were in all ten or eleven coaches and so I came to Dorset House where the Child met me in the gallery. The house was well dressed up against I came.

Upon the 23rd my Lady Manners[94] came in the morning to dress my head. I had a new black wrought taffeta gown which my Lady St John's[95] tailor made. She used often to come to me and I to her and was very kind one to another. About five o'clock in the evening my Lord and I and the Child went in the great coach to Northampton House, where my Lord Treasurer[96] and all the company commended her and she went down into my Lady Walden's[97] chamber. My cousin Clifford saw her and kissed her

---

91 Some of the nine daughters of Edmund Sheffield, later 1st Earl of Mulgrave, and his wife Ursula (d. 1617), daughter of Sir Thomas Tyrwhitt.

92 Frances (d. 1619), widow of Matthew Parker (d. 1573), wife of Tobie Matthew, Archbishop of York (1546–1628). She was one of five sisters all married to archbishops.

93 Possibly the wife of Sir Edward or Edmund Withypole, knighted in 1599; their home was near Oatlands, Surrey.

94 Katherine, daughter of Francis Manners (1578–1632), 6th Earl of Rutland, and Frances Knyvet. She married George Villiers, Duke of Buckingham on 16 May 1620.

95 Joan (d. 1631), wife of Sir Oliver St. John.

96 Thomas Howard (1561–1626), 1st Earl of Suffolk, Lord Chamberlain 1603–14 and Lord Treasurer 1614–18, when he and his wife were tried and convicted of embezzlement, as Clifford mentions later in the diary.

97 Elizabeth (d. 1633), wife of Theophilus, Lord Howard de Walden.

but I stayed with my Lady Suffolk.[98] All this time of me being at London I was much sent to and visited by many, being unexpected that ever matters should have gone so well with me and my Lord, everybody persuading me to hear and to make an end since the King had taken the matter in hand, so as now I had a new part to play upon the stage of this world.

Upon the 26th I dressed myself in my green satin night gown.

Upon the 27th I dined at my Lady Elizabeth Gray's lodgings in Somerset House where I met my Lady Compton and my Lady Fielding and spoke to them about my coming to the King. Presently after dinner came my Lord thither and we went together to my Lady Arundel's where I saw all the pictures in the gallery and the statues in the lower rooms.[99]

Upon the 28th I dined above in my chamber and wore my night gown because I was not very well which day and yesterday I forgot that it was fish day and eat flesh at both dinners. In the afternoon I played at glecko with my Lady Gray and lost 27lb and odd money.

Upon the 31st this night I sent Thomas Woodgate with a sweet bag[100] to the Queen for a New Year's gift, and a standish[101] to Mrs Hanno, both which cost me about 16 or 17lb.

---

98 Catherine (d. 1633), daughter and co-heiress of Sir Henry Knyvett or Knevet (d. 1598); widow of Richard Rich; wife of Thomas Howard, Earl of Suffolk. She was famous for her beauty, until a bout with smallpox in 1619, which is noted in the diary. She was blamed for corrupting her husband, mentioned above.

99 As mentioned above, the Arundels had the first important collection of European classical and Renaissance art in England. As women, including aristocratic women, rarely traveled outside of the British Isles, the collection gave Clifford and her peers a rare opportunity to see work of this sort. Clifford was an important patron of painters and was painted many times. Although she enjoyed the style of the European high Renaissance, she preferred a more "English" style for her own commissioned portraits: front-facing subjects in shallowly defined spaces, often surrounded by significant objects, and always symbolically, rather than naturalistically, composed in time and space.

100 A fragrant sachet.

101 An inkstand or pot.

As the King passed by he kissed me. Afterwards the Queen came out into the drawing chamber where she kissed me and used me very kindly. This was the first time I either saw the King, Queen or Prince since my coming out of the north.

This was the last time I ever saw my Lady of Northumberland.

1617

January 1617

Upon New Year's Day presently after dinner I went to the Savoy to my Lord Carey's.[1] From thence he and I went to Somerset House to the Queen where I met Lady Derby,[2] my Lady Bedford, and my Lady Montgomery and a great deal of other company that came along with the King and the Prince. My Lord Arundel had much talk with me about the business and persuaded me to yield to the King in all things. From Somerset House we went to Essex House to see my Lady of Northumberland. From thence I went to see my Lady Rich[3] and so came home. After supper I went to see my sister Beauchamp and stayed with her an hour or two for my Lord was at the play[4] at Whitehall that night.

Upon the 2nd I went to the Tower to see my Lady Somerset and my Lord. This was the first time I saw them since their arraignment.

Upon the 5th I went into the Court. We went up into the King's Presence Chamber where my Lord Villiers was created

---

1 Robert Carey (1560–1639), later first Earl of Monmouth. He had a long career as a public servant and became Chamberlain to Prince Charles (that is, master of his household) in 1617. This and other visits made in this month are part of Clifford's campaign to assess and influence opinion of her suits.

2 This is "my young Lady Derby" of the memoir; her husband, William Stanley, inherited the earldom of Derby from his brother, Ferdinando, who died in 1594. William and Ferdinando's mother was Margaret Clifford, George's sister; her portrait is included in *The Great Picture* as one of Clifford's illustrious aunts.

3 This is Frances Wray (d. c. 1634), married to Robert Rich (1559–1619), 3rd Baron Rich; they were married in December of 1616. She is stepmother-in-law to Lady Rich (see note 63n1, above). After her husband was made first Earl of Warwick (of the second creation) in 1618, she is known as "Lady Warwick"—not to be confused with Clifford's "aunt of Warwick" in the memoir.

4 Possibly *The Poor Man's Comfort* by Robert Daborne, performed by Queen Anne's Men.

Earl of Buckingham, my Lord, my Lord of Montgomery[5] and diverse other Earls bringing him up to the King. I supped with my Lord of Arundel and my Lady and after supper I saw the play of the mad lover[6] in the hall.

Upon the 6th being Twelfth Day I went about four o'clock to the Court with my Lord. I went up with my Lady Arundel and ate a scrambling supper[7] with her and my Lady Pembroke[8] at my Lord Duke's[9] lodging. We stood to see the masque[10] in the box with my Lady Ruthven.[11]

Upon the 8th we came down from London to Knole. This night my Lord and I had a falling out about the land.

Upon the 9th I went up to see the things in the closet[12] and began to have M[r] Sandys his Book read to me about the Gov-

---

5 Philip Herbert (1584–1650), 1st Earl of Montgomery and later 4th Earl of Pembroke, younger son of Henry Herbert and Mary Sidney. His brother was Lord Chamberlain to James, and he would be to Charles upon his accession. He and Clifford married in 1630.

6 *The Mad Lover* by John Fletcher, performed by the King's Men.

7 What we would call a buffet, where guests help themselves.

8 Mary (1580–1649), daughter of Gilbert Talbot, 7th Earl of Shrewsbury, and Mary Cavendish; sister of Alethea, "Lady Arundel" and Elizabeth, "Lady Gray"; wife of William Herbert, 3rd Earl of Pembroke. She was an heiress and a patron. Her marriage was unhappy and childless.

9 Lodovic Stuart (1574–1672), Duke of Lennox and later Duke of Richmond. Before James' sons were born, Stuart was next in line for the Scottish throne. He held positions in the Scottish court from a young age and accompanied the King to England when Elizabeth died. In England he was given grants of land, and offices including ambassadorships, and Steward of the Household (1616). His lodgings were at Whitehall.

10 "The Vision of Delight" by Ben Jonson.

11 Although Lady Elizabeth Grey, mentioned above, held the title of Lady Ruthven or Ruthen, this Lady Ruthen is Barbara, daughter of William, 4th Lord Ruthven and 1st Earl of Gowrie, and Dorothea Stewart (a daughter or granddaughter of Margaret Tudor). Her father and her brother Alexander conspired separately against the King and were executed. Despite the forfeiture of her family's estates and honours, Barbara retained her position in Queen Anne's bedchamber, and in 1603 was given a pension of £200. She married Sir John Hume but is not the Lady Hume referred to above.

12 A private room or inner chamber used for devotion and study.

The Queen gave me warning to take heed of putting my matters absolutely to the King lest he should deceive me.

ernment of the Turks,[13] my Lord sitting the most part of the day reading in his closet.

Upon the 10th my Lord went up to London upon the sudden, we not knowing it till the afternoon.

Upon the 16th I received a letter from my Lord that I should come up to London the next day because I was to go before the King on Monday next.

Upon the 17th when I came up my Lord told me I must resolve to go to the King the next day.

Upon the 18th, being Saturday I went presently after dinner to the Queen to the drawing chamber, where my Lady Derby told the queen how my business stood and that I was to go to the King, so she promised me she would do all the good in it she could. When I had stayed but a little while there, I was sent for out, my Lord and I going through my Lord Buckingham's chamber who brought us into the King being in the drawing chamber. He put out all that were there and my Lord and I kneeled by his chair side when he persuaded us both to peace and to put the matter wholly into his hands, which my Lord consented to, but I beseeched His Majesty to pardon me for that I would never part with Westmorland while I lived upon any condition whatsoever. Sometimes he used fair means and persuasions, and sometimes foul means but I was resolved before so as nothing would move me. From the King we went to the Queen's side and brought my Lady St John to her lodging and so went home. At this time I was much bound to my Lord for he was far kinder to me in all these businesses than I expected, and was very unwilling that the King should do me any public disgrace.

Upon the 19th my Lord and I went to the Court in the morning thinking the Queen would have gone to the Chapel, but she did not, so my Lady Ruthen and I and many others stood in the closet[14] to hear the sermon. I dined with my Lady Ruthen. Presently after dinner she and I went up to the drawing chamber,

---

13 *A relation of a journey begun an: Dom: 1610 ... Containing a description of the Turkish Empire, of Aegypt, of the Holy Land, of the remote parts of Italy, and ilands adjoyning* by George Sandys (1615). Sandys translated Ovid's *Metamorphoses* (1621) and wrote paraphrases of the *Psalms*. This work is a travelogue which surveys the cultures, religions, and antiquities of the east, the highlight of which is the journey to the Holy Land, which Sandys describes as despoiled and corrupt by tyrannous rulers and licentious rule.

14 In this case, a private chapel.

where my Lord Duke, my Lady Montgomery, my Lady Burleigh[15] persuaded me to refer these businesses to the King. About six o'clock my Lord came for me so he and I and Lady St John's went home in her coach. This night the masque was danced at the Court but I would not stay to see it because I had seen it already.

Upon the 20th I and my Lord went presently after dinner to the Court. He went up to the King's side about his business. I went up to my Lady Bedford in her Lodgings where I stayed in Lady Ruthen's chamber till towards three o'clock about which time I was sent for up to the King into his drawing chamber when the door was locked and nobody suffered to stay there but my Lord and I, my Uncle Cumberland, my cousin Clifford, my Lord of Arundel, my Lord of Pembroke,[16] my Lord of Montgomery and Sir John Digby. For lawyers there were my Lord Chief Justice Montagu and Hobart, Yelverton[17] the King's solicitor, Sir Ranulphe Crew[18] that was to speak for my Lord of Cumberland and Mr Ireland[19] that was to speak for my Lord and me. The King asked us all whether we would submit to his judgment in this case, to which my Uncle of Cumberland, my cousin Clifford and my Lord answered they would, but I would never agree to it without Westmorland at which the King grew into a great chaff,

---

15 Elizabeth (1579–1654), daughter of Sir Robert Drury and Elizabeth Stafford; 2nd wife of William Cecil (1566–1640), father of Lord Roos mentioned above. Cecil was styled Lord Burleigh or Burghley until suceeding as Earl of Exeter in 1623.

16 William Herbert (1580–1630), 3rd Earl of Pembroke. Tutored by Samuel Daniel (as was Clifford), he was a patron of Jonson, Massinger, and Inigo Jones; and a dedicatee, as Lord Chamberlain, of the 1623 folio edition of Shakespeare's works. His brother Philip, the Earl of Montgomery, would be Clifford's second husband. As he had inherited the title by that time, she is known to history as the dowager Countess of Dorset, Pembroke, and Montgomery.

17 Sir Henry Yelverton (1566–1629); Solicitor General in 1613; he succeeded Francis Bacon as Attorney General in 1617. He was imprisoned in 1620 and again in 1621 on corruption charges, but by 1625 was a judge in the Court of Common Pleas.

18 Sir Ranulphe Crew (1558–1646); judge and MP who helped prosecute Yelverton. In 1625 he was Lord Chief Justice of the King's Bench, but lost his position for refusing to support forced loans (this was one of the issues causing conflict between Parliament and the King, prior to the Civil Wars).

19 Thomas Ireland, a lawyer who was knighted by King James in 1617.

my Lord of Pembroke and the King's solicitor speaking much against me. At last, when they saw there was no remedy, my Lord, fearing the King would do me some public disgrace, desired Sir John Digby to open the door, who went out with me and persuaded me much to yield to the King. My Lord Hay[20] came out to me to whom I told in brief how this business stood. Presently after my lord came from the King where it was resolved that if I would not come to an agreement, there should be an agreement made without me. We went down, Sir Robert Douglas[21] and Sir George Chaworth[22] bringing us to the coach. By the way my Lord and I went in at Worcester House to see my Lord and my Lady,[23] and so came home. This day I may say I was led miraculously by God's providence and next to that I must attribute all my good to the worth and nobleness of my Lord's disposition for neither I nor anybody else thought that I should have passed over this day so well as I thank God I have done.

Upon the 22nd the Child had the sixth fit of her ague.[24] In the morning Mr Smith[25] went up in the coach to London to my Lord to whom I wrote a letter to let him know in what case the Child was, and to give him humble thanks for his noble usage towards me at London. The same day my Lord came down to Knole to see the Child.

---

20 James Hay (d. 1636), later first Earl of Carlisle, husband of Lucy Percy, mentioned below. One of James' Scottish favourites, he is referred to later as "my Lord of Doncaster," which title he received in 1619 when he was sent as ambassador to Germany.

21 Robert Douglas (1574?–1639), later Viscount Belhaven; another Scottish companion of the King's, and at present a Gentleman of the Bedchamber.

22 Sir George Chaworth was knighted by James in 1605 and was later made Viscount Chaworth of Armaugh. He was employed as an ambassador on at least one occasion, so is also a trusted and loyal servant of the King's.

23 Edward Somerset (1553–1628), 4th Earl of Worcester, and his wife Elizabeth Hastings (d. 1621). He held various posts under Elizabeth and James; she was a waiting woman to Elizabeth. Again, Clifford and Sackville are "networking." The Scottish gentlemen and nobles (such as Hay, Douglas, and Chaworth) around the King may be less than favourably disposed towards the squabbles of the English aristocrats, but the Worcesters—loyal to Queen Elizabeth in memory, and resolutely English—provide a counterbalance.

24 An "ague" is a fever; a fit of ague is one of a series of feverish episodes, possibly seizures. They were expected to come with regularity, and they were thought to rid the body of its illness.

25 A physician.

All the time of my being in the country there was much ado at London about my business insomuch that my Lord, my uncle of Cumberland, my cousin Clifford, both the Chief Justices and the counsel of both sides were diverse times with the King about it and that the King hearing it go so directly for me he said there was no law in England to keep me from the Land. There was during this time much cockfighting at the Court, where my Lord's cocks did fight against the King's, although this business was somewhat chargeable to my Lord, yet it brought him into great grace and favour with the King, so as he useth him very kindly and speaketh very often to him and better of him than any other man. My Lord grew very great with my Lord of Arundel.

Upon the 23rd my Lord went up betimes to London again. The same day the Child put on her red baize^{26} coat.

Upon the 25th I spent most of the time in working and going up and down to see the Child. About five or six o'clock her fits took her which lasted six or seven hours.

Upon the 28th at this time I wore a green plain flannel gown that William Dunn made me and my yellow taffeta waistcoat. Rivers used to read to me in Montaigne's Essays and Moll Neville in the Fairy Queen.^{27}

Upon the 30th Mr Amherst the preacher came hither to see me with whom I had much talk. He told me that now they began to think at London that I had done well in not referring this business to the King and that everybody said God had a hand in it.

February 1617

Upon the 4th should have been the Child's fit, but she missed it.

Acteon came presently after dinner with a letter to Tom the groom to meet my Lord at Hampton Court with his hunting horses. At night Thomas Woodgate came from London and brought a squirrel to the Child. My Lord wrote me a letter by which I perceived my Lord was clean out with me and how my enemies have wrought much against me.

Upon the 6th the Child had a kind of grudging of her ague again.

At night Mr Osberton came from London and told me that the Baron de Joiners came out of France and had great entertainment both of the King and Queen and was lodged at Salisbury House.

Upon the 7th presently after dinner Mr Osberton and I had a great deal of talk, he telling me how much I was condemned in the world and what strange censures most folks made of my courses, so as I kneeled down to my prayers and desired God to send a good end to these troublesome businesses, my trust being wholly in him that always helped me.

Upon the 8th the Child had a great fit of her ague again insomuch I was very fearful of her that I could hardly sleep all night, so I beseech God Almighty to be merciful to me and spare her life.

---

26 Fine woolen cloth.
27 Edmund Spenser's epic poem, first published in 1590. The 1615 and 1617 issues of the 1609 edition include a dedicatory verse to George Clifford.

My sister Compton and her husband were now on terms of parting so as they left Horsely, she lying in London. It was agreed that she should have a 100^{lb} a year and he to take the children from her.

My Lord did nothing so often come to my Lord William as he did heretofore for the friendship between them grew cold, my Lord beginning to harbour some ill opinion of him.

He told me the Earl of Buckingham[1] was sworn a Privy Councillor and that my Lord Willoughby's brother, Mr Henry Bertie,[2] was put into the Inquisition at Ancona.

About this time there was much ado between my Lord of Hertford[3] and my Lord Beauchamp about the assurances of lands to Mr William

---

1 I.e., George Villiers.
2 Henry Bertie, younger son of Sir Peregrine Bertie (1555–1601), 12th Lord Willoughby de Eresby, and Mary Vere; brother of Robert mentioned above. The Spanish Inquisition persecuted supposed heretics. In this case, Bertie was probably taken in for his protestant views and allegiances; his later release is connected with him having "turned Papist."
3 Edward Seymour (1539?–1621), 1st Earl of Hertford, eldest son of Edward Seymour (d. 1552), 1st Duke of Somerset, who was executed for treason, and Anne, sole heiress of Thomas of Woodstock. He was married first to Catherine Grey (1539–68), second to Frances Brandon (d. 1598), and third to Frances Howard (d. 1639), who is mentioned below, 177.

Upon the 12th the Child had a little grudging of her ague. Rivers came down presently from London and told me that the Judges had been with the King diverse times about my business but as yet the Award is not yet published, but it is thought it will be much according to the Award formerly set down by the Judges. He told me that he had been with Lord William, who as he thought did not very well like of the agreement considering how he had heretofore showed himself in this business. After supper the Child's nose fell a-bleeding which as I think was the chief cause she was rid of her ague.

Upon the 13th the King made a speech in the Star Chamber about duels and combats,[28] my Lord standing by his chair where he talked with him all the while, he being in extraordinary grace and favour with the King.

Upon the 14th I sent Mr Edwards' man to London with a letter to my Lord, to desire him to come down hither. All this day I spent with Marsh who did write the Chronicles of the year 1607[29] who went in afterwards to my prayers desiring God to send me some end of my troubles, that my enemies might not still have the upper hand of me.

Upon the 16th my Lord came hither from London before dinner and told me how the whole state of my business went and how things went at Court.

Upon the 17th about eight o'clock in the morning my Lord returned to London.

At night Mr Askew[30] came and brought me a letter from my Lady Grantham and told me a great deal of news from London. I signed a bill to give him 7^{lb} at his return from Jerusalem. This day I gave the Child's old clothes to Legge for his wife.

Upon the 21st the Child had an extreme fit of her ague and the Doctor set by her all the afternoon and gave her a salt powder to put in her beer.[31]

---

28 On the occasion of sentencing two duellists.

29 These do not survive. They may have been like the 1603 memoir and the later annual accounts for 1650–75, but they may have been records of the legal proceedings as they began. Clifford gives the impression that she is working her way through her family's history, year by year. The name "chronicles" alludes to the Biblical book of that name, and to works such as Holinshed's history of England.

30 Possibly Egeon Askew (1576–?), a divine and preacher; his family was from Cumberland.

31 Children were commonly given "small" beer, which was low in alcohol, but high in nutrition and calories. It was thought to have medicinal value as well.

Seymour,[4] but my sister Beauchamp grew great with my Lord of Hertford and so got the upper hand.

About this time the curtain in the Child's chamber window was let up to let in the light which had been close shut up for three weeks or a month before.

About this time the King and my Lord Chancellor delivered the seals to Sir Francis Bacon[5] and he was Lord Keeper.

4 Edward, Lord Beauchamp ("my brother Beauchamp") and William Seymour (1588–1660), later 2nd Duke of Somerset, are both grandsons of Hertford. The settlement of lands on the younger man would diminish the value of Beauchamp's estate.
5 Francis Bacon (1561–1626), Attorney General (1613–17), author, and philosopher.

Upon the 22nd Basket went up with the great horses to my Lord because my Lord intended to ride a day with the Prince. Legge came down and brought me word how that the King would make a composition and take a course to put me from my rights to the lands, so as if I did not consider of it speedily it would be too late and how bitter the King stood against me. My sister Compton sent to borrow 12^{lb} so I sent her ten twenty shilling pieces.

Upon the 24th, 26th, 27th, I spent my time in working and hearing Mr Ran[32] read the Bible[33] and walking abroad. My Lord writ me word that the King had referred the drawing and perfecting of the business to the solicitor.

My soul was much troubled and afflicted to see how things go, but my trust is still in God and compare things past with things present and read over the Chronicles.

March 1617

Upon the 1st after supper Mother Dorset[34] came hither to see me and the Child.

Upon the third Petley[35] and Tom[36] went to Buckhurst with my Lord's horses and hounds to meet my Lord there by whom I wrote a letter to my Lord to beseech him that he would take Knole in his way as he goes to London.

Upon the 6th Coach puppied in the morning.

---

32 A chaplain in Sackville's service. He spends much of the next month reading with Clifford, but on 27 March, Sackville forbids him to continue.

33 Both Bibles that Clifford used regularly (the Authorized Version and the Geneva) were Protestant ones. The Russell family was staunchly Protestant, but much of the nobility of the period were Catholic, more or less secretly. Later in the diary Clifford expresses her resolve "never to be a papist."

34 Sackville's stepmother, Anne (d. 1618), dowager Countess of Dorset, daughter of Sir John Spencer of Althorp and Katherine Kyston. According to Clifford, "[s]he was a lady of great wit and spirit" (*Lives* 44). She was also at this time a woman of some substance, as she enjoyed the revenues from three jointures, having married three times.

35 Thomas Petley is listed twice in the Knole catalogue, once as Under Farrier (shoer of horses) and once as Brewer; William Petley is a Footman.

36 Probably Thomas Leonard, Master Hunstman, but possibly Thomas Giles, Groom of the Stables.

The 14th, being Friday, my uncle of Cumberland and my cousin Clifford came to Dorset House to my Lord where he and they signed and sealed the writings and made a final conclusion of my business and did what they could to cut me off from my right, but I referred my cause to God.

Upon this Friday or Saturday died my Lord Chancellor Egerton my Lady Derby's[6] husband.

This day I put on my grogram[7] mourning gown and intend to wear it till my mourning time come out because I was found fault with with all for wearing such ill clothes.[8]

Upon the 17th the women made an end of the sheet of my Lady Sussex[9] her work that is for the Palace which was begun in April, presently after I came out of the north from my mother.

---

6 Alice (d. 1637), daughter of Sir John Spencer of Althorpe (d. 1586) and Katherine Kyston; dowager Countess of Derby and wife of Thomas Egerton (1540?–1617). Milton's *Arcades* was produced in her honour in 1634. Anne, Sackville's stepmother, is her sister, and her first husband was a cousin of Clifford.

7 Probably grosgrain, a densely woven silk with a fine ribbed texture.

8 She has been criticized for not wearing formal enough clothes in respect of her mother's death.

9 Bridget Morison (d. 1623), wife of Robert Radcliffe (1569–1629), 5th Earl of Sussex, whom she left in 1601. Several works of literature by authors such as Robert Greene, Thomas Kyd, and George Chapman were dedicated to her. The sheet is an embroidered piece of fabric.

Upon the 8th I made an end of Exodus with Mr Ran. After supper I played at glecko with the steward, as I often do after dinner and supper.

Upon the 9th Mr Ran said service in the chapel but made no sermon in the afternoon. I went abroad in the garden, and said my prayers in the standing. I was not well at night so I ate a posset[37] and I went to bed.

Upon the 11th we perceived that the Child had two great teeth come out, so as now she had in all 18. I went in the afternoon and said my prayers in the standing in the garden and spent my time in reading and working as I used to. The time grew tedious so as I used to go to bed about eight o'clock and lie abed till eight the next morning.

Upon the 12th I wrote to my Lord, to Sir Walter Raleigh, to Marsh etc.

Upon the 13th I made an end of Leviticus with Mr Ran. I sent by Willoughby a little jewel of opal to my Lady Trenchard's[38] girl.

Upon the 14th I made an end of my Irish stitch cushion. This afternoon Basket came from London and told me that my Lord and my Uncle of Cumberland were agreed and that the writings were sealed.[39]

The King set forward this day on his journey to Scotland, the Queen and the Prince going with him to Theobalds.

Upon the 15th my Lord came down to Buckhurst and was so ill by the way he was fain to alight once or twice and go into a house. All the household were sent down from London to Knole.

The 16th my Lord sent for John Cook to make broths for him and Josiah to wait in his Chamber by whom I wrote a letter to entreat him that if he were not well I might come down to Buckhurst to him. This day I spent walking in the Park with Judith and carrying my Bible with me thinking on my present fortunes and what troubles I have passed through.

Upon the 19th Willoughby brought me very kind messages from my sister Compton, my sister Beauchamp and the rest of the Ladies I sent her to.

---

37 Hot milk curdled with liquor and flavoured with sugar and spices, a remedy for colds.
38 The wife of Sir Thomas Trenchard (1582–1657), Sheriff of Dorset.
39 The writings referred to here are known as the "King's Award"; see Introduction, 25.

About this time my Lord Hay was sworn a Privy Councillor.

About this time my Lord took Adam a new barber to wait on him in his chamber.

Upon the 20th I spent most of the time in walking abroad and playing at cards with the steward and Basket and had such ill luck that I resolved not to play in three months. After supper I wrote a letter to my Lord to entreat him that he would come and see me and the Child as soon as he could.

The 21st Ned footman came from Buckhurst and told me that my Lord was reasonable well and that he had missed his fit which did much comfort me.

The 22nd my cook Hortelius came down from London to me by Dr Layfield. The steward came from Buckhurst and told me [my] Lord had not been well so as his going to London had been put off till the next week and that he had lent out his house to my Lord Keeper[40] for two terms until my Lady Derby was gone out of York House and my brother Sackville had written to my Lord to lend him the litter to bring up my sister Sackville to London who was 13 weeks gone with child. This day I began a new Irish stitch cushion not one of those for Lady Rich but finer canvas.

Upon the 24th we made rosemary cakes.

Upon the 26th my Lord came hither with Thomas Glemham from Buckhurst. He was troubled with a cough and was fain to lie in Leicester Chamber.

Upon the 27th my Lord told me that he had acknowledged no statutes on his lands and that the matter was not so fully finished but there was a place left for me to come in.[41] My Lord found me reading with Mr Ran and told me that it would hinder his study very much so as I must leave off reading the Old Testament until I can get somebody to read it with me. This day I made an end of reading Deuteronomy.

Upon the 28th I walked with my Lord abroad in the Park in the garden, where he spake to me very much of this business with my Uncle Cumberland. I wrought very much within doors and strived to set as merry a face as I could upon a discontented heart, for I might easily perceive that Mathew and Lindsay had got a great hand of my Lord and were both of them against me, yet by this means they put my Lord William clean out of all grace

---

40 I.e., Francis Bacon.
41 The King's Award required Sackville to put lands up as guarantee that Clifford would not resume legal action. Here he tells her he has not done that yet, which means he hasn't agreed to the settlement yet. He would like Clifford to renounce the possibility of future action, so that the settlement will be larger, and so that he doesn't have to tie up lands in assurance. She never acquiesces to this demand.

Upon the 29th the possession of Brougham Castle was delivered by my Lord's warrant to Thomas Taylor etc. of my uncle Cumberland's servants, most of the gentlemen and justices being there present.

About this time the Marquis of D'Ancre[10] was slain in France which bred great alterations abroad.

About this time Lady Robert Rich was brought to bed of her third son which was her fifth child called Henry.

Captain Manwaring and these folks told me that for certain the match with Spain and our Prince would go forward. The King of Spain was

---

10 Concino, Marechal d'Ancre (1575–1617), a Florentine. A politician and favourite of Marie de Medici, he was assassinated with the consent of Louis XIII in 1617; his body was disinterred by a mob of people and then mutilated. An anonymous play on the topic of the "Marquis d'Ancre" was played on 22 June in London and ordered suppressed.

and trust with my Lord which I hope may be the better hereafter for me and my child knowing that God often brings things to pass by contrary means.

Upon the 29th my Lord went to London, I bringing him down in his coach. I found this time that he was nothing so much discontented with this agreement as I though he would have been and that he was more pleased and contented with all the passages at London than I imagined he would have been.

Upon the 30th I spent in walking and sitting in the Park having my mind much more contented than it was before my Lord came from Buckhurst.

April 1617

Upon the 2nd my Lord came down from London with Tom Glemham with him. My Lord told me how the King was gone with so few company as he had but one Lord went with him through Northamptonshire.

Upon the 4th my Lord told me that he had as yet passed no fines and recoveries of my land but that my Uncle Cumberland had acknowledged statutes for the payment of the money, and that all writings were left with my Lord Keeper and my Lord Hobart till the next Term, at which time they were fully to be concluded on. This was strange news to me, for I thought all matters had been finished. This day we began to leave the little room and dine and sup in the great chamber.

Upon the 5th my Lord went up to my closet and saw how little money I had left, contrary to all that they had told him. Sometimes I had fair words from him and sometimes foul but I took all patiently and did strive to give him as much content and assurance of my love as I could possibly yet I always told him that I would never part with Westmorland upon any condition whatsoever.

Upon the 6th after supper because my Lord was sullen and not willing to go into the nursery I made Mary bring the Child to him into my chamber which was the first time she stirred abroad since she was sick. Upon the 7th my Lord lay in my chamber.

Upon the 8th I sat by my Lord and my brother Sackville in the drawing chamber and heard much talk about many businesses and did perceive that he was entered into a business between my Lady of Exeter and my Lord Roos of which he will not easily quit himself.

Upon the 11th my Lord was very ill this day and could not sleep so that I lay on a pallet. Upon the 12th Mrs Watson came grown so gracious to English folks that he had written his letter in behalf of Lord Willoughby's brother to get him out of the Inquisition.

hither with whom I had much talk of my Lord's being made a Knight of the Garter.[42] This night I went into Judith's chamber where I mean to continue until my Lord be better.

Upon the 13th my Lord sat where the gentlewomen used to sit. He dined abroad in the great chamber and supped privately with me in the drawing chamber and had much discourse of the humours of the folks at Court.

Upon the 14th I was so ill with lying in Judith's chamber that I had a plain fit of a fever.

Upon the 15th I was so sick and my face so swelled that my Lord and Tom Glemham were fain to keep the table in the drawing chamber as I sat within. Marsh came in the afternoon to whom I gave directions to go to M[r] Davys and M[r] Walter about the drawing of letters to the tenants in Westmoreland, because I intend to send him thither. This night I left Judith's chamber and came to lie in the chamber where I lay when my Lord was in France in the green cloth of gold bed where the Child was born.

Upon the 16th my Lord and I had much talk about these businesses, he urging me still to go to London and to sign and seal but I told him that my promise was so far passed to my mother and to all the world that I would never do it whatsoever became of me and mine. Yet still I strived as much as I could to settle a good opinion in him towards me.

Upon the 17th in the morning my Lord told me he was resolved never to move me more in these businesses because he saw how fully I was bent.

Upon the 18th being Good Friday I spent most of the day in hearing Kate Buxton read the Bible and a book of Preparation to the Sacrament.[43]

Upon the 19th I signed 33 letters with my own hand which I sent by him[44] to the tenants in Westmoreland. The same night after supper my Lord and I had much talk and [he] persuaded me to yield to these businesses, but I would not, and yet I told him I was in perfect charity with the world. All this Lent I ate flesh and observed no day but Good Friday.

---

42 There were (and are) only 25 living members of the Order of the Garter at any one time. Sackville was never actually made a Knight of the Order. The honour was conferred on the most favoured nobles by the King; the duties of a Knight of the Garter were purely ceremonial. It is not known what the origin of the name of the Order is, but it has been awarded since 1348 and is still awarded today.

43 *A preparation to the receiving of the sacrament*, 5th ed., by William Bradshaw (1615).

44 I.e., Marsh.

This day we came to dine abroad in the great chamber.

About the 20th being Easter Day my Lord and I and Tom Glemham and most of the folks received the communion by Mr Ran yet in the afternoon my Lord and I had a great falling out, Mathew continuing still to do me all the ill offices he could to my Lord. All this time I wore my white satin gown and my white waistcoat.

Upon the 22nd this night we played at barley break[45] upon the bowling green.

Upon the 23rd my Lord Clanrihard[46] came hither. After they were gone my Lord and I and Tom Glemham went to Mr Lane's house to see the fine flowers that is in the garden. This night my Lord should have lain with me in my chamber, but he and I fell out about Mathew.

Upon the 24th my Lord went to Sevenoaks again. After supper we played at barley break upon the green. This night my Lord came to lie in my chamber.

Upon the 25th, being Friday, I began to keep my fish days which I intend to keep all the year long. After dinner I had a great deal of talk with Richard Dawson that served my Lady, he telling me all the manner how the possession of Brougham Castle was delivered to my Uncle of Cumberland's folks, and how Mr Worleigh and all my people are gone from home except John Raivy who kept all the stuff in the Baron's chamber, the plate being already sent to Lord William Howard's.

Upon the 26th I spent the evening in working and going down to my Lord's closet where I sat and read much in the Turkish History[47] and Chaucer.[48]

---

45 A game played in couples. One was in the middle, or "hell" and tried to capture others, who were permitted to "break" or charge the middle couple if they saw the need.

46 Richard de Burgh (d. 1635), 4th Earl of Clanrihard or Clanicarde, later Baron Somerhill, Viscount Tunbridge, Earl of St. Albans, Baron of Imanney, and Viscount Galway; husband of Frances Walsingham (1567–1632), who was widow of Sir Philip Sidney and Robert Devereux, 1st Earl of Essex. He was Irish and also held various positions in the colonial government.

47 Suzuki identifies this title as *The General History of the Turks* by Richard Knolles, published in 1610, but it is possibly the work by George Sandys mentioned above (111).

48 There are two sixteenth-century editions of Chaucer's works to which this could refer. Clifford's love of Chaucer continued through her life: in 1649 she wrote in a letter from Appleby that "if I had not excellent Chaucer's book here to comfort me I were in a pitiful case, having so many troubles as I have, but when I read in that I scorn and make light of them all, and a little part of his divine spirit infuses itself in me."

Upon the 28th was the first time the Child put on a pair of whalebone bodice.[49] My Lord went a-hunting the fox and the hare. I sent William Dunn to Greenwich to see my Lady Roxborough[50] and remember my service to the Queen.

About this time my Lord made the steward alter most of the rooms in the house and dress them up as fine as he could and determined to make all his old clothes in purple stuff for the gallery and drawing chamber.[51]

May 1617

Upon the 1st I cut the Child's strings[52] off from her coats and made her use to go about so as she had two or three falls at first but had no hurt from them.

Upon the 2nd the Child put on her first coat that was laced with lace being of red baize. Upon the 3rd my Lord went from Buckhurst to London and rid it in four hours, he riding very hard and hunting all the while. He was at Buckhurst and had his health exceeding well.

The 7th my Lord Keeper rode from Dorset House to Westminster in great pomp and state amongst by wish my Lord was one.

Upon the 8th I spent the day in working the time being very tedious unto me as having neither comfort nor company only the Child.

---

49 A bodice was the top part of a gown. By the late sixteenth century whalebone was used to stiffen bodices and give them the distinctive shape of a typical gown of the period. Little Margaret is being dressed as an adult woman. Remarkably, she is still considered enough of a child to have the "strings" attached to her coat; see 133n53, below.

50 Jane (d. 1643), daughter of Patrick, Lord Drummond. She was governess to the royal children.

51 In the list of Sackville's clothes made in 1619, several outfits are described, including one of blue velvet embroidered all over with globes, hearts, and flames of gold. In addition to cloak, hose, girdles, etc., the ensemble included banners, "cordalls" for trumpets, and two caparisons with which to deck out his horses. It is noted in the margin that the caparisons were taken in March 1619 to make a canopy, chair coverings, and cushions for Knole. The outfit probably referred to here included a cloak of purple uncut velvet and a purple satin suit, both embroidered with gold and silver.

52 These are strips of fabric hanging down the back of her dress from the shoulders, evidently to steady a toddler. In *The Great Picture* there are strings depicted on Robert Clifford's gown.

Mr Ryder came hither and told me Lord Sheffield's wife was lately dead since the King went from York.

This term my Lord's mother-in-law did first of all sue out of her thirds which was an increase of trouble and discontent to my Lord.[11]

---

11 Anne Spencer, dowager Countess of Dorset, Sackville's stepmother, mentioned above (121). As a widow, she is entitled to a third of the value of her husband's heirs' estate. Normally this is satisfied by the jointure properties. But here the widow has perceived that the value of the estate has increased markedly, so she is arguing to renew her entitlement and adjust the value of her share.

    Jointures could be a great burden on an estate. Clifford herself was a drain on the already indebted and overburdened Sackville estate, living as she did for 50 years longer than her first husband. She also outlived her second husband by 25 years, so enjoyed considerable wealth from her double jointure during her latter years.

Upon the 12th I began to dress my head with a roule[53] without a wire. I wrote not to my Lord because he wrote not to me since he went away. After supper I went with the Child who rode on the piebald nag that came out of Westmorland with M^{rs} [blank].

Upon the 13th the Child came to lie with me which was the first time that ever she lay all night in a bed with me ever since she was born.

Upon the 14th the Child put on her white coats and left off many things from her head, the weather growing extreme hot.

Upon the 17th the steward came from London and told me that my Lord was much discontented with me for not doing this business because he must be fain to tie land for the payment of the money which will much encumber his estate.

Upon the 18th Mr Woolrich came hither to serve me he bringing me news that all in Westmoreland was surrendered to my Uncle of Cumberland.

Upon the 19th came my cousin Sir Edward Gorge who brought me a token from my Lady Somerset.

Upon the 24th we set up a great many of the books that came out of the north in my closet this being a sad day with me thinking of the troubles I have passed. I used to spend much time in talking with Mr Woolrich about my dear mother and other businesses in the north.

Upon the 26th my Lady St John's tailor came hither to me to take measure of me and to make me a new gown. In the afternoon my cousin Russell wrote me a letter to let me know how my Lord had cancelled my jointure he had made upon me last June when I went into the north and by these proceedings I may see how much my Lord is offended with me and that my enemies have the upper hand of me but I am resolved to take all patiently casting all my care upon God. This footman told me that my cousin Russell and my Lady Bedford were agreed, and my Lord Herbert and his Lady[54] and that next week they

---

53 A round cushion or pad of hair or other material, forming part of a hair arrangement.
54 Henry Somerset (1577–1646), Lord Herbert and later 5th Earl and 1st Marquess of Worcester, and his wife Anne, daughter of John (d. 1584), Lord Russell (one of Margaret Clifford's brothers), and Elizabeth Cooke (1528–1609). The agreement concerns the inheritance by Francis Russell of the Bedford titles and estates.

were to seal the writings and the agreement which I little expected.[55]

Upon the 27th I wrote a letter to my Lord to let him know how ill I took his canceling of my jointure but yet told him I was content to bear it with patience whatsoever he thought fit.

Upon the 29th I wrote a letter to my sister Beauchamp and sent her a lock of the Child's hair. I wrote a letter to my sister Compton and my aunt Glemham[56] I being desirous to win the love of my Lord's kindred by all the fair means I could.

The 31st Mr Hodgson told me how my cousin Clifford went in at Brougham Castle and saw the house but did not lie there and that all the tenants were very well effected towards me and very ill towards them.

June 1617

Upon the 3rd Mr Heardson came hither in the morning and told me that as many did condemn me for standing out so in this business, so on the other side many did commend me in regard that I have done that which is both just and honourable. This night I went into a bath.

Upon the 6th after supper we went in the coach to Goodwife Sislye's and ate so much cheese there that it made me very sick.

Upon the 8th being Whitsunday we all went to church but my eyes were so blubbered with weeping that I could scarce look up and in the afternoon we fell out about Mathew. After supper we played at barley break upon the bowling green.

Upon the 9th I wrote a letter to the Bishop of London[57] against Mathew. The same day Mr Hodgson came home who had been with my cousin Russell at Chiswick and what a deal of care he had of me and my cousin Russell and my cousin Gorge sent me word that all my businesses would go well [and] that they could not find that the agreement was fully concluded in regard there was nothing had passed the great seal.

---

55 This has nothing directly to do with Clifford's interests, but concerns an agreement to allow Francis Russell (her first cousin) to inherit the title of Earl of Bedford.

56 Anne Sackville, wife of Sir Henry Glemham; Sackville's aunt.

57 John King (1559?–1621), son of Philip King and Elizabeth Conquest; chaplain to Queen Elizabeth, Dean of Christ Church, Vice Chancellor of Oxford; consecrated Bishop of London in 1611. This entry implies that Matthew held a degree in theology.

Ever since the King's going in to Scotland the Queen lay at Greenwich, the Prince being often with her till about this time she removed to Oatlands.

Upon the 13th I sayed[58] on my sea water green satin gown and my damask embroidered with gold, both which gowns the tailor which was sent down from London made fit for me to wear with open ruffs after the French fashion.

Upon the 16th Mr Woolrich came home and brought me a very favourable message from the Court.

Upon the 19th I wrote a letter to the Queen of thankfulness for the favours she had done me and enclosed it to Lady Ruthven desiring her to deliver it.

Upon the 20th I received a letter from my cousin Gorge which advised me of many proceedings and showed me the care my cousin Russell had of all my business and within it a letter from my Lady Somerset. I returned a present answer to both these letters and sent my cousin Gorge half a buck which my Lord had sent me half an hour before with an indifferent kind letter.

Upon the 21st I spent the time as I did many wearisome days besides, in working and walking. After supper I walked in the garden and gathered cherries and talked with Josiah who told me he thought all of the men in the house loved me exceedingly well, except Mathew and two or three of his consorts.

Upon the 23rd my Lord sent Adam to trim the Child's hair and sent the dowsets[59] of two deer, and wrote me a letter between kindness and unkindness.

Upon the 25th my Lord went up to London to christen Sir Thomas Howard's child with the Prince, my Lord being exceeding great with all them, and so with my brother Sackville he hoping by their means to do me and my Child a great deal of hurt.

Upon the 30th still working and being extremely melancholy and sad to see things go so ill with me, and fearing my Lord would give all his land away from the Child.

July 1617

Upon the 1st still working and sad.

Upon the 2nd I received a letter from Sir George Rivers who sent me word that my Lord was settling his land upon his brother and that the value of the fines I released to my Lord by all likelihood was very great which did much perplexed me.

Upon the 3rd I rode on horseback to Withyham to see my Lord

---

58 Essayed, i.e., tried.
59 Pie filled with meat sweetened with honey.

About this time there was a great stir about my Lady Hatton's daughter, my brother Sackville undertaking to carry her away with men and horses,[12] and he had another squabble about a man that was arrested in Fleet Street.

After this he went to the Spa and left my sister Sackville to keep my sister Beauchamp company.

About this time my Lord keeper and all his company went away from Dorset House.

About this time my Lord Roos went over beyond the sea there being a great discontentment between him and his wife.

About this time Lord Zouch[13] went by sea into Scotland to the King and Sir John Digby set out on his long expected journey to Spain.

---

12 Another great scandal of the time. Frances (then aged fourteen), daughter of Sir Edward Coke and Elizabeth Cecil, Lady Hatton, was promised in marriage to the Earl of Buckingham's brother, John Villiers, by her father. This was an attempt to raise Coke's fortunes at Court by helping to marry off Villiers, who was a thoroughly unattractive person. Lady Hatton opposed the match, and she and Frances went into hiding. Coke found them and kidnapped Frances. Lady Hatton continued to seek opportunities to seize her daughter, and it seems this "stir" involving Edward Sackville is one of these. Finally the King ordered Lady Hatton taken into custody until after the wedding in September 1617. The marriage was not a success; Frances returned to her mother's house, where she fell in love with Sir Robert Howard. She and Robert had a son in 1624 and were arrested for adultery.

13 Edward (1556?–1625), 11th Lord Zouche; a patron of Ben Jonson. Presently he held the office of Lord Warden of the Cinque Ports.

Treasurer's tomb and went down into the vault and came home again, I weeping the most part of the day seeing my enemies had the upper hand of me.

My Lady Rich sent a man hither with a letter of kindness, by whom I sent a letter to my Lord desiring him to come hither because I found myself very ill.

Upon the 7th and 8th still I kept in, complaining of my side which I took to be the spleen.

Upon the 9th Marsh brought me the King's Award.

Upon the 10th [and] 11th I spent the time in perusing that and other writings the Award being as ill for me as possible.

Upon the 12th Mr Davys came hither to whom I showed the Award desiring him to make an abstract of it to send down to the tenants. Presently after my Lord came down hither, he being somewhat kinder to me than he was, out of pity, in regard he saw me so much troubled.

Upon the 15th at night Mrs Arundel's[60] man brought me a dapple grey horse which she had long promised me.

Upon the 16th my Lady Wotton came hither on horseback, she and my Lord having lain that night at Sir Percival Hart's, and so hunted a deer as far as Otford. She stayed not above an hour in regard she saw I was so resolutely determined not to part with Westmoreland.

Upon the 26th I sent letters into Westmorland and sent to Hugh Hartley's wife a bored angel[61] and to Lady Lowther[62] a pair of Willoughby's gloves. The same night Dr Donne[63] came hither.

---

60 Blanche (1583–1649), daughter of Edward Somerset, 4th Earl of Worcester, and Elizabeth Hastings; wife of Thomas Arundel (1586?–1643), later 2nd Lord Arundel, of Wardour, Wiltshire. In 1643 she held Wardour Castle for a short time with 25 men, against 1300 Republican troops. Her son Henry married Richard Sackville's niece, Cecily Compton.

61 An angel was a coin showing the angel Michael piercing a dragon on the obverse. The coins were bored to show the metal inside was gold.

62 Eleanor, daughter of William Musgrave, widow of Sir Christopher Lowther (1557–1617).

63 John Donne, poet and divine. He was ordained in 1615, and in 1621, and at the behest of Sackville, obtained the rectory of Sevenoaks, near Knole, which he kept until his death. In Clifford's funeral sermon, Bishop Rainbow reported that Donne said of her that she could converse on matters "from predestination to slea [embroidery]-silk."

She told me that Mr Henry Bertie was out of the Inquisition house and was turned papist and that Sir Henry Goodyear was turned papist.

Upon the 4th, being Wednesday, the King came to Brougham and upon the 7th hunted all day in Whinfield and upon the 8th he went from Brougham. Both my uncle of Cumberland and my cousin Clifford was there and gave him great entertainment and there was music and many other devices.

The 27th being Sunday I went to church forenoon and afternoon Dr Donne preaching and he and the other strangers dining with me in the great chamber.

Upon the 31st I sat still thinking the time to be very tedious.

August 1617

Upon the 1st I rode on horseback, with Moll Neville, Kate Buxton and as many horses as I could get. I alighted at Sir Percival Hart's and afterwards went to Lady Wroth,[64] whither my Lady Rich came from London to see me.

Upon the 2nd my brother Compton came hither. Before supper my Lord came from London, this time of his being here he lying in my chamber.

Upon the 3rd in the afternoon we had much falling out about the keeping of the house[65] which my Lord would have me undertake which I refused, in regard things went so ill with me. This night the child lay all night with my Lord and me, this being the first night she did so.

Upon the 4th in the morning my Lord went to Penshurst but would not suffer me to go with him, although my Lord and my Lady Lisle[66] sent a man on purpose to desire me to come. He hunted and lay there all night there being my Lord Montgomery, my Lord Hay, my Lady Lucy[67] and a great deal of other company yet my Lord and I parted reasonable good friends he leaving with me his grandmother's wedding ring.

Upon the 8th I kept my chamber all day.

At night Mr Ran came and persuaded me to be friends with Mathew, but I told him that I had received so many injuries from him that I could hardly forget them.

Upon the 10th, being Sunday, I kept my chamber being very troubled and sad in mind.

---

64 Mary Sidney (1586–1640), daughter of Sir Robert Sidney (1563–1636) and Barbara Gamage (1562–1621), wife of Sir Robert Wroth, mistress of William Herbert, Earl of Pembroke. A writer; she published, but then had to withdraw, *The Countesse of Mountgomeries's Urania* in 1621, which includes the sonnet sequence "Pamphilia to Amphilanthus." There is an extensive body of criticism about her work.

65 I.e., paying to run and supply the house.

66 Robert Sidney (1563–1626) and Barbara Gamage (1562–1621), parents of Lady Mary Wroth and Robert Sidney, mentioned above.

67 I.e., Lucy (Harington) Russell; see above.

About this time I began to think much of religion and do persuade myself that this religion in which my mother brought me up in is the true and undoubted religion so as I am steadfastly purposed never to be a papist.

About this time my Lady Roxburrow that had been so great with the Queen many years, being great with child, went to Scotland in a litter.

Upon the 31st my Lord returned to London from his Sussex progress where he had been extraordinary [blank] by all the gentlemen and did go with two or three hundred horse in his company.

Upon the 11th my Lord went from Buckhurst beginning his progress into Sussex, my Uncle Neville,[68] my brother Compton, Tom Glemham, Coventry and about 30 horse more, they being all very gallant, brave and merry. M[r] Ran brought me a message from Mathew how willing he would be to have my favour, whereto I desired M[r] Ran to tell him as I was a Christian I would forgive him and so had some hours' speech with M[r] Ran.

Upon the 12th or 13th I spent most of the time in playing at glecko and hearing Moll Neville read the Arcadia.[69]

Upon the 19th my Lord wrote me a very kind letter from Lewes to which I wrote an answer. Presently in the afternoon I went to Penshurst on horseback to my Lady Lisle where I found my Lady Dorothy Sidney, my Lady Manners with whom I had much talk, and my Lady Norris,[70] she and I being very kind. There was my Lady Wroth who told me a great deal of news from beyond sea, so we came home at night, my cousin Barbara Sidney bringing me a good part of the way.

Upon the 28th Marsh came hither. He told me of a rumour of my brother Sackville's fighting and many other businesses of my Lord of Essex and my Lady Paget.[71]

Upon the 29th D[r] Carter[72] came hither and told me that my brother Sackville was slain.

---

68 Henry Neville, later 7th Lord Abergavenny, widower of Mary Sackville; father of Bess, Cecily, Mary or Moll, and Tom.

69 *The Countess of Pembroke's Arcadia* by Philip Sidney. First published in 1590, there were at least ten editions by this date.

70 Bridget (1584–1620), another daughter of Edward de Vere, 17th Earl of Oxford, and Anne Cecil; wife of Francis Norris (1579–1623), later Earl of Berkshire. At this time she was separated from her husband.

71 Lettice Knollys (1541–1634), twice widowed, and at this time wife of William (1572–1629), 4th Baron Paget of Beaudesert. She was notorious for her sexual conduct; for the suspicious deaths of her first two husbands after she had begun affairs with the next ones; for her ambition; and for her resemblance, which she exploited, to Queen Elizabeth. Essex is Lady Paget's grandson.

72 John Carter (1554–1635), puritan divine, or his son John (d. 1655), who was also a divine.

September 1617

Upon the 1st Sr Thomas Wroth and his wife[73] came and sat with me most part of the afternoon, they telling me a great deal of news of my Lady Cary the widow. Duck came from London and told me there was no such thing as my brother Sackville's fighting with Sr John Wentworth.[74]

Upon the 15th we rid on horseback to my Lady Selby's. All this week I being at home and was sad to see how ill things went with me, my Lord being in the midst of his merry progress far out of Sussex where he had hunted in many gentlemen's parks then he went to Woodstock to meet the King, and he stayed up and down at several gentlemen's houses a good while. From thence he went to the Bath where he stayed not above two days but yet returned not to London till about Michaelmas.

Upon the 29th my Lord came home to Knole from his long journey. At this Michaelmass did my Lord receive five thousand pounds of my uncle the Earl of Cumberland which was the first penny that ever I received of my portion.

October 1617

Upon the 4th came Sir Percival Hart and Sir Ed. [blank] to dine and after dinner my Lord showed them his stables and all his great horses.

Upon the 25th being Saturday came my Lady Lisle, my Lady [blank], my cousin Barbara Sidney etc. I walked with them all the wilderness over and had much talk with her of my cousin Clifford and many other matters. They saw the child and much commended her. I gave them some marmalade of quinces for about this time I made much of it.

Upon the 28th I strung my chains and bracelets with Willoughby.

Upon the 30th fell the child to be something ill and out of temper like a grudging of an ague which continued with her about a month or six weeks after.

Upon the 31st my brother Sackville spent the day in playing at cards with my cousin Howard.

---

73 Sir Thomas Wroth (1584–1672), eldest son of Thomas Wroth and Joan Bulmer, and Margaret (d. 1635), daughter of Richard Rich. He was parliamentarian, writer, and colonial administrator.
74 Sir John Wentworth of Gosfield, married to Catherine, daughter of Sir Moyle Finch (d. 1614).

Which cost me five score pounds besides the satin.

These three days was the last time that ever I was in my mother's chamber in St Augustine Friars, which was the same chamber I was married in to Richard Lord Buckhurst who was Earl of Dorset three days after I was married to him.

The 4th day King James kissed me when I was with him, and that was the last time ever I was so near King James as to touch him.

November 1617

Upon the 1st my brother Sackville and I, my cousin Charles Howard went up to London. My Lord stayed behind but went upon Monday after to Buckhurst so stayed there and at Lewes till I came hither again. I left Moll Neville and Kate Buxton here to keep the child company.

Upon the 2nd, being Sunday, I went to church with my sister Sackville to St Bride's, and afterwards my cousin Gorge and I went and dined with my Lady Ruthven, where I met my Lady Shrewsbury. In the afternoon I saw her Lord there. All this time I was at the court I wore my green damask gown embroidered, without a farthingale.[75] The same day I sent the Queen by my Lady Ruthen the skirts of a white satin gown all pursled[76] and embroidered with colours.

Upon the 3rd I went to see my Lady St John's. From thence I went to Austin Friars where I wept extremely to remember my dear and blessed mother. I was in the chamber where I was married and went into most of the rooms in the house, but found very little or nothing of the stuff and pictures remaining there. From thence I went to my Lord [blank] and so to Whitehall where my Lady Arundel told me that the next day I should speak to the King for my Lady Arundel was exceeding kind with me all this time.

Upon the 4th I carried my Lady Rich to dine with me to Mrs Watson's where we met my cousin Russell and my cousin Gorge and had an extreme great feast. From thence I went to the court, where the Queen sent for me into her own bedchamber and here I spoke to the King. He used me very graciously and bid me go to his attorney, who should inform him more of my desires. All the time of my being in London I used to sup privately and to send for Mr Davys to confer with me about my law business.

Upon the 5th I carried Mr Davys to Gray's Inn[77] to the King's attorney, when I told him His Majesty's pleasure. From thence I went to Mr Walter's advice and help in this business and so I

---

75 A framework of hoops made of whalebone worn under a skirt.
76 If this means "pursed," then drawn into close folds or pleats. Possibly instead "pearled."
77 One of the inns of court, where lawyers had their "chambers" or offices.

came down this night to Knole. The next day my Lord Hay was married to my Lady Lucy Percy.[78]

Upon the 17th in the morning my Lord brought my cousin Clifford (though much against my will) into my bedchamber where we talked of ordinary matters some quarter of an hour and so he went away.

Upon the 19th came John Taylor with whom I had some two hours talk of ancient matters, of my father and the north.

Upon the 20th I came down to Knole leaving my Lord behind me in London.

Upon the 30th I do not remember whether my Lord went to the church or stayed at home.

December 1617

Upon the 8th I was not very well and Mr Thomas Cornwallis the groom porter came hither.

Upon the 9th I spent time with him talking of Queen Elizabeth and of such old matters at the Court.

Upon the 10th my Lord went away to Buckhurst where all the country gentlemen met my Lord with their greyhounds. All the officers of the house went to Buckhurst where my Lord kept great feasting till the 13th, at which time all the gentlemen went away. This time Sir Thomas Parker was there when my brother Sackville and he had much squabbling. From this day to the 20th my Lord lived privately[79] at Buckhurst having no company with him but only Mathew.

Upon the 15th came Sr Henry Neville's Lady.[80] I carried her up into my closet and showed her all my things and gave her a pair of Spanish leather gloves.

Upon the 22nd my Lord and I and all the household removed from hence to London, the child going two hours before in a litter.

Upon the 25th being Christmas Day Mr [blank] preached in the chapel and my Lord and I dined below, there being great housekeeping[81] kept all this Christmas at Dorset House.

---

78 Lucy (1599–?), daughter of Henry Percy (1564–1632), 9th Earl of Northumberland, and Dorothy Devereux (1564–1619).

79 Meaning that he had no groups of friends staying with him, and did not entertain.

80 Elizabeth, daughter of Sir John Smith (of Kent), wife of Sir Henry Neville mentioned above.

81 Meaning the house was well-prepared for entertaining large parties of guests.

Upon the 28th I went to church in my rich night gown and petticoat, both my women waiting upon me in their liveries but my Lord stayed at home. There came to dine Mrs Lindsay and a great company of neighbours to eat venison.

Now I had a great desire to have all my father's sea voyages written so I did set Jones etc. to inquire about these matters.[82]

---

82 The account of George Clifford's voyages against the Spanish fleets from 1986 to 1598 survives, in the handwriting of a professional scribe.

The 2nd the child grew ill with a cough and a pain in her head so as we feared the smallpox, but it proved nothing for within eight or ten days she recovered.

About this time my Lady Rich was brought to bed of a son her sixth child. I should have christened it but it died in three or four days.

About this time my Lady Lisle was brought to bed of her first son at Baynards's Castle and within a little while after fell sick of the smallpox.

About this time died Tom Robins my brother Sackville's man, but he left his master no remembrance for they were fallen out.

This month died my Lord Cobham[1] he being lately come out of the Tower, he being the last of the three that was condemned for the first conspiracy against the King at his first coming to England.

---

1 Henry Brooke (d. 24 January 1619), 8th Lord Cobham. He was imprisoned in 1603 for a plot to put Arabella Stuart on the throne. He was allowed out of the Tower in 1617 to go to Bath to improve his health, but was seized with paralysis on his return and remained in a semicoma until his death.

1619

The first of this month I began to have the curtain drawn in my chamber and to see light.[1] This day the Child did put on her crimson velvet coat laced with silver lace, which was the first velvet coat she ever had. I sent the Queen a New Year's gift, a cloth of silver cushion embroidered richly with the King of Denmark's arms, and all over with slips of tentstitch.[2]

The 2nd, 3rd, 4th and 5th I sat up and had many Ladies come to see me, and much other company and so I passed away the time. My Lord went often to the Court and abroad, and upon Twelfth Eve my Lord lost 400lb pieces playing with the King.

Upon the 6th the Prince had the masque at night in the Banqueting House.[3] The King was there, but the Queen was so ill she could not remove from Hampton Court. All this Christmas it was generally thought she would have died.

The 11th my Lord went down to Knole.

The 12th the Banqueting House at Whitehall was burnt to the ground, and the writings in the Signet Office were all burnt.

The 16th came my Lord of Arundel and his Lady. The same day I sent my cousin Hall of Gilford a letter and my picture with it which Larkin[4] drew at Knole this summer.

The 18th my Lady Wotton came to see me and stayed most part of the afternoon with me [with] whom I had much conference of old matters, and of the northern business.

The 19th my Lady Verulamia[5] came, my Lord Cavendish,[6] his

---

1 Clifford was pregnant in 1617, and gave birth in 1618; the child did not survive. She has been in mourning, and may also have been depressed. This is presumably why 1618 is not included in these accounts.

2 Petit-point embroidery.

3 This masque—and its title—are lost.

4 William Larkin, who painted portraits of several members of the Court between 1609 and 1619. The portrait for which this drawing must have been a study is of Clifford in a decorated gown trimmed with lace, a ruff and an ear-string (a kind of earring, but made of thread) of silk, from which a pearl is suspended. It hangs at Knole, with the companion portrait of her husband.

5 Alice Barnham (d. 1650), wife of Francis Bacon, who was created Baron Verulamia on 12 July 1618.

6 William Cavendish (1591?–1628), son and heir of William Cavendish, 1st Earl of Devonshire, and Anne Keighley; an intimate friend of the King.

I brought down with me my Lady's great trunk of papers to pass away the time which trunk was full of writings of Craven and Westmoreland and other affairs with certain letters of her friends and many papers of philosophy.

My lord came into my chamber and told me the news of my sister Beauchamp's child's death.

Lady, my Lord Bruce, his sister and much other company, my Lady Herbert,[7] my old Lady Dormer,[8] my young Lady Dormer,[9] with whom I had much talk about religion.

The 20th came my Lord Russell, Sir Edward Gorge, my sisters Beauchamp, Compton and Sackville, and dined with me and in the afternoon came my Lady Bridgewater[10] and much other company, and my Lady of Warwick who told me a great deal of good news.

The 22nd here supped with me my sister Sackville, my sister Beauchamp, Bess Neville, Tom Glemham and my brother Compton and his wife. I brought them to sup there of purpose, hoping to make them friends.

The 23rd I came from London to Knole in a litter, the Child riding all the way in her coach. I went through the City and over the bridge but she crossed the water. We found my Lord at Knole who had stayed there all this time since his coming from London.

The 24th, being Sunday, here dined Sir William Selby and his Lady and Sir Ralph Boswell.

All this week I kept my chamber because I found myself ill and weak.

The 29th in the morning died my sister Beauchamp's daughter M[rs] Anne Seymour[11] in the same house her father died five months before. The child was opened, it having a corrupt[12] body,

---

7 There were several Ladies Herbert at this time. This is probably Anne, wife of Henry Somerset, mentioned in May 1617.

8 Elizabeth (d. 1631), daughter of Anthony Browne, 1st Viscount Montagu, and Magdalen Dacre; widow of Robert, Lord Dormer of Wyng (d. 1616).

9 Alice, daughter of Richard Molyneux and widow of Sir William Dormer (d. 1616). By "old Lady," Clifford means the dowager Countess or Baroness. The "young" lady is married to the Earl or Baron's heir, and hence is the current Countess or Baroness.

10 Frances, daughter and co-heiress of Fredinando Stanley, 5th Earl of Derby, and Lady Alice Spencer; wife of John Egerton (1579–1649), first Earl of Bridgewater, son of Sir Thomas Egerton and his wife Elizabeth.

11 One of the children of Anne Sackville and Edward Seymour, Lord Beauchamp (d. 15 September 1618).

12 I.e., infected by bacteria and therefore a potential health hazard.

About this time my sister Compton was reconciled to her husband and went to his house in Finch Lane where they stayed some ten or twelve days and then he brought her into the country to Brambletie.

About this time my Lord William caused my cousin Clifford to come before the Lords of the Council about northern business, so as the spleen increased more and more betwixt them and bred faction in Westmoreland which I held to be a very good matter for me.

My Lady of Suffolk at Northampton House about this time had the smallpox which spoiled that good face of hers which had brought to others much misery and to herself greatness which ended with much unhappiness.

The 13th Wat Conniston made an end of reading the King's book upon the Lord's Prayer[2] which was dedicated to my Lord of Buckingham.

About the 20th the King fell into an extreme fit of the stone at Newmarket so as many doubted of his recovery and the Prince rid down post to him. The 22nd the King came to Royston and there voided a stone[3] and so grew reasonable well.

This business was one of the foulest matters that hath fallen out in our time, so as my Lady Roos was counted a most odious woman.

---

2 James I's *A Meditation upon the Lord's Prayer* was published in 1619.
3 I.e., a kidney stone.

so it was put in lead and the day following Legge brought it to Knole which day was my birthday I being now 29 years old.

The 31st my cousin Russell's wife[13] was brought to bed of a son, it being her fourth child, at Chiswick, which was christened in the church privately and named Francis.

February 1619

The 1st carried my Lord Beauchamp's child from Knole where it had stood in his chamber to Withyham where it was buried in the vault so that now there was an end of the issue of that marriage which was concluded presently after mine.

The 3rd my Lord went to Buckhurst meaning to lie there private a fortnight or thereabouts.

The 8th my Lady Wotton sent her page to see me, and that day I made pancakes[14] with my women in the great chamber.

The 10th Wat Conniston began to read St Austin of the City of God[15] to me and I received a letter from Mr Davys with another enclosed in it of Ralph Conniston whereby I perceived things went in Westmorland as I would have them.[16]

The 15th Sir Thomas Lake, his Lady and Lady Roos were sent to the Tower. There was nothing heard all this term but this matter between the Countess of Exeter and them, at which hearing the King sat for several days. It was censured on my Lady Exeter's side against them who were fined at great fines both to the King and her. There was spoken extraordinary foul matters of my Lady Roos, and reports went that among others she lay with her own brother so as these foul matters did double the miseries of my Lady Lettice Lake, in her unfortunate match. Sara Swarton was fined and censured to be whipped, which answer was not executed by reason she con-

---

13 Catherine, daughter of Giles, 3rd Lord Chandos; wife of Clifford's cousin Francis Russell, with whom she had eight children.

14 For Shrove Tuesday, the day before Ash Wednesday, or the first day of Lent.

15 This translation of St. Augustine's *City of God* was published in 1610.

16 By 1619, it had become apparent that there would be problems enforcing the King's Award. The tenants questioned its validity (as Anne had not agreed to it), and the security of their leases was therefore dubious. The tenants had brought actions against Francis; William Howard was competing with Francis for local authority and influence (Spence 72–73), as Clifford mentions in the entry of 28 February.

I began and kept this Lent very strictly not eating butter or eggs till the 18th of February. Moll Neville kept it with me, but my Lord persuaded me and Mr Smith wrote unto me so as I was content to break it. Besides, I looked very pale and was weak and sickly.

The old Queen dowager of Denmark[4] was alive when her daughter Queen Anne of England died.

About this time I caused the book of the Cliffords to be newly copied out.

The 9th the Queen's corpse was brought from Hampton Court to Denmark House by water in the night in a barge with many Lords and Ladies attending it.

---

4 Sophia, daughter of Ulric III and widow of King Frederick II of Denmark and Norway.

fessed all she knew. In Sir Thomas Lake's place Sir George Calvert was sworn Secretary.[17]

My Lord should have gone to London the 24th of this month but I entreated him to stay here the 25th because on that day 10 years I was married, which I kept as a day of jubilee to me so my Lord went not up till the 27th at which time he rid on horseback by reason of the great snow, and was so ill and sick after his journey so that whereas he intended to have returned in two or three days he stayed nine or ten days.

The 28th, being Sunday, the Judges came to Sevenoaks. I did often receive letters from Mr Davys and Marsh by which I perceived my motion to Sir John Suckling[18] on his behalf took good effect and that businesses went well to my liking in Westmorland by reason of differences between my Lord William and my cousin Clifford.

March 1619

Upon the 2nd the Queen died at Hampton Court between two and three in the morning. The King was then at Newmarket. Legge brought me the news of her death about four o'clock in the afternoon, I being in my bed chamber at Knole where I had the first news of my mother's death. Legge told me my Lord was to take some physic of Mr Smith so as he could not come from London these four or five days yet. She died in the same chamber that Queen Jane,[19] Harry the 8th's wife, died in. The Prince was there when the pangs of death came upon her but went into another chamber some half an hour before she died.

The 4th my Lord Sheffield was married at Westminster in St Margaret's Church to one Anne Erwin, daughter of Sir William Erwin, a Scottish man, which was held a very mean match and indiscrete part of him.

---

17 Sir George Calvert (1580?–1632), later 1st Lord Baltimore. A favourite of George Villiers, the Earl of Buckingham; later a colonial administrator. See 12 February 1616, 65-67n19, for a summary of this scandal. Lady Lettice Lake, is married to Arthur Lake, Anne's brother. Sara Swarton must have been a servant involved in the affair.

18 Sir John Suckling (1569–1627). An ambitious courtier, he held many lucrative posts and became Master of Requests in 1620 (the Master of Requests was in charge of bringing private suits to the attention of the monarch).

19 Jane Seymour (1509?–37), 3rd wife of Henry VIII and mother of Edward VI.

When my Lord was at London my brother Sackville fell sick of a fever and was dangerously ill. At length it turned to a second ague which continued most of the month so as it was generally reported that he was dead.

The 10th Wat Conniston made an end of reading St Austin of the City of God.

The 24th there was no running at tilt by reason of the Queen's death which I held a good fortune for my Lord because he meant not to run, which I think would have given the King some distaste.

Most of the great Ladies about the town put themselves in mourning and did watch the Queen's corpse at Denmark House which did lay there with much state.

The 5th at night about nine of the clock the Queen's bowels,[20] all saving her heart, were buried privately in the Abbey at Westminster in the place where the King's mother's tomb is. There were none came with it but three or four of her servants and gentlemen ushers which carried it and a herald before it. The Dean of Westminster and about ten others were by.

About the 9th my Lord came down to Knole and continued taking physic and diet.

The 17th my Lord went to Buckhurst to search for armour and provision, which should be laid up by the papists. This day I made an end of my Lady's book in the praise of a Solitary Life.[21]

The 18th I compared the two books of the Cliffords that Mr Knisden[22] sent me down. The 20th I made an end of reading the Bible over which was my Lady my mother's. I began to read it the 1st of February so as I read all over the whole Bible in less than two months.

The 24th my Lord of Warwick[23] died in Allington House leaving a great estate to my Lord Rich and my good friend his Lady[24] and leaving his wife which was my Lady Lampwell[25] a widow the second time. This day Wat Conniston made an end of reading Mr Saragoll's book of the Supplication of Saints[26] which my Lord gave me.

The 26th, being Good Friday, after supper I fell into a great passion of weeping in my chamber, and when my Lord came in I told him I found my mind so troubled as I held not myself fit to receive the communion this Easter which all this Lent I intended to have done.

The 27th in the morning I sent for Mr Ran and told him I found not my self fit to receive the communion. The next day

---

20 Her internal organs, the removal of which was a routine part of the embalming process.

21 Spence identifies this as a manuscript by Harrington called "In Praise of a Solitary Life."

22 According to Spence, this is St. Loe Kniveton, an antiquary employed by Margaret in the research undertaken to support their legal claims (165).

23 I.e., Robert Rich. He was created Earl of Warwick in 1618.

24 I.e., Robert Rich and Frances Hatton.

25 I.e., Frances Wray.

26 *Supplications of the saints* by Thomas Sorocold. One of the editions published between 1612 and 1619.

when my Lord heard I had told Mr Ran so much, he sent for him and told him the communion could be put off both for himself and the household except any of them would receive at the church.

The 28th, being Easter Day, Mr Ran preached in the chapel but there was no communion in the house but at the church. In the afternoon I began to repent that I had caused the communion to be put off till Whitsuntide, my Lord protesting to me that he would be a very good husband to me, and that I should receive no prejudice by releasing my thirds.[27]

The 29th my Lord went to Buckhurst, and so to Lewes to see the muster,[28] which the country prepared in much the better fashion by reason of their affection for him, which was as much as any Lord hath in his own country or can have.

April 1619

The first day in the morning I writ in the Chronicles.

The 4th there was a general thanksgiving at Paul's Cross for the King's recovery at which were most of the Privy Council and the Bishop of London preached.

The 5th my Lord Hume[29] died in Channel Row, who married Mrs Mary Dudley my old companion, and left her as well as he could possibly.

The 6th my Lord came from Buckhurst to Knole. At his being at Lewes there was great play between my Lord of Hunsdon,[30] my Lord of Effingham, and my Lord who lost there 200^{lb}, and the town entertained him with fireworks.

The 8th there came a letter to my Lord to advise him to come to Royston to the King, because most of the Lords had been with him in the time of his sickness.

---

27 That is, sign away her claim to a third of the value of his estate in the event of his death. She is reluctant to do so until he has made arrangements to ensure her jointure.

28 The assembly of armed men for inspection. Although England had no standing army at this time, men were obliged to be prepared to fight under the command of local leaders.

29 Alexander Home or Hume (1566?–1619), 1st Earl of Home; a Scottish favourite of the King's who had accompanied him south in 1603. His wife, here called Mary Dudley, is referred to as "Lady Hume" above.

30 Henry Carey, 4th Lord Hunsdon and later Earl of Dover.

The 9th my Lord went from Knole to London. The next day he went to Royston to the King with whom he watched that night, my Lord of Warwick[31] and my Lord North[32] watched with him. The King used him very well so that my Lord came not back till the 13th to London. There he stayed till I came up.

The 17th I came to London. Moll Neville, the gentlewomen, and most of the house came with me, so that I left none to wait on the Child but Mary Hutchins.

Sunday the 18th I went to Warwick House to see my young Lady of Warwick[33] where I met my Lord of Warwick, Mr Charles Rich, Mr Nathaniel Rich, Lady Harry Rich.[34] After all the company were gone to the sermon my Lord came in thither.

This day I put on my black mourning attire and went to my sister Beauchamp where I spake with Mrs Bathurst and told her I did both forgive and forget any thing she had done against me and that I had spoken to my Lady of Warwick in her behalf.

Monday the 19th I went to Somerset House and sat a good while there by the Queen's corpse and then went into the privy[35] galleries and showed my cousin Mary those fine delicate things there. From thence I went to Bedford House and stayed with my Lady of Bedford a little while and she and I went to Channel Row to see my Lady Hume the widow. This day my Lord, my Lord Hunsdon and my sister Sackville christened Hamon's child at St Dunstan's Church.

The 20th I went to Parsons Green to my Lady St John's, where I met the Spanish friar,[36] that is the agent here. This day and the next my Lord had cocking at the cockpit where there met him an infinite company.

---

31 I.e., Robert Rich, who succeeded his father.
32 Dudley (1582–1666), 3rd Baron North; a favoured courtier, famous invalid, and later Parliamentarian.
33 I.e., Frances Hatton.
34 Charles Rich (d. 1627), son of Robert Rich (1559–1619), Earl of Warwick, and Penelope Devereux (1562–1607); Nathaniel Rich (1586?–1636), the eldest son of Richard Rich (illegitimate son of Richard, 1st Baron Rich) and a daughter of John Machell, Sheriff of London; he and Robert Rich (2nd Earl of Warwick) had business ventures together in the West Indies. Lady Harry Rich is Isabel, daughter and heiress of Sir Walter Cope, and wife of Henry Rich.
35 I.e., private.
36 Possibly the Duke de Frias, Constable of Castille, who was Spanish Ambassador to England.

The 20th the King was brought in a litter from Royston to Ware and the next day to Theobalds, being carried the most part of the way in a chair by the Guard, for that he was so ill he could not endure the litter.

Thursday the 22nd I went in the morning to see my sister Compton and found my brother Compton there. I was in the room where my Lord's mother in law[37] died, the Countess of Dorset, and went up and down the rooms. Afterwards my sister Beauchamp and my sister Sackville came to see me.

Friday the 23rd I went to Blackfriars to see my Lady Cavendish and my Lady Kinloss[38] in that house where my Lady Somerset was brought to bed[39] in her great troubles. Then I went to Denmark House and heard prayers there and this night I watch'd all night with the Queen's corpse. There watched with me my Lady Elizabeth Gorge[40] and diverse other ladies and gentlewomen, besides there sat up my brother Compton, my cousin Gorge, my cousin Thatcher and M[r] Renolds. At the beginning of the night there came thither my Lord of Warwick and his Lady, Sir Harry Rich,[41] Charles Rich, my Lord Carew[42] and Sir Thomas Edmonds,[43] but all these went away before twelve o'clock. I came not away till five o'clock in the morning.

Saturday the 24th my Lord went to Theobalds to see the King, who used him very graciously.

This night my cousin Clifford came out of the north where matters went more to my content and less to his than was expected. Either this night or the next morning Sir Arthur Lake's Lady was brought to bed of a son.

---

37 This is Sackville's stepmother, not a mother-in-law in the modern sense.
38 Magdalene (d. after 1631), daughter of Alexander Clerk; widow of Edward (1549–1611), 1st Lord Bruce of Kinloss, and wife of Sir Edward Fullerton (d. 1631); mother of Lord Bruce and Lady Cavendish, mentioned above (157).
39 I.e., gave birth.
40 The sister of Sir Edward Gorge.
41 Henry Rich, 1st Earl of Holland (1590–1649), son of Robert Rich, 1st Earl of Warwick, and Penelope Devereux. He was one of the leaders of the Royalist forces in the Civil Wars and was executed in 1649 for treason.
42 George Carew (1555–1629), Baron Carew of Clopton and later 1st Earl of Totnes; a civil servant.
43 Sir Thomas Edmonds (1563?–1639), Treasurer of the Royal Household.

Sunday the 25th, after dinner, I, my Lady of Warwick, and [blank] went to the sermon in the great hall. After Sermon my Lord came thither to fetch me so we went to Hyde Park and took the air. After my Lord came home he went to see my brother Sackville who still continueth to look ill, and is very sickly and out of temper in his body.

Monday the 26th my Lord's cocks fought at Whitehall, where my Lord won five or six battles. I went in the afternoon to see my Lady Windsor⁴⁴ and my Lady Raleigh in her house which is hard by Austin Friars; then I went to Clerkenwell to that house that Sir Thomas Challoner⁴⁵ built.

Tuesday the 27th I put on my new black mourning night gown and those white things which Nan Horne made for me. This day Mr Orfeur brought unto me two of the tenants of Westmoreland who craved my assistance in their behalf against my Uncle of Cumberland.

The 28th my Lord and I, my cousin Sackville and my Lady Windsor went to see my Lady Somerset where we saw her little child. My Lord went to see the Earl of Northumberland and I and Lady Windsor went to see my Lady Shrewsbury and after supper my Lord and I went by water to Channel Row to see my Lord of Hertford and his Lady where we found my Lady Beauchamp and my Lord of Essex's sister.⁴⁶ Then I went to Arundel House and met with her and talked with her about my Lord's being made Knight of the Garter.

The 30th my Lord Southampton was sworn a Privy Councillor to the King at Theobalds.

May 1619

The 1st after supper Mr Davys came and did read to my Lord and me the bill my Uncle of Cumberland and my cousin Clif-

---

44 Catherine (d. 1654), daughter of Edward Somerset, 4th Earl of Worcester, and Elizabeth Hastings; sister of Blanche and Henry mentioned above; wife of Thomas Windsor (1591–1641), 6th Lord Windsor of Stanwell.

45 Sir Thomas Challoner (1521–65), diplomat and author. He built a great house in Clerkenwell.

46 Dorothy Devereux (1600–36), sister of Robert, Earl of Essex.

This 3rd Monsieur Barnevelt[5] was beheaded at the Hague which is like to breed great alteration for the best for this man hath long been a secret friend to the Spaniards and an enemy to the English.

About this time Monsieur Trinnel[6] came over to condole for the death of the Queen out of France.

---

5 Johann von Oldenbarnevelt, formerly Ambassador to England, executed by order of a Calvinist tribunal in Holland on 3 May 1619.
6 François Juvenal, Marquis de Tresnel, Ambassador Extraordinary from France to England.

ford put in the Chancery against the tenants of King's Meaborne.[47]

The 2nd when I returned home I found Mr Hammon and his wife here. I told her that she had made so many scorns and jests of me that for my part she was nothing welcome to me.

The 3rd about two or three o'clock in the morning Sir Arthur Lake's wife died, having been grievously tormented a long time with pains and sores which broke out in blotches so that it was commonly reported that she died of the French disease.[48]

This day one Williams a lawyer was arraigned and condemned at the King's Bench of treason and adjudged to be hanged, drawn and quartered for a certain book he had made and entitled Balaam's ass, for which book one M[r] Cotton[49] was committed to the Tower and long time kept prisoner there upon a suspicion to have made it, but of late he was gotten out upon bail and now well quitted. Williams being condemned was carried to Newgate and the 5th of this month was hanged, drawn and quartered, according to his sentence, at Charing Cross.

The 5th my Lord of Kent's daughter my Lady Susana Longville and her husband[50] came and dined with me.

The 6th my Lord sat up playing at cards and did not come home till twelve o'clock at night.

The 7th presently after dinner my cousin Clifford came and sat in the gallery half an hour or an hour and so my Lord and he went abroad.

The 8th this afternoon John Dent and Richard Dent were before my Lord Chancellor, my cousin Clifford and John Taylor being present where my Lord Chancellor told them that for tenant rights he meant utterly to break them, willing them to be good tenants to my uncle of Cumberland, whereat the poor men were much perplexed and troubled; but I gave them the best comfort and encouragement I could.

The 9th being Sunday my Lord and I went not to the church

---

47 These lands are part of the disputed estates. The tenants are presumably the ones she mentions late in the previous month, and refers to by name (John and Richard Dent) on the 8th of this month.

48 I.e., syphilis.

49 Possibly John Cotton (1584–1652), Puritan clergyman in England and Massachusetts.

50 Susana, daughter of Henry Grey (c. 1623), 6th Earl of Kent, and Mary Cotton (d. 1580), and Michael Longueville, later Lord Grey of Ruthin.

About this time went my Lord of Doncaster of his embassage into Germany being sent by the King both to the Emperor and the Palsgrave to mediate those stirs which was like then to fall amongst them.

This 13th day it is just 13 years and two months since my father his funeral was kept and solemnized in the Church at Skipton as Queen Anne her body was this night buried in the Abbey church at Westminster.

This was the last time I saw my old Lady of Pembroke.

in the morning because Skinne was married that day there to
Sara. In the afternoon I was not well so neither my Lord nor I
went to church. My sister Beauchamp came hither and sat here
and my brother Compton, whom I made promise me to give me
his hand upon it that he would keep his house in Finch Lane until
Lady Day[51] next because my sister Compton might sometimes
come up to London. After I was gone to bed Sir John Suckling,
M[r] Davys and M[r] Sherborne came hither, and I had them into
the chamber. Sir John Suckling was very forward to do me all the
pleasure he could, and M[r] Sherborne promised to speak to my
Lord Chancellor in the behalf of the poor tenants.

The 10th Sir John North[52] came and told me much news from
beyond the sea.

The 11th in the morning my Lord William Howard came up to
me in my Lady Margaret's chamber and conferred with me about
an hour promising me to do all the good he could in the northern business. This day my Lord went to Salisbury House to see
my cousin Clifford, there being ordinary passages of kindness
betwixt them, so that he useth to keep my Lord company at
running at the ring and going to Hyde Park and those places.

The 13th I was one of the mourners at the Queen's funeral and
attended the corpse from Somerset House to the Abbey at Westminster; my Lord also was one of the Earls that mourned at this
time. I went all the way hand in hand with my Lady of Lincoln.[53]
After the sermon and all the ceremonies ended my Lord, my self,
my Lord of Warwick and his Lady came home by barge. Being
come home I went to my sister Beauchamp to show her my
mourning attire. At this funeral I met with my old Lady of Pembroke,[54] and diverse others of my acquaintance, with whom I had

---

51 Lady Day is the Feast of the Annunciation, 25 March.
52 Sir John North, son of Sir John North (1551?–97) and Dorothy Dale;
   brother of Lord North mentioned above.
53 Elizabeth Knyvett (1574?–1630), widow of Thomas Clinton, 3rd Earl of
   Lincoln (d. 15 January 1619). She bore 18 children and was also the
   author of *The Countess of Lincoln's Nursery*, a treatise on breast-feeding.
54 Mary Sidney (1561–1621), dowager Countess of Pembroke, and the
   mother of Clifford's future husband Philip Herbert. She was the most
   important female author of her era and also a significant patron. Her
   works include prose additions to her brother's *Arcadia*, verse translations
   of the *Psalms*, and closet drama (plays performed in private places, such
   as large country homes). There is an extensive body of scholarship about
   her work and the circle of writers she gathered round her.

This was the last time I saw my Lord of Hertford.

The 15th after the shower was past my Lady Dudley[7] which was my mother's old friend came to see me and brought her daughter Margaret with her.

---

7 Theodesia (d. 1650), daughter of Sir James Harington and Lucy Sidney, wife of Edward Sutton (1567–1643), 5th Baron Dudley; Margaret must have died before her father, as Edward and Theodesia had no direct heirs.

much talk. My cousin Clifford was also a mourner and bore the banner before the Lords. When all the company was gone and the church doors shut up the Dean of Westminster, the Prebends[55] and Sir Edward Zouch who was Knight Marshall,[56] came in a private way and buried the corpse at the east end of King Henry 7th chapel about seven o'clock at night. There was 180 poor women mourners.[57]

The 14th my Lord Chancellor made an order which did much affright the tenants but I gave them all the comfort I could.

I went to see my Lady of Hertford[58] in Channel Row and spoke very earnestly to my Lord of Hertford in Wood's behalf but I could not prevail and his answer was that he would not pay any of his grandchildren's debts after his death.

This night my Lord made a great supper to two or three of the Frenchmen that came over with the Ambassador. After supper there was a play and then a banquet at which my Lady Pennyston[59] and a great many Lords and Ladies were.

The 15th I went by water to the Savoy to my Lord Carew and spoke to him very earnestly in the behalf of Peter Cooling and his son, for a Gunner's place in Carlisle[60] and received a reasonable good answer from him.

My Lord and I intended to have gone home into the country and had sent the coach and horses. About then there came a sudden great shower which stayed our going.

My Lord brought me to Westminster Abbey where I stayed to see the tombs and the place where the Queen was buried in an angle in Henry 7th chapel.

---

55 Church officials.
56 A judicial post with jurisdiction covering the King's house as well as a twelve-mile radius of the palace.
57 These, and the money to pay them, were usually specified in the will of the deceased.
58 Frances Howard (1578–1639), daughter of Thomas Howard, first Viscount Howard of Bindon, and Mabel Burton. She secretly wed Edward Seymour, 1st Earl of Hertford, in 1600, and later married Lodovic Stuart, Duke of Lennox. She was an accomplished poet.
59 Sackville's mistress, the wife of Sir Thomas Pennyston. Sackville is thought to have had several affairs, none of which were conducted with great discretion. This one produced two daughters who were supported by Clifford after Sackville's death.
60 One whose office was to work a cannon, in this case at the fortress castle at Carlisle (a city in the north of England, very close to the Scottish border). The Master Gunner was an office of the Crown.

Within a day or two after I came out of town my Lord Chancellor had the tenants before him and willed them to yield to my uncle of Cumberland at which time he gave Mr Davys hard words.

The 27th my Lord, my brother Sackville and I, Moll Neville and Mr Langworth rid abroad on horseback in Whitby wood and did not sup till eight or nine o'clock. After supper my Lord and I walked before the gate, where I told him how good he was to everybody else and how ill to me; in conclusion he promised me in a manner that he would make me a jointure of 4000^lb a year whereof part should be of the land he has assured to my uncle of Cumberland.

This term there was great expectation that my Lord of Suffolk his Lady and that faction should have been proceeded against in the Star Chamber but their suit was put off till Michaelmas term.

This term my Lord William Howard put in a bill into the Star Chamber against Sir William Hutton[8] and others of my cousin Clifford's faction.

This term my Lord kept an exceeding great table and at dinner had much company. He had often cocking and sometimes with the King at Greenwich and won a great deal of money.

The 19th my Lady Roos' submission was read in the Star Chamber but Sir Thomas Lake and his Lady refused to submit for which their contempt they were committed close prisoner to the Tower.

---

8 Possibly a son of Sir Richard Hutton (1561?-1639), a Judge, and Agnes Briggs; or a son of Matthew Hutton (1529–1606), Archbishop of York, and his wife Beatrice Fincham. Both of these families lived in the north near the Clifford estates.

The 17th my Lord and I and all the household came down to Knole. I took my leave also of the two tenants and gave them gold and silver.

The 24th, 25th, 26th and 27th I went abroad with my brother Sackville sometimes early in the morning and sometimes after supper, he and I being kind, and having better correspondence than we have had.

The 31st I stayed at home and was sad and melancholy.

June 1619

The 2nd I rose about four o'clock in the morning and rid abroad on horseback and my cousin Mary with me. I was sad and melancholy and at night I broke off a piece of my tooth. Right before the 4th I and Moll Neville rode about three or four o'clock in the morning and up to the beacon and sent into my Lady Selby's for some bread and butter. This day at night was the first time that my Lady Margaret lay alone, Mary having a bed made hard by her.

The 6th being Sunday I heard neither sermon nor prayers, because I had no coach to go to church.

All this week I spent at my work and sometimes riding abroad and my cousin Mary reading Ovid's Metamorphoses[61] to me.

The 12th Mr Heardson came to me. I spent that day in keeping him company and talking of old matters he being a very sad man for the death of his wife.

The 18th my Lord came down from London after supper from the term.[62]

The 20th my Lord and I went to church at Sevenoaks.

The 23rd my Lord went to London to take up certain bonds, which he did discharge with part of my portion.[63]

The 24th my Lord received the last payment of my portion which was 6000^{lb} so that he received in all 17000^{lb}. John Taylor required of my Lord an acquittance which he had refused to give in regard he had delivered in the statutes, which were a sufficient discharge.

---

61 Probably the translation by A. Golding, of which there were seven issues or editions between 1567 and 1612; possibly the translation by J. Brinsley, published in 1618.

62 I.e., now that the term is over.

63 The money for her dowry that he has received from Francis.

The 21st Sir Thomas Glemham married Sir Peter Vavasour's daughter with whom he had a great portion. The marriage was at her father's house and private.

About this time my cousin Mary made an end of reading Parson's resolution and Burney's resolution[9] all over to me.

The first of July my sister Beauchamp took her journey to Glemham where she intends to sojourn two or three years, so as her household is dispersed only some necessary attendants remaining and Mrs Batters came into Kent.

---

9 A Protestant adaptation of a book of Christian exercise, of which there were 19 editions or issues between 1582 and 1589. Again this is one of her mother's books, part of the collection of religious and alchemical works which Clifford inherited.

The 25th the King dined at Sir Thomas Watson's and returned to Greenwich at night.

The 26th my Lord came down from London to Knole.

The 28th my Lady Hatton borrowed my Lord's coach and went to London for altogether as I think for as I conceive she came not thither to drink the water of the Well but to avoid the King's importunity for the passing of Purbeck whereof her son-in-law was made Viscount.[64]

The 30th my brother Compton came hither and all his mother's plate was delivered to him, so after dinner he returned to Brambletie where his wife lives with him but with many discontents.

July 1619

The 2nd my Lord and Sir Henry Vane played at bowls. This day at night my Lady Margaret was five years old, so as my Lord caused her health to be drunk throughout the house.

The 4th Mr Chantrell preached at Sevenoaks my Lord having sent for him purposely from Lewes to that end.

The 19th my Lady of Devonshire[65] came back from the Wells and dined at Sevenoaks and came not hither but sent her woman to see me.

The 22nd my Lady Margaret began to sit to Mr Van Somer[66] for her picture.

The 27th about this time my Lady of Bedford had the small-pox and had them in that extremity that she lost one of her eyes. About this time my cousin Clifford's wife[67] was brought to bed at Lonesborrow of a son which lived not seven hours and was christened Francis and was buried at Lonesborrow. The same day

---

64 Further to the scandal mentioned on 7 July 1617, 140n12: the Isle of Purbeck was part of the inheritance of Lady Hatton. Villiers is here made Viscount Purbeck, and the King wants her to give the property of the same name to him.

65 Elizabeth Boughton (d. 1642), widow of Sir Richard Wortley, and wife of William Cavendish (d. 1626), 1st Earl of Devonshire.

66 Paul van Somer (1558–1622). This exquisite portrait is reproduced in Spence (78).

67 Frances (1590–1644), daughter of Robert Cecil (1563–1612) and Elizabeth Brooke (1565–97). She married Clifford's cousin Henry in 1610. Clifford felt the marriage had been made to draw on the power of the Cecil family.

This Sunday my cousin Olsworth[10] was here and showed me those remembrances that are to be set up at Cheyneys for my great grandfather of Bedford and my grandfather of Bedford and my aunt of Warwick.

About this time my Lady Lowther was married to secretary Naunton.[11] All this summer Lady Pennyston was at the Wells near Eridge drinking the water.

This coming hither of my Lady Pennyston's was much talked of abroad in the world and my Lord was much condemned for it.

About this time my Lord, intending to keep a more sparing house, put away Thomas Waste and Gifford and took in one in that place which was Sir John Suckling's man.

The 11th I paid M[r] Give 10 pieces upon his return from Jerusalem who told me much news from Rome, Naples and other places.

Upon the 2nd I began to think I was quick with child,[12] so as I told it to my Lord, my sister Sackville and my sister Compton.

---

10 Probably Arnold Oldisworth, Steward to Anne (Russell) Dudley, "my aunt of Warwick" (d. 1603).

11 Sir Robert Naunton (1563–1635), son of Henry Naunton and Elizabeth Ashby. He became Secretary of State in January 1618.

12 She can feel the movement of the foetus; she would be about four months pregnant.

Lady Rutland[68] and Lady Katherine Manners came and dined here from the Wells and in the evening went to London.

August 1619

The 14th my cousin Mary and I had a bitter falling out.

The 15th being Sunday I went not to church at all and I fell out with Kate Buxton and swore I would not keep her and caused her to send for her father.

The 18th Sir Edward Buxton came hither and I told him I was determined not to keep his daughter.

The 24th after supper came Sir Thomas Pennyston and his Lady, Sir Maximilian Dallison[69] and his Lady. The 25th they stayed here all day there being great entertainment and much stir about them.

The 26th they all went away.

The 27th my Lord rid abroad betimes in the morning and came not in till night.

This night the two green beds in my chamber were removed.

The 30th my Lord sat much to have his picture drawn by Van Somer and one picture was drawn for me.[70]

September 1619

The 21st all this week I spent with my sister Compton and my sister Sackville being sad about an unkind letter my Lord sent me.

October 1619

The first came my Lord Dacres, his new wife my Lady Wildgoose and M[rs] Pembroke Lennard to see me and sat here two or three hours with me in the afternoon.

---

68 Cicely (d. 1653), daughter of Sir John Tufton and widow of Sir Edward Hungerford; wife of Francis Manners (1578–1632), 6th Earl of Rutland. She is the stepmother of Katherine Manners.

69 Sir Maximilian Dallison, High Sheriff of Ken in 1612, knighted in 1603.

70 The portrait for which this drawing was probably a study is a full-length oil painting, in which Clifford is shown wearing a dress worn without a farthingale (a hooped petticoat) but with a transparent apron, embroidered shoes, and ear-strings.

The 7th Bess of the laundry went away and one Nell came in her room.

About this time I kept my chamber and stirred not out of it till the latter end of March so as most of my friends thought I would not have escaped it.

About this time the gallery was hung with all my Lord's caparisons[13] which Edwards the upholsterer made up.

The 25th the Palsgrave was crowned King of Bohemia at Prague and the 28th the Lady Elizabeth was crowned Queen at the same place.

About the end of this month my sister Beauchamp came from Glemham for altogether and came to live with my sister Sackville at the end of Dorset House which end of the House my brother Sackville and my Lord did lately repair and made very fine.

---

13 A covering for a horse; in this case, of rich, ornamented fabric.

The 2nd Kate Buxton went away from serving me to her father's house in Sussex.

The 6th my Lady Selby was my deputy in christening Sir Henry Vane's child. Mr Walter Stuart and Sir Robert Yeakesly were godfathers. The child was named Walter.

Upon the 10th Mary was brought to bed of a boy. The same night I began to be ill.

The 14th came Sir Francis Slingsby who brought his daughter Mary to serve me who came that night and lay in Judith's chamber, so that I mean to keep her continually about me.

Upon the 15th at night the fire dog played with fire[71] so as I took cold with standing at the window.

Upon the 24th my Lady Margaret christened Mary's child with Sir William Selby and my cousin Sackville and called it Richard but neither my Lord nor I was at the church.

Upon the 25th came down hither to see me my Lord Russell and my cousin Sir Edward Gorge. My Lord made very much of them and showed them the house and the chambers and my closet but I did not stir forth of my chamber.

The 26th I kept James Wray a day or two who told me of many old matters and the certain day of the death of my brother Robert.[72]

Upon the 29th came little Sir Henry Neville[73] and dined here and went the same night to Penshurst. This night the drawing chamber chimney was on fire so that we were all afraid so that I supped in the new drawing room with my Lord. After

---

71 A meteor shower.

72 Robert (1585–91), Lord Clifford. He died when he was six. According to Clifford he was "a child of rare wit and parts and of a sweet nature, and had many perfections in him far above his years" (Lives, 5). Of her grief at Robert's death, Margaret Clifford wrote (in her autobiographical letter to Dr. Layfield), "Oh miserable woman, wretched in the hope of my life, to lose a child of that hope, of that love, to me a rose, that sweet Robin pulled before the time, the only son of his mother, tormented with sickness, so many weeks before. Oh troubles come in by floods, my dear Lord, in dangers unknown for number, myself sonless, my honour brought down, my poverty increased, my misfortunes to my enemies laid open: they gain, when I lose" (Portland Papers XXIII, f. 7).

73 Probably the first son of Sir Henry Neville (d. 1629); and Elizabeth Smith. Their second son, also named Henry (1620–94), was born the next year, so the first must have died by then.

All this term there was much sitting in the Star Chamber by all the Lords of the Council about my Lord of Suffolk's business. In the end the censure was given that he should pay fifteen thousand pounds to the King and that he and his Lady should remain prisoners in the Tower during the King's pleasure.

Upon the 16th at night Willoughby came to lie in the Child's chamber and Penn is to do all the work in the nursery.

All the time of my Lord's being at London he kept a great table having a great company of Lords and gentlemen that used to come and dine with him.

All this winter my Lady Margaret's speech was very ill so strangers could hardly understand anything she spoke; besides she was so apt to take cold and so out of temper that it grieved me to think of it, and I do verily believe all these inconveniences proceeded from some distemper in her head.

The 29th of November was the last time my Lord saw Lady Penniston at her mother's lodging in the Strand.

Upon the 30th, being Tuesday, my Lord of Suffolk and his Lady came out of the Tower.

this I never stirred out of my own bedchamber till the 23rd of March.[74]

November 1619

Upon the 2nd I had such ill luck with playing with Legge and Basket at glecko that I said I would not play again in six months.

Upon the 8th shortly after supper when I came into my chamber I was so ill that I fell into a swoon which was the first time that I ever swooned.

Upon the 20th my Lord of Suffolk and his Lady were sent to the Tower.

Upon the 24th Sir Francis Slingsby came hither to me and read to me in the sea papers upon my father's voyages.

Upon the 28th though I kept my chamber altogether, yet methinks the time is not so tedious to me as when I used to be abroad. About this time I received letters from Mr Davys by which I perceive how ill things were likely to go in Westmoreland, especially with Mr Hilton and Michael Brunshall.

Upon the 29th all the Ladies and gentlewomen hereabout being very kind to me all this time of me not being well. This day I received a letter and a box of sweetmeats from my cousin Hall which was brought me by one of her tenants, to whom I gave a good reward and returned her a letter of many thanks.

December 1619

Upon the 2nd Wat Conniston made an end of reading a book called Leicester's Commonwealth[75] in which there are many things of the Queen of Scots concerning her arraignment and her death which was all read to me.

Upon the 7th I gave Sir Robery Jaxley my sable muff.

Upon the 12th being Sunday my Lord neither went to church nor had no sermon here because Mr Ran was at Oxford. Sir Ralph Boswell dined here and played and sung to me in the afternoon.

Upon the 13th my Lord gave me three of his shirts to make clouts[76] of.

---

74 Clifford gave birth to Thomas, Lord Buckhurst, on 2 February 1620. He died on 6 July.
75 A pro-Catholic pamphlet attacking the rebellion planned by the Earl of Leicester, first published in 1584.
76 Diapers.

Upon the 14th Wat Conniston began to read the book of Josephus to me of the Antiquities of the Jews.[77]

Upon the 15th my Lord and I by M[r] Amherst's direction set our hands to a letter of attorney for Ralph Conniston to receive those debts which were due to my Lady of the tenants and this day Ralph Conniston went away towards his journey into the north. After supper my Lord and I had a great falling out, he saying that if ever my land came to me, I should assure it as he would have me.

Upon the 18th my Lord came and supped with me in my chamber which he had not done before since his coming from London for I determined to keep my chamber and did not so much as go over the threshold of the door.

Upon the 26th there dined below with the gentlewomen M[rs] Care, Goody Davis and Goody Crawley. I writ a letter to my Lord to thank him for the pedigree of the Sackvilles which he sent me down.

Upon the 29th Judith and Bromedish aired the furs which were come down from London and I spent the time as before in looking at the chronicles.

Upon the 30th and 31st I spent the time in hearing of reading and playing at tables with the steward. About this time my Lord of Doncaster came home from his long embassage in to Germany.

---

77 The first English translation of this work was published in 1602.

Appendix A: Aemilia Lanyer, "To the Lady Anne, Countess of Dorset" and "The Description of Cooke-ham"

[These two poems were included in Lanyer's 1611 publication, *Salve Deus Rex Judaeorum*. The centrepiece of the volume is a 1,500 line poem about the passion of Christ, with a special emphasis on the role of women in that story. There are eight dedicatory prefaces to noblewomen, and one to "All Virtuous Women in General." One of the dedications is to Clifford's mother Margaret, and the one included here is to Anne. The other dedicatees are the most influential and highly placed women in courtly society: they include Queen Anne, Princess Elizabeth, Arabella Stuart, and four more aristocratic women, all mentioned in the pages of Clifford's 1616–1619 diary. "The Description of Cookeham" is one of the additional pieces collected at the end of the volume. It is addressed to Margaret Clifford, and represents Anne as a young woman.

As Barbara K. Lewalski writes, "Aemilia Lanyer (1569–1645) was the first Englishwoman to publish a substantial volume of original poems, and to make an overt bid for patronage as a male poet of the era might, though in distinctively female terms" (213). She was the daughter of an Italian court musician and his English mistress, and was raised within households close to the courtly centre. She became the mistress of Henry Cary, Lord Hunsdon (mentioned in the 1619 diary, 65), a man much older than herself. Soon after marrying a court musician, Lanyer gave birth to a son named Henry, making little secret of the likelihood that it was Cary's child. Upon her husband's death, she engaged in lawsuits to recover some of his income, and later opened a school, which did not flourish.

It is clear from her writing that Lanyer hoped that Margaret Clifford would be her patron—support her, that is, as a poet, in her household—and that Anne Clifford would continue or enhance that patronage. Certainly, Lanyer stayed with the family at some time (probably between 1603 and 1605) at Cookham Dean (a house leased by Margaret's brother William and referred to as "Cookham" in the 1603 memoir). But no records survive showing a relationship of patron to client (Lewalski 216). We have no record of any poetry written by Lanyer after the publication of *Salve Deus*, so it appears that Lanyer did not receive the patronage she hoped for from the Cliffords, or indeed from the other ladies to whom the volume is dedicated. Why this was the case is not clear: Lanyer's poetry is skillful and compelling, and while it artfully refigures Christian myth and poetic genres to emphasize women's role in the history of virtue, it does so in ways which should have been acceptable to the women to whom it was addressed. Perhaps Lanyer's personal life made her unwelcome in that circle: while we think of her as a learned and talented poet, they may have thought of her first as the middle-class mistress of a nobleman, and therefore socially unacceptable. It is also possible that the women to whom she appealed for support did not want to support her as a *poet*, although there would have been ways to frame the patronage, such as by employing her as a servant or governess. Whatever the reason, it is sadly true that had Lanyer been male, she would likely have received the patronage she sought, and therefore been able to leave us with a more extensive body of work.

The dedicatory epistle to Anne Clifford shows all the conventional features of epideictic poetry, or the poetry of praise. This poetic style is aimed at reflecting its subject's virtues back to the subject: "Then in this mirror let your fair eyes look,/To view your virtues in this blessed book" (7–8). As a mirror or witness, the poem provides the subject with better knowledge of herself. More importantly, the poem will immortalize the subject—the praise will live on long after its subject's death:

> So shall you show from whence you are descended,
> And leave to all posterities your fame,
> So will your virtues always be commended,
> And every one will reverence your name;
> So this poor work of mine shall be defended
> From any scandal that the world can frame:
>   And you a glorious actor will appear
>   Lovely to all, but unto God most dear. (Stanza 11)

The terms of the praise are the ones the subject values, in this case Christian virtue and family continuity. Using these structures, the poet imagines a cycle of recognition, in which the subject of the poem is as needy of the poet and his or her praise as the poet is of the subject's support.

Envisioning the relationship between the patronized and the patron as cyclical and reciprocal (rather than hierarchical and dependent) gives the poet the opportunity to imagine that the social distance between the two is radically diminished. As an equal, the poet is "deserving" of material support comparable to that enjoyed by the patron—or at least not *undeserving*. To this conventional trope Lanyer adds the Christian belief that all are equal in the eyes of God:

> Greatness is no sure frame to build upon,
> No worldly treasure can assure that place;
> God makes both even, the cottage with the throne,
> All worldly honours there are counted base. (17–21)

Lanyer sustains this argument throughout the poem, drawing upon various theological precepts: that Christ's love is equally accessible to all, that death comes to all, and that worldly wealth is not recognized in the immaterial world of the soul and afterlife. As well as the traditional appeal to the patron's sense of self-worth (and even vanity) Lanyer adds an appeal to Christian conscience and virtue. Through this combination, she promises to immortalize Clifford as a noble and moral woman.

In "The Description of Cooke-ham" Lanyer also describes her subject, Margaret Clifford, as a devout Christian. She depicts her walking with her Bible, the books of which are personified as Christ and the apostles, Moses, David, and Joseph. As in the dedicatory verse to Anne, Lanyer also draws upon theological teachings to diminish the distance between herself and her potential patron:

> Unconstant fortune, thou art most to blame,
> Who casts us down into so low a frame:
> Where our great friends we cannot daily see,
> So great a difference is there in degree.
> Many are placed in those orbs of state,
> Partners in honour, so ordained by fate;
> Nearer in show, yet farther off in love,
> In which, the lowest always are above.
> But whither am I carried in conceit?
> My wit too weak to conster[1] of the great.
> Why not? although we are but born of earth,
> We may behold the heavens, despising death;

---

1 Construe

And loving heaven that is so far above,
May in the end vouchsafe us entire love. (103–16)

Lanyer also speaks of her own conversion at Cookham, where she "first obtained/Grace from that grace where perfect grace remained" (1–2), and depicts her poetry as a kind of offering that has religious resonance (5–6). To this set of images she adds selected references to classical mythology that stress the poem's potential to eternalize the memory of the patron, such as the phoenix and Echo—the nymph who died of grief at the death of Narcissus, and who remained a bodiless voice, responding to the words spoken by others.

"The Description of Cooke-ham" shares with Ben Jonson's "To Penshurst" (another example of the country-house poem) the construction of an idealized world in which man is the head of the natural and social worlds, and yet is also a harmonious part of both. This is part of the accepted tradition of the pastoral elegy, which mourns the loss of the harmony of man and society with nature. But Lanyer's poem is longer than "To Penshurst" or the typical pastoral elegy; and she depicts these relationships more extensively and intensively than is usual. The landscape leaps to respond to Margaret, and to serve her pleasure as she walks within it; the house dresses for her arrival, and is desolate at her departure. Most singular about this aspect of the poem, however, is that it does not depict the relationship between man, nature, and society, but rather between a *woman*, nature, and her society. That society is female: the other figures in the poem are her daughter Anne, and the poet. It has only implicit relations with the male society: at its most direct about such matters, the poem mentions that Anne is "To honourable Dorset now espoused" (95). But there are no fathers or husbands or patriarchs figured in the poem, and Lanyer depicts the lost ideal as both socially and genealogically female. Moreover, although this society is idealized, it is not radically simplified and rusticated, as is some pastoral poetry, but is rich with culture and learning. In its representation of a rich, complex, and civilized—but female-only—society, the poem is unprecedented and unequalled in English verse of the period.

The poem is also distinguished by its vivid depiction of melancholy. Pastoral elegy is always about loss, but it is not always about melancholy, which can be defined as insatiate grief. While the loss of place in "Cooke-ham" is mourned, it is the loss of the relationship that is the source of the melancholy. That relationship does not seem to conform to our expectations for the kind of friendship that Lanyer might have had with Clifford and with Margaret, according to the social norms and codes by which they lived. There are erotic elements to her affection for Anne ("yet it grieves me that I cannot be/Near unto her" [99–100]), and the depiction of the kiss exchanged on the tree belongs more comfortably in a love poem than it does here:

> To this fair tree, taking me by the hand,
> You did repeat the pleasures which had past,
> Seeming to grieve they could no longer last.
> And with a chaste, yet loving kiss took leave,
> Of which sweet kiss I did it soon bereave:
> Scorning a senseless creature should possess
> So rare a favour, so great happiness.
> No other kiss it could receive from me,
> For fear to give back what it took of thee:
> So I ungrateful creature did deceive it,
> Of that which you vouchsafed in love to leave it. (162–72)

In the last line, it is the poet's "heart" that will be tied, by the lines of poetry, to Margaret, rather than her fame, or her life, or her reputation. Part of the power of the poem comes from the sense that the speaker has lost not just a means of sustenance, and not simply a location or even a group of friends, but the object of her heart's desire. While same-sex desire and even relations between women were not unknown at the time, it was not conventional to the depiction of the relations between patrons and their clients to represent them as such "great friends" (105).

Finally, "Cooke-ham" offers us a portrait of Anne Clifford in her youth and young adulthood. It is extremely flattering, another convention of such poetry. Nonetheless, Lanyer selects certain compliments from among the many available, and these give us an idea of the young Clifford's character and pastimes. The poem praises Clifford's "well framed mind" (98), her "virtues" (100), her sense of "love and duty" (102); it frames the praise in terms of the continuity of her family's traits (93–94), and it mentions "sports" (119) which could be games, or playacting of some sort. And in the poem as a whole, she depicts a mother and daughter pair, isolated from the world but united together. These are all terms which feature in Clifford's evaluation of her self and her relationship with her mother, as we see in the excerpt from her autobiography printed later in this volume.

This text of "To the Lady Anne, Countess of Dorset" is a modernized version of the 1611 publication. The text of "The Description of Cooke-ham" is from *The Broadview Anthology of Seventeenth-Century Verse and Prose* (Peterborough, ON: Broadview Press, 2001).]

"To the Lady Anne, Countess of Dorset"

To you I dedicate this work of grace,
This frame of glory which I have erected,
For your fair mind I hold the fittest place,
Where virtue should be settled and protected;
If highest thoughts true honour do embrace,
And holy wisdom is of them respected:
     Then in this mirror let your fair eyes look,
     To view your virtues in this blessed book.

Blessed by our Saviour's merits, not my skill,
10   Which I acknowledge to be very small;
Yet if the least part of his blessed Will
I have perform'd, I count I have done all:
One spark of grace sufficient is to fill
Our lamps with oil, ready when he doth call
     To enter with the bridegroom to the feast,
     Where he that is the greatest may be least.[1]

Greatness is no sure frame to build upon,
No worldly treasure can assure that place;
God makes both even, the cottage with the throne,
20   All worldly honours there are counted base;
Those he holds dear, and reck'neth as his own,
Whose virtuous deeds by his especial grace
     Have gain'd his love, his kingdom, and his crown,
     Whom in the book of life he hath set down.

Titles of honour which the world bestows,
To none but to the virtuous doth belong;

---

1 Reference to the parable of the ten virgins, five of whom had oil for their lamps and were prepared to meet the bridegroom. See Matthew 25:1–13.

As beauteous bowers where true worth should repose,
And where his dwellings should be built most strong:
But when they are bestow'd upon her foes, 30
Poor virtue's friends endure the greatest wrong:
For they must suffer all indignity,
Until in heav'n they better graced be.

What difference was there when the world began,
Was it not virtue that distinguished all?
All sprang but from one woman and one man,
Then how doth gentry come to rise and fall?
Or who is he that very rightly can
Distinguish of his birth, or tell at all,
In what mean state his ancestors have been, 40
Before some one of worth did honour win?

Whose successors, although they bear his name,
Possessing not the riches of his mind,
How do we know they spring out of the same
True stock of honour, being not of that kind?
It is fair virtue gets immortal fame,
'Tis that doth all love and duty bind:
If he that much enjoys, doth little good,
We may suppose he comes not of that blood.

Nor is he fit for honour, or command, 50
If base affections over-rules his mind;
Or that self-will doth carry such a hand,
As worldly pleasures have the power to blind
So as he cannot see, nor understand
How to discharge that place to him assign'd:
God's steward must for all the poor provide,
If in God's house they purpose to abide.

To you, as to God's steward I do write,
In whom the seeds of virtue have been sown,
By your most worthy mother, in whose right, 60
All her fair parts you challenge as your own;
If you, sweet lady, will appear as bright
As ever creature did that time hath known,
Then wear this diadem I present to thee,
Which I have framed for her eternity.

You are the heir apparent of this crown
Of goodness, bounty, grace, love, piety,
By birth it's yours, then keep it as your own,
Defend it from all base indignity;
70   The right your mother hath to it, is known
Best unto you, who reaped such fruit thereby:
      This monument of her fair worth retain
      In your pure mind, and keep it from all stain.

And as your ancestors at first possessed
Their honours, for their honourable deeds,
Let their fair virtues never be transgressed,
Bind up the broken, stop the wound that bleeds,
Succour the poor, comfort the comfortless,
Cherish fair plants, suppress unwholesome weeds;
80   Although base pelfe[1] do chance to come in place,
      Yet let true worth receive your greatest grace.

So shall you show from whence you are descended,
And leave to all posterities your fame,
So will your virtues always be commended,
And every one will reverence your name;
So this poor work of mine shall be defended
From any scandal that the world can frame:
      And you a glorious actor will appear
      Lovely to all, but unto God most dear.

90   I know right well these are but needless lines,
To you, that are so perfect in your part,
Whose birth and education both combines;
Nay more than both, a pure and godly heart,
So well instructed to such fair designs,
By your dear mother, that there needs no art:
      Your ripe discretion in your tender years,
      By all your actions to the world appears.

I do but set a candle in the sun,
And add one drop of water to the sea,
100   Virtue and beauty both together run,
When you were born, within your breast to stay;

---

1 Weeds; waste.

Their quarrel ceased, which long before begun,
They live in peace, and all do them obey:
    In your fair madam, are they richly plac'd,
    Where all their worth by eternity is grac'd.

You goddess-like unto the world appear,
Enriched with more than fortune can bestow,
Goodness and Grace, which you do hold more dear
Than worldly wealth, which melts away like snow;
Your pleasure is the word of God to hear,   110
That his most holy precepts you may know:
    Your greatest honour, fair and virtuous deeds,
    Which from the love and fear of God proceeds.

Therefore to you (good madam) I present
His lovely love, more worth than purest gold,
Who for your sake his precious blood hath spent,
His death and passion here you may behold,
And view this lamb, that to the world was sent,
Whom your fair soul may in her arms enfold:
    Loving his love, that did endure such pain,   120
    That you in heaven a worthy place might gain.

For well you know, this world is but a stage
Where all do play their parts, and must be gone;
Here's no respect of persons, youth, nor age,
Death seizeth all, he never spareth one,
None can prevent or stay that tyrant's rage,
But Jesus Christ the just: by him alone
    He was overcome, He open set the door
    To eternal life, ne'er seen, never known before.

He is the stone the builders did refuse,   130
Which you, sweet lady, are to build upon;
He is the rock that holy church did choose,
Among which number, you must needs be one;
Fair shepherdess, 'tis you that He will use
To feed his flock, that trust in him alone:
    All worldly blessings he vouchsafes to you,
    That to the poor you may return his due.

And if deserts a lady's love may gain,
Then tell me, who hath more deserv'd than He?

140   Therefore in recompense of all his pain,
       Bestow your pains to read, and pardon me,
       If out of wants, or weakness of my brain,
       I have not done this work sufficiently;
            Yet lodge him in the closet of your heart,
            Whose worth is more than can be show'd by art.

"The Description of Cooke-ham"

       Farewell (sweet Cooke-ham) where I first obtained
       Grace from that grace where perfect grace remained;
       And where the muses gave their full consent,
       I should have power the virtuous to content:
       Where princely palace willed me to indite,
       The sacred story of the soul's delight.
       Farewell (sweet place) where virtue then did rest,
       And all delights did harbour in her breast:
       Never shall my sad eyes again behold
10   Those pleasures which my thoughts did then unfold:
       Yet you (great lady) mistress of that place,
       From whose desires did spring this work of grace;
       Vouchsafe to think upon those pleasures past,
       As fleeting worldly joys that could not last:
       Or, as dim shadows of celestial pleasures,
       Which are desired above all earthly treasures.
       Oh how (methought) against you thither came,
       Each part did seem some new delight to frame!
       The house received all ornaments to grace it,
20   And would endure no foulness to deface it.
       The walks put on their summer liveries,
       And all things else did hold like similes:
       The trees with leaves, with fruits, with flowers clad,
       Embraced each other, seeming to be glad,
       Turning themselves to beauteous canopies,
       To shade the bright sun from your brighter eyes:
       The crystal streams with silver spangles graced,
       While by the glorious sun they were embraced:
       The little birds in chirping notes did sing,
30   To entertain both you and that sweet spring.
       And Philomela[1] with her sundry lays,

---

1   Philomela was turned into a nightingale before she could be captured
    and killed by the man who had raped her. As a woman, she had her

Both you and that delightful place did praise.
Oh how methought each plant, each flower, each tree
Set forth their beauties then to welcome thee:
The very hills right humbly did descend,
When you to tread upon them did intend.
And as you set your feet, they still did rise,
Glad that they could receive so rich a prize.
The gentle winds did take delight to be
Among those woods that were so graced by thee.   40
And in sad murmur uttered pleasing sound,
That pleasure in that place might more abound:
The swelling banks delivered all their pride,
When such a Phoenix once they had espied.[1]
Each arbour, bank, each seat, each stately tree,
Thought themselves honoured in supporting thee.
The pretty birds would oft come to attend thee,
Yet fly away for fear they should offend thee:
The little creatures in the burrow by
Would come abroad to sport them in your eye;   50
Yet fearful of the bow in your fair hand,
Would run away when you did make a stand.
Now let me come unto that stately tree,
Wherein such goodly prospects you did see;
That oak that did in height his fellows pass,
As much as lofty trees, low growing grass:
Much like a comely cedar straight and tall,
Whose beauteous stature far exceeded all:
How often did you visit this fair tree,
Which seeming joyful in receiving thee,   60
Would like a palm tree spread his arms abroad,
Desirous that you there should make abode:
Whose fair green leaves much like a comely veil,
Defended Phoebus[2] when he would assail:
Whose pleasing boughs did yield a cool fresh air,
Joying his happiness when you were there.

---

tongue cut out by her attacker, but revealed him by weaving the story
into a tapestry. As the bird of poetry, she sings the most beautiful of all
songs.

1 In Greek mythology, the beauty of the Phoenix's song stopped the sun
   god in his chariot. The Phoenix is unique, there being only one alive at
   any one time. It is also a symbol of resurrection, as is Philomela.
2 The sun god.

Where being seated, you might plainly see,
Hills, vales, and woods, as if on bended knee
They had appeared, your honour to salute,
70 Or to prefer some strange unlooked for suit:
All interlaced with brooks and crystal springs,
A prospect fit to please the eyes of kings:
And thirteen shires appeared in all your sight,
Europe could not afford much more delight.
What was there then but gave you all content,
While you the time in meditation spent,
Of their Creator's power, which there you saw,
In all his creatures held a perfect law;
And in their beauties did you plain descry,
80 His beauty, wisdom, grace, love, majesty.
In these sweet woods how often did you walk,
With Christ and his Apostles there to talk;
Placing his holy writ in some fair tree,
To meditate what you therein did see:
With Moses you did mount his holy hill,
To know his pleasure, and perform his will.
With lovely David you did often sing,
His holy hymns to heaven's eternal King.
And in sweet music did your soul delight,
90 To sound his praises, morning, noon, and night.
With blessed Joseph you did often feed
Your pined brethren,[1] when they stood in need.
And that sweet lady sprung from Clifford's race,[2]
Of noble Bedford's blood, fair stream of grace;
To honourable Dorset now espoused,
In whose fair breast true virtue then was housed:
Oh what delight did my weak spirits find
In those pure parts of her well framed mind:
And yet it grieves me that I cannot be
100 Near unto her, whose virtues did agree
With those fair ornaments of outward beauty,
Which did enforce from all both love and duty.
Unconstant fortune, thou art most to blame,
Who casts us down into so low a frame:

---

1 Joseph fed the Israelites, who were "pined," or wasted by suffering and
  hunger.
2 I.e., Anne.

Where our great friends we cannot daily see,
So great a difference is there in degree.
Many are placed in those orbs of state,
Partners in honour, so ordained by fate;
Nearer in show, yet farther off in love,
In which, the lowest always are above. 110
But whither am I carried in conceit?
My wit too weak to conster of the great.[1]
Why not? although we are but born of earth,
We may behold the heavens, despising death;
And loving heaven that is so far above,
May in the end vouchsafe us entire love.
Therefore sweet memory do thou retain
Those pleasures past, which will not turn again:
Remember beauteous Dorset's former sports,[2]
So far from being touched by ill reports; 120
Wherein myself did always bear a part,
While reverend love presented my true heart:
Those recreations let me bear in mind,
Which her sweet youth and noble thoughts did find:
Whereof deprived, I evermore must grieve,
Hating blind fortune, careless to relieve.
And you sweet Cooke-ham, whom these ladies leave,
I now must tell the grief you did conceive,
At their departure; when they went away,
How everything retained a sad dismay: 130
Nay long before, when once an inkling came,
Methought each thing did unto sorrow frame:
The trees that were so glorious in our view,
Forsook both flowers and fruit, when once they knew
Of your depart, their very leaves did wither,
Changing their colours as they grew together.
But when they saw this had no power to stay you,
They often wept, though speechless, could not pray you;
Letting their tears in your fair bosoms fall,
As if they said, "Why will ye leave us all?" 140
This being vain, they cast their leaves away,
Hoping that pity would have made you stay:

---

1 I.e., "where is this thought taking me? I'm not capable of analyzing
   those above me."
2 I.e., Clifford, and the games that she and Lanyer played together.

Their frozen tops like Age's hoary hairs,
Shows their disasters, languishing in fears:
A swarthy rivelled ryne[1] all overspread,
Their dying bodies half alive, half dead.
But your occasions called you so away,
That nothing there had power to make you stay:
Yet did I see a noble grateful mind,
150   Requiting each according to their kind,
Forgetting not to turn and take your leave,
Of these sad creatures, powerless to receive
Your favour when with grief you did depart,
Placing their former pleasures in your heart;
Giving great charge to noble memory,
There to preserve their love continually:
But specially the love of that fair tree,
That first and last you did vouchsafe to see:
In which it pleased you oft to take the air,
160   With noble Dorset, then a virgin fair:
Where many a learned book was read and scanned
To this fair tree, taking me by the hand,
You did repeat the pleasures which had past,
Seeming to grieve they could no longer last.
And with a chaste, yet loving kiss took leave,
Of which sweet kiss I did it soon bereave:
Scorning a senseless creature should possess
So rare a favour, so great happiness.
No other kiss it could receive from me,
170   For fear to give back what it took of thee:
So I ungrateful creature did deceive it,
Of that which you vouchsafed in love to leave it.
And though it oft had giv'n me much content,
Yet this great wrong I never could repent:
But of the happiest made it most forlorn,
To show that nothing's free from nature's scorn,
While all the rest with this most beauteous tree,
Made their sad consort sorrow's harmony.
The flowers that on the banks and walks did grow,
180   Crept in the ground, the grass did weep for woe.
The winds and waters seemed to chide together,
Because you went away they know not whither:

---

1 Shrivelled bark.

And those sweet brooks that ran so fair and clear,
With grief and trouble wrinkled did appear.
Those pretty birds that wonted were to sing,
Now neither sing, nor chirp, nor use their wing;
But with their tender feet on some bare spray,
Warble forth sorrow, and their own dismay.
Fair Philomela leaves her mournful ditty,
Drowned in dead sleep, yet can procure no pity: 190
Each arbour, bank, each seat, each stately tree,
Looks bare and desolate now for want of thee;
Turning green tresses into frosty grey,
While in cold grief they wither all away.
The sun grew weak, his beams no comfort gave,
While all green things did make the earth their grave:
Each brier, each bramble, when you went away,
Caught fast your clothes, thinking to make you stay:
Delightful Echo wonted to reply
To our last words, did now for sorrow die: 200
The house cast off each garment that might grace it,
Putting on dust and cobwebs to deface it.
All desolation then there did appear,
When you were going whom they held so dear.
This last farewell to Cooke-ham here I give,
When I am dead thy name in this may live,
Wherein I have performed her noble hest,
Whose virtues lodge in my unworthy breast,
And ever shall, so long as life remains,
Tying my heart to her by those rich chains.   210

property or
margaret?

Appendix B: Anthony Stafford, "To the Admired Lady, Anne, Countess of Dorset," dedication to the second part of Stafford's Niobe, or His Age of Tears (1611)

[This dedication was printed with the second part of Anthony Stafford's theological treatise, *Stafford's Niobe, or His Age of Tears*, published in 1611, but was removed from most copies before they were bound. There is only one known copy of the dedication that survives, although two other copies have torn first pages (obscuring the dedicatee of the volume) (Williamson 329–32).

Niobe is an invective against the perceived sins of the times, as well as a call to discipline lust and desire: "to a discerning judgment the world is turned topsy-turvy, with the heels upwards; and nothing stands in his own place, but, what nature hath placed lowest, that the violence of vice hath carried highest" (*Niobe* 2.8). Stafford (1587–1645?) is known as a minor Catholic polemicist; none of his works were popular, and this one was no exception. He is probably, however, the addressee of Thomas Randolph's fine poem "An Ode to Master Anthony Stafford, to Hasten Him into the Country" (1638).

We believe that Clifford and her husband had the dedication removed from the volume. It is likely that it was offensive to Sackville and Clifford because of their loyalty to the state religion, which was Protestantism. Throughout this period it was important for community leaders to show their support for the English church, and to be perceived as resisting Catholicism, which was the religion of hostile foreign powers. This was true whatever their personal beliefs and forms of worship: England was officially a Protestant nation, and Catholic ritual was not permitted in churches or in private homes.

This is a modernized version of Williamson's copy of the dedication, printed in his biography of Clifford.]

To the admired lady, Anne, Countess of Dorset, daughter to the right honourable George, late Earl of Cumberland.

Lady (for no word can express your worth) I cannot but wonder at mine own admiration; that I who am hardly drawn into the admiration of any man should so easily be driven into amazement by a woman. I am astonished, Madame, I am astonished, and could find it in my heart to pray you, and such as you are (if there by any such) to desist from doing well: for I am afraid that (ere long) you will disable my sex, falsify the scriptures, and make woman the stronger vessel. But it is not I alone whom you have troubled and amazed: you grow cruel, and disquiet the first of your own sex, Eve, whose grieved ghost methinks I see rising out of her low-built bed, looking upon you with an envious blush, for doing her a never departing disgrace. For whereas she was created in perfection, and made her self imperfect, you being created in imperfection, have almost made your self perfect: and whereas she came first to know evil by doing evil, you know it, by doing good. Nay, which is more, Madam, you seem (but do but seem) to wrong God himself, and to disallow of his providence. For, whereas He hath thought it fit to place you in one of the highest degrees of honour, you creep downwards to the lowest degree of humility, as if you meant to steal from your title, and give it the slip, Lady, neither can I, neither dare I, praise you like a poet, but like a divine; for I know that the reason why we honour God no better is not only because we seek honour, one of another, but because we transfer his honour, one to another. No, no, Madam: I will not tell you, that you are without sin; though indeed, it seems to the world that you are: for sin, who is valiant in others, is a coward in you, and dare not come out, nor show himself. I am not therefore to be blamed, in giving you such short pinioned praises (which cannot soar so high as your long-winged worth) by reason that divinity curbs me, and forbids me to ascribe as much honour, and praise, to the architecture as to the architect. Which some, of late, have done and, to make ostentation of the strength of their wits, have made withall a declaration of the weakness of their judgments. I could tell you, Madam, that virtue wanted a beautiful lodging, and therefore commanded nature to build you, and that nature was content to fulfill her command, with this condition: that virtue should make you her principal palace. But, I will spare those praises, as needless, for your soul sits in the superficies [surface] of your face, and inward-you are seen in outward-you. And indeed, to say the truth, I have greater need to excuse the rash dedication of my book, than to extol you. But I hope, Lady, I shall deserve an excuse, by reason you have amazed and distracted me, by attracting the best parts of my mind from me, to honour the true honour which is in you. I beseech your ladyship then, to let my ecstasy excuse me, and gently to pronounce pardon to a gentleman, that here proclaims to the world he honours your virtues, not your fortunes, and commands posterity to post this small packet of your many virtues from one generation to another. Accept, then, Madam, this book, as from him, who can no longer smother the unexpressible honour he owes you. The favour, Madam, if you deign to me, I vow, that if I live after you, you shall live after me; and I will try if I can limne [draw] your soul, as curiously with the pen as the limner doth your body with the pencil. If Madame, you live after me, do me so much right as to say, "He is dead, who, amongst the few he honoured, honoured me most."

While you live, he that died for you, live and dwell in you, and grant, that you may glory as much that you shall be one of that other world, as we glory that you are one of this; and that as we are happy in you here, so you may be most happy there.

Your Ladyship's most
observant servant,
Anthony Stafford

Appendix C: The Great Picture of the Clifford Family, attributed to Jan van Belcamp (1610–53), dated 1646

[While Clifford's writing is *sui generis* ("of its own kind"), perhaps the single most extraordinary document she left behind is the massive family portrait known as *The Great Picture*.[1] In it she is depicted visibly twice, and invisibly one more time, as the centre tableau shows her family only days after her conception. It deserves as much attention as a text as do her written works, and rewards the student more readily than *The Great Books* with information about how she constructed her image in later years. There were two copies made, one for Appleby Castle and one for Skipton Castle: in these original locations, the portrait would have influenced more people, given the limited access to her written materials. Viewers would have included all of the residents of and visitors to the castles, including those who came for court hearings (and other official proceedings) held there. If we accept Richard Spence's assertion that "No one in the Stuart era appreciated better than Lady Anne the power of publicity in projecting an image and propounding a cause" (118), then this is the single most important example of that appreciation in her historical legacy.

The Skipton version of the painting does not survive. The Appleby version of the triptych, now at the Abbot Hall Art Gallery in Kendal, Cumbria, measures 18 feet wide and nine feet high, with the wings fully extended. The central panel depicts Clifford's brothers Francis and Robert, and her parents. The image represents the family in an imaginary tableau, gathered before George's departure to the Azores, and including Anne *in utero* (Spence 183). Portraits hanging on the wall of the painted space depict her aunts Margaret Clifford, Countess of Derby, George's half-sister; Frances Clifford, Baroness Wharton; Anne

---

1   We do not know for certain who painted this impressive and detailed family portrait: it has been attributed to Jan Van Belcamp and to Remigius Van Lemput, both Dutch (Spence 185).

Russell, Countess of Warwick, and Elizabeth Russell, Countess of Bath. The left hand panel shows Anne at the age 15, when (according to her own understanding) she should have inherited the property. The right hand panel shows her at the age (56) at which she did inherit the Westmorland estates. The left-hand panel contains inset portraits of her educators, Anne Taylor and Samuel Daniel; the right-hand panel depicts her husbands, Richard Sackville and Philip Herbert. Below each of these is an inscription giving a brief biography and summary of his or her relation to Clifford. Surrounding the panels are coats-of-arms and miniature biographies of her ancestors. These biographies reflect the researches done for the lawsuits and used in preparation of *The Great Books*. They cover six centuries of genealogy, and document the accretion of the assets of her inheritance, and the path of transmission that justified her claims.

The painting also gives us probably the most extensive record of a female-owned library from the period. There are fifty works depicted; each is identified with a short title. Works represented in the left-hand panel include William Camden's *Britannia*, Cornelius Agrippa's *The Vanity of the Arts and Sciences*, Miguel Cervantes' *Don Quixote*, Baldesar Castiglione's *Courtier*, Daniel's *Chronicles of England*, Michel de Montaigne's *Essays*, John Gerard's *Herbal*, Philip Sidney's *Arcadia*, Edmund Spenser's *Works*, Ovid's *Metamorphoses*, St. Augustine's *City of God*, Guillaume de Salluste Du Bartas' *Divine Weeks and Works*, and Chaucer's *Works*. In the right-hand panel, we see Plutarch's *Lives* and *Morals* (in French), Henry Wotton's *The Elements of Architecture*, Ben Jonson's *Works*, John Donne's *Poems*, George Herbert's *Poems*, several theological and meditational works about mortality, and John King's *Sermons*.

The collection is diverse, and includes works of poetry and fiction, devotion, philosophy, natural history and science, theology, geography, history, architecture, and social conduct. It is a miniature library of the English Renaissance, but it is not simply a selection of the books that any learned aristocrat should posses. The collection is distinctly modern, and includes many works published for the first time in Clifford's lifetime. It has no works of classical philosophy or rhetoric—no Aristotle, no Plato, no Cicero; and includes only Ovid's poetry—no Virgil or Horace. It has few works by church fathers (with the exception of St. Augustine): this implies, in part, the family's commitment to the reformed religion, as Protestants rejected many of the teachings of patristic writers in favour of direct reading of the Bible. It has more English works than a collection of this size might normally have, and also more works of English poetry. Her mother's interest in natural history and botany is clear in the selections on those topics, as is her father's experience in travel and navigation in geographical works such as Ortelius' *Theatre of the Whole World.* The collection's preponderance of historical works, from Plutarch to Daniel, reflects Cliffords' sustained interest in history-writing. As Spence points out, many of the authors whose works are depicted in the painting had social or familial connections to Clifford and her extended family (189), so the choices are also ones that reinforce the sense of her family's sphere encompassing all that was great about English culture.

The painting also artfully expresses Clifford's faith in the assertion of individual female rights and privileges within a patriarchal familial, social, and governmental system. The coats-of-arms and genealogies assert the primacy of male primogeniture, but also emphasize female inheritance within that system. While the figures themselves show a patrilineal line of inheritance from George to his heirs, it is Margaret who is pointing the way. Clifford herself dominates the visual tableau, and frames the rest of the genealogical diorama. She describes her distinctive resemblance to both her parents in the opening of her autobiography; but this resemblance is made even more explicit here. The manner of her dress in the right-hand portrait resembles that of her father. Other details also suggestively draw out this resemblance, such as the fact that her mother's pearls are draped like her father's sword-belt in the older portrait of herself. The size and opulence of *The Great Books* is a testament to her cultural authority and wealth, and the lavishness and expanse of this painting is an even more forceful witness to her prestige and power.]

Appendix D: From Anne Clifford, "A Summary of the Records and a True Memorial of the Life of Me the Lady Anne Clifford" (1652)

[This excerpt is from an early twentieth-century edition of one of the abridged versions of *The Great Books of the Records of Skipton Castle* (1652), more usually known as *The Great Books of the Clifford Family*, three large volumes illuminated with genealogical trees and decorative borders that were compiled under Clifford's direction. It is presumed that she wrote or dictated the lives of her immediate family, and possibly much of the rest of the volumes. There were three copies of the complete books made in her lifetime, and additional abridgements of these were made during the next two centuries, usually for family members. The records and accounts included in the books were intended to present proof of her claims to the Westmorland and Skipton titles. Her mother Margaret began the research for these volumes; both Margaret and later Clifford hired professional scholars and antiquaries to search for documents among the estate and state papers (Spence 164). In her diary of March 1619 Clifford mentions one of these men, saying "the 18th I compared the two books of the Cliffords that Mr Knisden sent me down."

The Great Books of the Clifford Family begins with biographical accounts of Clifford's ancestors from the eleventh and twelfth centuries, and continues through her own generation. The excerpt included here, written in 1652, is taken from her narrative autobiography, which covers the years from her conception to her inheritance and precedes the annual accounts.

Compared to the memoir and diary, this account is compact. Also, the events Clifford is describing are now many years removed, and there is less emotional immediacy than in her earlier accounts. Another difference is that this account was written to be read by others—not the public at large, but her family, descendants, and others within her circle of influence. The autobiography was written after Clifford's great deliverance by what she calls "a happy genius," as she looked back upon the conflicts of her earlier years from the comfortable perspective of a secure and happy outcome. She often reiterates her sense of having been delivered from her enemies by divine providence, as well as from the misfortunes they caused her. This sense is often expressed in Biblical quotations, through which she depicts herself as having been rewarded after long years of suffering and deprivation. Hindsight has not only eased the pain and softened the edges of earlier conflicts, but has bolstered her faith and her use of the commonplaces of that faith. One of the most interesting Biblical references, however, is not to her suffering and deliverance, but rather this passage from *Revelations* (14: 13), with which she describes her relationship with the memory of her mother: "And I heard a voice from heaven saying unto me, Write. Blessed are the dead which die in the Lord from henceforth: Yea, saith the Spirit, that they may rest from their labours; and their works do follow them."

This is a modernized version of the text, from *The Lives of Lady Anne Clifford and of Her Parents*, ed. J.P. Gilson. London: The Roxburghe Club, 1916.]

A summary of the records and a true memorial of the life of me the Lady Anne Clifford, who by birth being sole daughter and heir to my illustrious father, George Clifford, the 3rd Earl of Cumberland, by his virtuous wife Margaret Russell, my mother, in right descent from him, and his long continued noble ancestors the Veteriponts, Cliffords and Veseys, Baroness Clifford, Westmorland and Vesey, High Sheriffess of Westmorland, and Lady of the Honour of Skipton in Craven, was by my first marriage Countess Dowager of Dorset, and by my second marriage Countess Dowager of Pembroke and Montgomery.

I was, through the merciful providence of God, begotten by my valiant father, and conceived with child by my worthy mother, the first day of May in 1589 in the Lord Wharton's house in Channell Row in Westminster, hard by the river of Thames, as *Psalms* 139.[1] Yet I was not born 'til the 30th day of January following, when my blessed mother brought me forth in one of my father's chief houses called Skipton Castle in Craven, *Ecclesiastes* 3;[2] for she

---

1 See 139: 13–14, "For thou hast possessed my reins: thou hast covered me in my mother's womb. I will praise thee; for I am fearfully and wonderfully made: marvelous are thy works; and that my soul knoweth right well."

2 "To everything there is a season, and a time to every purpose under heaven," etc.

came down into the north from London with her two sons, being great with child with me, my father then being in great peril at sea in one of his voyages. For both a little before he begat me and a little after, it was ten thousand to one but that he had been cast away on the seas by tempests and contrary winds; yet it pleased God to preserve him, so as he lived to see my birth, and a good while after, for I was fifteen years and nine months old when he died. And some seven weeks before my mother was delivered of me died her eldest son, the Lord Francis Clifford, in the said Castle of Skipton, and the 22nd of February after my birth was I christened by the name of Anne in the parish church at Skipton; Philip, Lord Wharton, my aunt's husband, being then my godfather, my father being then at London, as he was also when I was born. For he landed in England the 29th of December before I was born, by reason of his great business of giving account to the Queen of his sea voyages, he lying then at Bedford House in the Strand, where Ambrose, Earl of Warwick, died the day before I was christened, who was husband to my mother's eldest sister, the excellent Anne Russell, Countess of Warwick.

About the last of March my father came down to Skipton Castle to us, which was the first time he ever saw me, I being then near eight weeks old. And the 2nd of April following my father and mother, carrying my brother Robert and myself along with them, went quite away from thence towards London. And I never came into that castle after that time 'til the 18th of July in 1649, when my second lord was then living, for he died not 'til the 13th of January following. And about six months before my then coming thither the said Castle had been demolished, and the principle buildings thereof quite pulled down by order of Parliament, having been made and kept as a garrison in the time of the late Civil Wars. *Ecclesiastes* 8:6.[1]

I was but some ten weeks old when I first came up to London, yet did not I nor my mother return again into the north 'til after the death of my father, remaining both of us in the southern parts, as Northamptonshire, Hertfordshire, Kent, Berkshire, and Surrey, and in and about the court and city of London, all that time. When I was about a year and four months old died my second brother Robert, then Lord Clifford, in North Hall in Hertfordshire, the 24th of May in 1591; and ever after that time

---

1 "Because to every purpose there is time and judgment, therefore the misery of man is great upon him."

I continued to be the only child to my parents, nor had they any other daughter but myself.

I was very happy in my first constitution both in mind and body, both for internal and external endowments, for never was there child more equally resembling both father and mother than myself. The colour of mine eyes were black like my father, and the form and aspect of them was quick and lively like my mother's; the hair of my head was brown and very thick, and so long that it reached to the calf of my legs when I stood upright, with a peak of hair on my forehead, and a dimple in my chin, like my father, full cheeks and round face like my mother, and an exquisite shape of body resembling my father. But now time and age hath long since ended all those beauties, which are to be compared to the grass of the field. *Isaiah* 40: 6, 7, 8;[1] *1 Peter* 1: 24.[2] For now when I cause those memorables of myself to be written I have passed the 63rd year of my age. And, though I say it, the perfections of my mind were much above those of my body; I had a strong and copious memory, a sound judgment and a discerning spirit, and so much of a strong imagination in me, as that many times even my dreams and apprehensions before hand proved to be true; so as old M[r] John Denham, a great astronomer, that sometime lived in my father's house, would often say that I had much in me in nature to show that the sweet influences of the Pleiades and the bands of Orion, mentioned in that 38th chapter of *Job*, verses 31, 32, 33, were powerful both at my conception and nativity.

But happy births are many times attended on by cross fortunes in this world, which nevertheless I overcame by the divine mercy of almighty God, *Psalms* 121.[3] And from my childhood, by the bringing up of my said dear mother, I did, as it were, even suck the milk of goodness, which made my mind grow strong against the storms of fortune, which few avoid that are greatly born and matched, if they attain to any number of years; unless they betake themselves to a private retiredness, which I could

---

1 "All flesh is grass, and all the goodliness thereof is as the flower of the field. The grass withereth, the flower fadeth: because the spirit of the Lord bloweth upon it: surely the people is grass. The grass withereth, the flower fadeth; but the word of our God shall stand forever."

2 "For all flesh is as grass, and all the glory of man as the flower of grass. The grass withereth, and the flower thereof falleth away."

3 "I will lift up mine eyes unto the hills, from whence cometh my help. My help cometh from the Lord, which made heaven and earth" (1–2).

never do 'til after the death of both my two husbands. In my infancy and childhood, by the means of my said aunt of Warwick, I was much beloved by that renowned Queen Elizabeth, who died when I was about thirteen years and two months old, and my mother outlived that excellent Queen the same time of thirteen years and two months over.

And the 1st of September in 1605 was the last time I ever saw my father in the air abroad; for then I took my leave of him on Greenwich Heath in Kent, as he brought me so far on my way toward Sutton in Kent, where my mother then lay, after I had been and stayed the space of a month in the old house at Grafton in Northamptonshire, where my father then lived, by reason of some unhappy unkindnesses towards my mother, and where he entertained King James and Queen Anne with great magnificence. Which was a time of great sorrow to my saint-like mother 'til I returned back again to her from my father the 1st day of September. *Psalms* 90: 15, 16, 17.[1]

The 30th of October, being Thursday, 1605, in the 3rd year of the reign of King James, died my noble and brave father, George, Earl of Cumberland, in the Duchy House by the Savoy at London, near the river of Thames, when he was about three months past forty-seven years old, my mother and I being present with him at his death, I being then just fifteen years and nine months old the same day; where a little before his death he expressed with much affection to my mother and me a great belief that he had, that his brother's son would die without issue male, and thereby all his lands would come to be mine; which accordingly befell, about thirty-eight years after, for his brother's son Henry, Earl of Cumberland, died without heirs male in the city of York the 11th of December 1643.

My father, for the love he bore to his brother, and the advancement of the heirs male of his house, by his last will and other conveyances which he had formerly sealed, did leave to his brother Francis, who succeeded him in the Earldom of Cumberland, and to the heirs male of his body, all his castles, lands and honours, with a proviso that they should all return to me, his only daughter and heir, if the heirs male failed; which they afterwards did, as

---

1 "Make us glad according to the days wherein thou hast afflicted us, and the years wherein we have seen evil. Let thy work appear unto thy servants, and thy glory unto their children. And let the beauty of the Lord our God be upon us: and establish thou the work of our hands upon us: yea, the work of our hands establish thou it."

before is mentioned. And my father was the last heir male of the Cliffords who did rightfully enjoy those ancient lands and honours in Westmorland given by King John to Robert de Vateripont, the 28th of October in the 5th year of his reign [1204], and the Honour of Skipton in Craven, and the lands thereunto belonging, given to Robert de Clifford, by King Edward the 2nd the [blank] day of [blank] in the 5th year of his reign [1311]; for my father was the seventeenth in descent from the first Robert de Clifford that was rightfully possessed of those lands and honours of Skipton in Craven; in all which long time those lands descended still from father to son, except twice, that they descended to the younger brother, the elder dying without issue, which was in the 1st [1327] and in the 36th year [1363] of King Edward the 3rd, "for those were ancient times," as *1 Chronicles* 4: 22.

I must not forget to acknowledge that in my infancy and youth and a great part of my life I have escaped many dangers, both by fire and water, by passage in coaches, and falls from horses, by burning fevers, and excessive extremity of bleeding many times to the great hazard of my life, all which, and many cunning and wicked devices of my enemies, I have escaped and passed through miraculously, and much the better by the help of prayers of my devout mother, who incessantly begged of God for my safety and preservation. *James* 5: 16.[1]

Presently after the death of my father, I being left his sole daughter and heir, his widow, my dear mother, out of her affectionate care for my good, caused me to choose her my guardian; and then in my name she began to sue out a livery in the Court of Wards, for my right to all my father's lands, by way of prevention to hinder and interrupt the livery which my uncle of Cumberland intended to sue out in my name, without either my consent or my mother's. Which caused great suits of law to arise between her and my said uncle, which in effect continued, for one cause or other, during her life; in which she showed a most brave spirit, and never yielded to any opposition whatsoever. In which business King James began to show himself extremely against my mother and me. In which course he still pursued, though his wife Queen Anne was ever inclining to our part and very gracious and

---

1 "Confess your faults one to another, and pray one for another, that ye may be healed. The effectual fervent prayer of a righteous man availeth much."

favourable unto us; for in my youth I was much in the court with her, and in masques attended her, though I never served her.[1]

So about the 9th of June in 1607, in the fifth year of his reign, to show how much he was bent against my blessed mother and myself in my uncles' behalf, he then gave the reversion of all those lands in Westmorland and Craven out of the Crown by patent to my uncle Francis, Earl of Cumberland, and to his heirs for ever (as appears by the records), after they had continued in the Crown from the time they were given by King John and King Edward the 2nd to my ancestors, 'til after the death of my father, excepting some few times of attainder, which were still restored again, the last restoration being in the first year of King Henry the 7th.[2] The grant of which land out of the Crown to my said uncle and his heirs was done merely to defeat me, as hoping to get my hand to release it to the heirs male. But after, by the providence of God, it turned to the best for me, for if this patent had not been granted out of the Crown, I should not have had that power which now I have to dispose of my lands to whomsoever I please: *Job* 5: 11–17.[3]

---

1   In court masques, Clifford was one of the noble ladies dancing in attendance on the Queen, but she never served her as a waiting woman, an intimate servant, friend, and advisor.

2   Here her uncle and the King are trying to repair, after the fact, the problem presented by the fact that her father's lawyers had neglected to have the Crown's rights to the lands formally removed from the records of its ownership. Clifford's suits were based, in part, upon the fact that the lands were illegally bequeathed to her uncle—the Crown's reversionary rights, as explained in the Introduction (20-21), invalidated the bequest. The change did not affect the legal problems with George's will, but was a clear indication of the Crown's preferences in the matter and, as Clifford says, was intended to pressure her into agreeing to relinquish her claim. Ironically, the removal of the reversion rights were ultimately to her benefit, as she notes below, as she was then able to will the property according to her preferences.

3   "To set up on high those that be low; that those which mourn may be exalted to safety. He disappointeth the devices of the crafty, so that their hands cannot perform their enterprise. He taketh the wise in their own craftiness: and the counsel of the froward is carried headlong. They meet with darkness in the daytime, and grope in the noonday as in the night. But he saveth the poor from the sword, from their mouth, and from the hand of the mighty. So the poor hath hope, and iniquity stoppeth her mouth. Behold, happy is the man whom God correcteth: therefore despise not thou the chastening of the Almighty."

Now by reason of those great suits in law my mother and I were in a manner forced for our own good to go together from London down into Westmorland; and so we came into Appleby Castle the 22nd of July in 1607, to lie there for a while, it being the first time I came into that county or to any of my father's lands after his death. We lay also that summer for two or three nights in Brougham Castle in the chamber where my father was born, and wherein afterwards my mother died; and that was the first time I ever came into that castle. And about that time I lay for three or four nights in Naworth Castle in Cumberland, it being the first time I ever came into that country.

The 8th day of that October 1607 my dear mother and I went out of Appleby Castle on our journey towards London, it being the last time I was ever with her in the said castle, though I was after with her in Brougham Castle in the year 1616. And in our way through Craven, the 12th of October, my mother and I would have gone into the Castle of Skipton to have seen it, but were not permitted so to do, the doors thereof being shut against us by my uncle of Cumberland's officers in an uncivil and disdainful manner; to which castle I never came after that time 'til the 18th of July in 1649, as it is before mentioned. And the 13th of that October was the last time that my mother was in her hospital [almshouse] at Beamsley, and the first time of my being there; for then we lay in Mr. Clapham's house there, it being the last time my blessed mother ever lay in Craven or was in that country. And from thence she and I arrived safe at London the 23rd of that October at our house at Augustine Friars, where I was married about a year and four months after to my first lord, Richard, Earl of Dorset.

And the 18th day of April after our return in 1608, I being then a maid, was the great pleading in the Court of Wards concerning the lands of mine inheritance in Westmorland and Craven, which pleading is amongst the records of my mother's time when she was a widow.

I must confess with unexpressible thankfulness that though through the goodness of almighty God and the mercies of my saviour Christ Jesus, redeemer of the world, I was born a happy creature in mind, body and fortune, and that those two lords of mine, to whom I was afterwards by the divine providence married, were in their several kinds worthy noblemen as any then were in this kingdom; yet was it my misfortune to have contradictions and crosses with them both: with my first lord about the desire he had to make me sell my rights in the lands of my ancient inheritance for money, which I never did, nor never would consent unto, insomuch as this matter was the cause of a long contention betwixt us, as also for his profuseness in consuming his estate, and some other extravagancies of his; and with my second lord, because my youngest daughter, the Lady Isabella Sackville, would not be brought to marry one of his younger sons, and that I would not relinquish my interest I had in 5000 pounds, being part of her portion, out of my lands in Craven. Nor did there want diverse malicious illwillers to blow and foment the coals of dissension betwixt us, so as in both their life times, the marble pillars of Knole in Kent and Wilton in Wiltshire were to me often times but the gay arbour of anguish. Insomuch as a wise man that knew the insides of my fortune would often say that I lived in both these my lords' great families as the river of Roan or Rodamus runs through the lake of Geneva, without mingling any part of its streams with that lake; for I gave myself wholly to retiredness, as much as I could, in both those great families, and made good books and virtuous thoughts my companions, which can never discern affliction, nor be daunted when it unjustly happens. And by a happy genius I overcame all those troubles, *Psalms* 62,[1] the prayers of my blessed mother helping me therein. *Isaiah* 5:16;[2] *Isaiah* 26:20;[3] *Psalms* 57;[4] *Psalms* 43;[5]

---

1 Especially 3–5, "How long will ye imagine mischief against a man? Ye shall be slain all of you: as a bowing all shall ye be, and as a tottering fence. They only consult to cast him down from his excellency: they delight in lies: they bless with their mouth, but they curse inwardly. Selah. My soul, wait thou only upon God; for my expectation is from him."

2 "But the Lord of hosts shall be exalted in judgment, and God that is holy shall be sanctified in righteousness."

3 "Come, my people, enter thou into thy chambers, and shut thy doors about thee: hide thyself as it were for a little moment, until the indignation be overpast."

4 Especially 3–4, "He shall send from heaven, and save me from the reproach of him that would swallow me up. Selah. God shall send forth his mercy and his truth. My soul is among lions: and I lie even among them that are set on fire, even the sons of men, whose teeth are spears and arrows, and their tongue a sharp sword."

5 Which begins, "Judge me, O God, and plead my cause against an ungodly nation: O deliver me from the deceitful and unjust man."

Psalms 71;[1] *Isaiah* 30: 9, 10.[2]

The Course of Life of this Anne, Countess of Dorset, etc., while she was wife and widow to Richard Sackville, Earl of Dorset

The 25th day of February in 1609, as the year begins on New Year's day, I was married to my first lord, Richard Sackville, then but Lord Buckhurst, in my mother's house and her own chamber in Augustine Friars in London, which was part of a chapel formerly, she being then present at my marriage; and within two days after I was married died my said lord's father, Robert Sackville, Earl of Dorset, in Little Dorset House at Salisbury Court at London, by whose death my said lord and I came then to be Earl and Countess of Dorset. *Job* 7: 1;[3] *Ecclesiastes* 3: 1.[4]

And the 25th of July in 1610, a year and five months after my said first marriage, was my cousin german[5] Henry, Lord Clifford, only son of my uncle of Cumberland, married in Kensington near London to the Lady Frances Cecil, daughter to Robert, Earl of Salisbury, Lord High Treasurer of England, and then the greatest man of power in the kingdom. Which marriage was purposely made, that by that power and greatness of his the lands of mine inheritance might be wrested and kept by strong hand from me; which notwithstanding came not to pass, by the providence of God, for the issue male which they had between them all died, and they left one only daughter behind them, the Lady Elizabeth, who is now Countess of Cork.

About two years after I was married to my said Lord he went to travel into France and the Low countries for a year, upon a

---

1 Especially 4–8, "Deliver me, O my God, out of the hand of the wicked, out of the hand of the unrighteous and cruel man. For thou art my hope, O Lord God: thou art my trust from my youth. By thee have I been holden up from the womb: thou art he that took me out of my mother's bowels: my praise shall be continually of thee."

2 "That this is a rebellious people, lying children, children that will not hear the law of the Lord: Which say to the seers, see not; and to the prophets, prophesy not unto us right things, speak unto us smooth things, prophesy deceits."

3 "Is there not an appointed time to man upon earth? Are not his days also like the days of an hireling?"

4 "To every thing there is a season, and a time to every purpose under the heaven."

5 Meaning a cousin by blood, rather than by marriage.

pre-engagement to his grandmother and others of his friends before he married me. He stayed beyond sea about a year, and came to me in Knole in Kent the 8th of April 1612, and lived twelve years after that. And the 8th of August after his coming home in that year, and three years and six months after I was married unto him, died, the 30th of August in that year 1612, my worthy cousin german the Lady Frances Bourchier, of a burning fever, to my great grief and sorrow, in my mother's house called Sutton in Kent; and she was buried in the church at Cheneys in Buckinghamshire.

And in the time that I after lived his wife I had by him five children, three sons and two daughters. The three sons all of them died young at Knole in Kent, where they were born; but my first child the Lady Margaret, who was born in Dorset House the 2nd of July in 1614, is now Countess of Thanet and mother of ten children. She was born in the life time of my dear mother, who was then at London, though not present at her birth.

My youngest daughter was born at Knole House in Kent the 6th of October in 1622, who is now Countess of Northampton and hath been mother of two children, that were sons, and one of them is dead. When my eldest daughter was near a year old, the 16th of June in 1615, was the great trial for my lands in Craven at the Common Pleas bar in Westminster Hall, as appears in the records of my time when I was Countess of Dorset; but my first lord and my uncle of Cumberland and his son, being all three present, agreed together to put it to the arbitration of the four chief judges then in England; which though it never came to be effected, because my mother and I absolutely refused to consent to it, yet was it the ground of that award, which King James a little after did make to my prejudice for all the lands of mine inheritance, and the cause of many griefs, sorrows and discontents. *Psalms* 40: 15, 16, 17.[1]

And by reason of that intended arbitration of the four judges I went to Brougham Castle in Westmorland to my dear mother, to ask her consent therein, but she would never be brought to submit or agree to it, being a woman of a high and great spirit, in

---

1 "Let them be desolate for a reward of their shame that say unto me, Aha, aha. Let all those that seek thee rejoice and be glad in thee: let such as love thy salvation say continually, the Lord be magnified."

which denial she directed for my good, as *Psalms* 32: 8;[1] *Isaiah* 30: 21, 28;[2] *Isaiah* 42: 3.[3]

And the 2nd of that April 1616 I took my last leave of my dear and blessed mother with many tears and much sorrow to us both, some quarter of a mile from Brougham Castle in the open air; after which time she and I never saw one another; for then I went away out of Westmorland towards London and so to Knole House in Kent, whither I came the 11th day of that month to my first and then only child, the Lady Margaret, and her father, where I then lay 'til after my mother's death.

And the month following, the 24th day, that blessed mother of mine died, to my unspeakable grief, in that castle of hers of Brougham aforesaid in Westmorland, in the same chamber wherein my father was born, myself, at the time of her death, being at Knole House in Kent. And a little after her death I went down into Westmorland again, and was present at her burial in Appleby church the 11th of July following; the remembrance of whose sweet and excellent virtues hath been the chief companions of my thoughts ever since she departed out of this world. *Revelations* 14: 13.[4] And a while after her death, the 22nd of August 1616, my said lord came to me to Brougham Castle in Westmorland for a fortnight or three weeks, and that was the only time that he was in any part of the lands of mine inheritance.

And from thence for four or five nights my lord and I went to Naworth Castle, his uncle the Lord William Howard's house in Cumberland, it being the first and last time that ever he was in that county. The 13th of September following my said lord went from Brougham Castle from me to York, where he lay for four or five nights, and where, my said lord, my uncle of Cumberland and his son being present, the case was pleaded for my lands

---

1 "I will instruct thee and teach thee in the way which thou shalt go; I will guide thee with mine eye."

2 *Isaiah* 30: 28 is not a relevant passage. Gilson suggests 18 instead, but 20 and 21 are both relevant. "And though the Lord give you the bread of adversity, and the water of affliction, yet shall not thy teachers be removed into a corner any more, but thine eyes shall see thy teachers. And thine ears shall hear a word behind thee saying, this is the way, walk ye in it, when ye turn to the right hand, and when ye turn to the left."

3 "A bruised need shall he not break, and the smoking flax shall he not quench: he shall bring judgment unto truth."

4 "And I heard a voice from heaven saying unto me, Write. Blessed are the dead which die in the Lord from henceforth: Yea, saith the Spirit, that they may rest from their labours; and their works do follow them."

before Edmond, Lord Sheffield, then Lord President of the North, and afterwards Earl of Mulgrave, on the 19th of September; which pleading is extant in the records of my time, the said lord of mine coming well to London the 26th of that month.

And about the 9th of December following, some three months after, I myself went from Brougham Castle to York and from thence to London. And so the possession of that castle, which was only kept for me in Westmorland, was wholly delivered up to the use of my uncle of Cumberland and his son again, the 29th of March in 1617; which they kept from me 'til their deaths, the latter of whom died not 'til the 11th of December, 1643, in the city of York.

The 18th and 20th of January 1617, as the year begins on New Year's Day, I was brought before King James in Whitehall to give my consent to the award, which he then intended to make, and did afterwards perform, concerning all the lands of mine inheritance; which I utterly refused, and was thereby afterwards brought to many and great troubles.

But notwithstanding my refusal, the 14th of March following, at which time the said King James took his journey towards Scotland, did my said lord sign and seal that award in Great Dorset House, by which he resigned to Francis, Earl of Cumberland and Henry, Lord Clifford, his son, and to their heirs male, all his right in the lands of mine inheritance; which brought many troubles upon me, the most part of the time after that I lived his wife; but notwithstanding those great and innumerable difficulties and oppositions God protected and enabled me to pass through them all. *Psalms* 32: 8;[1] *Isaiah* 30: 21;[2] *Jeremiah* 42: 3;[3] *Psalms* 71.[4]

And for the most part, while I was his wife, I lived either in his houses at Knole in Kent, or at Bolebrook in Sussex, or in Great Dorset House or in Little Dorset House in London; but Great Dorset House came not to be his 'til the decease of his good grandmother, Cecily Baker, Countess Dowager of Dorset, who was above eighty years of age when she died there, whose jointure-house it was. She died the 1st of October, 1615. She was a woman of great piety and goodness. And the 22nd of September in 1618 died his mother-in-law [stepmother], Anne Spencer,

---

1 "I will instruct thee and teach thee in the way which thou shalt go: I will guide thee with mine eye."
2 See above, note 228n2.
3 "That the Lord thy God may show us the way wherein we may walk, and the thing that we may do."
4 See above, note 226n1.

Countess Dowager of Dorset, who had been first married to William Stanley, Lord Mounteagle, and secondly to Henry, Lord Compton, before she married his father. She was a lady of great wit and spirit.

On the 10th day of July 1623 did my said lord, in Great Dorset House, he being then very sickly, make over to me my jointure of those lands in Sussex, part whereof I now enjoy, and part thereof I have assigned and made over to my two daughters. And two days after the jointure was thus made died William Bourchier, Earl of Bath, in his house at Temistock in Devonshire, by whose decease his son Edward, then his only child, and my cousin german, came to be Earl of Bath, and lived so thirteen years and eight months, and died without issue male, leaving only three daughters behind him.

Though I was happy in many respects being his wife, yet was I most unhappy in having the malicious hatred of his brother, then Sir Edward Sackville, towards me, who after came to be Earl of Dorset, by my said Lord's decease without heirs male; and by the cunningness of his wit he was a great practiser against me, from the time that I married his brother till his own death; which happened not 'til the 17th of July 1652, for he outlived his brother twenty-eight years and almost four months. And I then lay at Skipton Castle in Craven, at the time of his death; but I, whose destiny was guided by a merciful and divine providence, escaped the subtlety of all his practices, and the evils which he plotted against me. *Psalms* 35;[1] *Psalms* 37;[2] *Psalms* 140;[3] *Psalms* 3: 10.[4]

My first lord, Richard Sackville, Earl of Dorset, died at Great Dorset House at London the 28th day of March, being Easter Sunday, in 1624, about 12 a clock at noon, and was buried unopened, the 7th of April following, in the vault at Withyham church in Sussex, by his son Buckhurst, my child, and many others of the Sackvilles, his ancestors, and their wives. He was then just thirty-five years old at his death, and I about ten months

---

1 This passage begins, "Plead my cause, O Lord, with them that strive with me: fight against them that fight against me."

2 This passage begins, "Fret not thyself because of evildoers, neither be thou envious against the workers of iniquity."

3 This passage begins, "Deliver me, O Lord, from the evil man: preserve me from the violent man."

4 This reference is not correct; possibly 33: 10, "The Lord bringeth the counsel of the heathen to nought: he maketh the devices of the people of none effect."

younger; but I was not with him when he died, being then very sick and ill myself at Knole House in Kent, where I and my two daughters then lay. *Job* 7: 1;[1] *Ecclesiastes* 3;[2] 8:6.[3]

This first lord of mine was born the 28th day of March in 1589 in the Charterhouse in London, now called Sutton's Hospital, his mother being the Lady Margaret Howard, only daughter to Thomas, Duke of Norfolk, who was beheaded the 2nd of June 1572. This first lord of mine was in his own nature of a just mind, of a sweet disposition, and very valiant in his own person.

He had a great advantage in his breeding by the wisdom and devotion of his grandfather Thomas Sackville, Earl of Dorset, and Lord High Treasurer of England, who was then held one of the wisest men of that time, by which means he was so good a scholar in all manner of learning that in his youth when he lived in the University of Oxford, his said grandfather being at that time Chancellor of that University, there was none of the young nobility then students there that excelled him. He was also a good patriot to his country, and generally well beloved in it, much esteemed of by all the Parliaments that sat in his time, and so great a lover of scholars and soldiers, as that with an excessive bounty towards them, or indeed any of worth that were in distress, he did much diminish his estate, as also with excessive prodigality in house-keeping, and other noble ways at court, as tilting, masquing, and the like; Prince Henry being then alive, who was much addicted to those noble exercises, and of whom he was much beloved.

This first lord of mine built from the ground the College or Hospital of East Grinstead in Sussex, and endowed the same with lands for the maintenance thereof, though his father by his last will had appointed the building thereof, but lived not to see any part of it performed, he dying presently after.

This noble lord of mine died in his house at Great Dorset House at London the 28th of March, 1624, as is aforesaid, leaving only two daughters behind him, which he had by me; for the sons which he had by me died in his life time, so as his brother Sir Edward Sackville succeeded him in the Earldom of Dorset, who was beyond sea at Florence in Italy at the time of his brother's death, but came through France into England about the latter

---

1 See above, note 226n3.
2 See above, note 226n4.
3 "Because to every purpose there is a time and judgment, therefore the misery of man is great upon him."

end of May following, and never went out of England after; but grew to be a great man at the court both in the little time that King James lived and reigned after, and in King Charles' time, so as he was Lord Chamberlain to his Queen, and Knight of the Garter, and continued still to be a powerful enemy against me.

Appendix E: *From Edward Rainbow, Bishop of Carlisle,* A Sermon Preached at the Funeral of the Right Honourable Anne, Countess of Pembroke, Dorset, and Montgomery, who Died March 22, 1676, and was Interred April the 14th the Following at Appleby in Westmorland. With Some Remarks on the Life of that Eminent Lady

[Anne Clifford died on 22 March 1676. According to Spence, "her express wish was for a quiet family funeral" (242), but hundreds attended and heard this sermon delivered by Edward Rainbow, Bishop of Carlisle. It is a classical oration that begins with the choice of a text "suitable to the occasion of our present meeting," and continues with a detailed analysis of both the text ("every wise woman buildeth her house") and the occasion, the life and death of Clifford. It is a panygeric, high-flying and overblown in its praise of the subject. Its artistry is intended to reflect on the quality of both the speaker, Rainbow, and his subject, Clifford. It shows Clifford as she wished to be remembered by her people: as the exemplary, pious, and authoritative leader of her community.

Rainbow's biography was written by Jonathan Banks and published in 1688, and from it we learn much about his life. Edward Rainbow was the son of Thomas Rainbow, a churchman, and his wife Rebecca, a learned, middle-class woman. He was educated at his local grammar school, followed by Westminster, and then Magdalen College, Oxford. He took his B.A., his M.A., and his doctorate in divinity at Magdalen, and was a fellow, Dean and finally Master of the College. He worked as a tutor to the sons of Theophilus Howard, Earl of Suffolk (mentioned in *The Diary*), who also preferred him to church offices. In the Civil War he sided with the Royalists, and as a result lost his mastership of Magdalen for refusing to agree to a petition against the crown in 1650; exiled from Oxford, he took a position as a village priest in the county of Essex. The fall of the republican government and the re-instatement of the monarchy in 1660 changed his fortunes for the better, and he was made Vice-Chancellor of Cambridge in 1662 and Bishop of Carlisle in 1664. He wrote a collection of divine poems, and Banks' 1688 biography notes that "In his youth he had a rich vein in poesy, in which appeared somewhat of Ovid's air and fancy, tempered with the judgment of Virgil" (84). Banks characterizes him, beyond the measures usual in laudatory biography, as a man of conscience and modesty. Neither Banks nor Clifford's biographers note any especial connection between Rainbow and Clifford.

The oration is an exemplary exercise in the analysis of the figurative potential of the simplest statements in the Bible. The doctor of divinity's training was all directed towards this activity: all of his speaking—from regular sermons, to occasional speeches such as this one—developed the import, for the Christian subject, of the word of God. "I must first remind you," writes Rainbow, "that the manner of expressing the great and important truths in this text ... is for the most part figurative, synecdochical, allegorical, by parables, proverbs and similitudes." Biblical language, that is, was understood to be the distillation of all possible meaning, and each word was an opening into a world of riches and plentitude. The fundamental figure of Biblical language was metaphor: the word was the vehicle, or signifier, and as a theologian, the divine developed the many tenors, or signifieds, of the word. As an orator, the divine organized the meanings thus produced, and presented them powerfully and persuasively.

Rainbow divides his analysis of the passage into three parts. First, he analyzes "woman." He begins with theological arguments about the sex of the soul, drawing on scriptures to argue that the soul is without gender. Turning to history, he notes that it was a woman who gave birth to Christ and women who praised Him; and that women throughout classical and Christian history have proved themselves to be models of virtue. He then looks to moral philosophy, where he finds that all that is good has been figured as female: "Lastly, all the virtues intellectual, moral, prudence, justice; nay, even the theological, faith, hope and charity, in the import of their names, the properties and things ascribed to them, are represented under the schemes and figures of women." By this analysis he has established that "woman" is an appropriate subject for the adjective "wise," which he then proceeds to examine in detail. He defines wisdom in Christian terms: it begins with "fear of the Lord," and the ability "to know and practice all things which conduce to his worship and glory, and to man's happiness." He defines wisdom as an active form of virtue, rather than contemplative or speculative, and in this way sets the stage for the third part of his analysis, the building of the house. The house is the richest figure in the statement he is analyzing, and he is most artful in his unfolding of its significance. It figures the material houses she built and lived in; her family; her household people, and her own body. Because the house is the distinctive territory of the exercise of woman's virtue, his analysis of the meaning of the word allows him to show Clifford as the master of her world, the material and spiritual head of her many households.

In the second half of the sermon, we learn more about Clifford's habits, inasmuch as they pertain to Rainbow's discourse. Her piety is stressed, which is consistent with how she viewed herself in her later years. In Clifford's 1603 memoir, her religious faith and practice are hardly mentioned. In the 1616 to 1619 diary, they are one of many of her concerns; but in her autobiography and her later annual accounts, she depicts herself more constantly living with the word of God beside her, in her head and heart.

Rainbow also emphasizes her charity and her building projects, both of which were important activities of her later years, after she inherited the means, the authority, and the need to exercise herself in those areas. Her Royalism is also underlined. But of particular interest to us is his description of her writing process and her obsessive self-documentation. So that "'her actions in passing might not pass away,'" he writes, "she did cast up the account of them, and see 'what every day had brought forth;' she did set down what was of more remark, or dictated, and caused much of it to be set down in writing, in some certain seasons, which she contrived to be vacant from addresses; judging her time to be better spent thus, than in that ordinary tattle, which custom has taught many (of her sex especially) who have no business, and know no greater duty of life, than to see and be seen, in formal visits, and insignificant parley." And, as is evident from the diary of the last year of her life (published in D.J.H. Clifford's collection), she read and re-read what she wrote, as "she had such a desire to know, review, and reflect, upon all the occurrences, passages, and actions of her life."

Throughout Bishop Rainbow's discourse he praises Clifford as a woman. He does not present her as a "masculine" soul who was, by an accident of nature, born female; but neither does he present her virtues in terms that fall safely within the stereotype of the feminine. Rainbow begins with a deft conflation of the masculine and the feminine: "The subject here, to whom this excellent work is ascribed, *woman*, we must allow to be so far figurative as, (to say no more) by a synecdoche, under one to comprehend both sexes (or the species)". However, he soon departs from such evasive tactics. In his defence of Clifford's sex, he employs many of the arguments used by the most aggressive of the century's "feminist" publications, such as those by Rachel Speght, Bathsua Makin, and Margaret Fell. He begins with a discussion of the women of the Bible, and proceeds through historical examples of exceptional women, aguing that women of virtue are leaders in their moral and material communities. He points out that Clifford's most important acts of charity and piety—the things he values the most—were conducted after she was widowed for the second time, and when her life "was wholly at her own disposal." He never offers up stereotypical feminine qualities as virtues (meekness or submissiveness, for example), even when they could be translated easily into apt theological terms. In this respect, as in others, Rainbow's sermon is at once an extraordinary and a very welcome document, which reinforces the impression given in Clifford's own writings: that she had an unusual ability to slide through cracks in the prejudices of her world, and that she has left us, as a consequence, with extraordinary records of a life lived outside the strictures of the stereotypes of her time.

This text is a modernized version of the first publication of the sermon.]

"A Sermon Preached at the Funeral of the Right Honourable Anne, Countess of Pembroke, Dorset, and Montgomery"

The occasion of our present meeting being to pay our duty to the memory of the great, and good, Anne, Countess of Pembroke, Dorset, and Montgomery, whose earthly relics now lie before us, I sought after a text which might give me scope pertinently to speak and recount such things, of this their noble Lady, a great pattern of virtue, and an eminent benefactor to her generation; as that thereby God may be glorified in his Saint, and such honour given to her memory, for all that was praiseworthy of her, that others may be inflamed with the love of all those virtues, which gained love and esteem to her in her life; and shall make precious her memory after her death.

Let me therefore desire that your attentions may accompany my meditations, while I treat on that short, but comprehensive portion of Scripture, which is contained in part of the first verse of the 14th chapter of the *Proverbs* of the wise King Solomon.

Proverb 14.1. *Every wise woman buildeth her house.*

These words are a full proposition, a clear assertion, and although there lies under the terms some figurative meaning, as in all proverbial or parabolical sentences there commonly doth (even throughout this book called the *Proverbs* or *Parables* of Solomon) yet these words in the text come in the plainest kind of assertion, the most regular form of a proposition, categorical and simple, open and affirmative, and with the most universal note of comprehension. So that if there be any difficulty by reason of the figurative sense, it may be cleared by the full scope of the text, and the business of it dispatched, by answering two short questions: Who? and What?

1. *Who* it is of whom the assertion in the text is verified? And,
2. *What* is the full scope of the assertion?

Who is the subject in the proposition. The wise woman. And *What* it is that is asserted? What, to build her house.

These being answered, then the copula, the connection of the parts, the truth of the proposition in the literal sense, and also in the figure, will be manifest, and made easy to our application, and suitable to the occasion of our present meeting. And so also the truth of the proposition will be amplified by one great instance, an evident example here before us; that both the subject of my meditations, and of your contemplations (what we hear and see) may also be the subject of what we read, the proposition in the text; a woman adorned with the adjunct *wise*; a wise woman presented to your memory. And being such, the assertion that she built her house (in the letter as well as in the figure), that is, did all things necessary, decent and convenient for the building of it, brought the greatest blessings desirable to her house, shall be manifested by many instances.

I must first remind you that the manner of expressing the great and important truths in this text (as in this book of the *Proverbs*) is for the most part figurative, synecdochical, allegorical,[1] by parables, proverbs and similitudes.[2]

Men of the greatest wisdom and spirit, even those who spake by the Holy Spirit, the pen-men of the Holy Writ, have thought it fit to cloth such truths, as of themselves are simple, and naked, with these kind of rhetorical ornaments, to draw men's more considerate attentions and researches, to fix the eyes of the mind more earnestly on them. By these goads and nails, as the wise preacher tells us, to rouse up dull affections, and to fasten the things in our mind, least at any time we should let them slip.[3] Thus holy Job and the prophets, thus holy David, as well as his wise son King Solomon, opened their mouths in parables; nay, a greater than Solomon here, our blessed Saviour did open to the people his Wisdom in parables so frequently, that St. Matthew 13.34, we are told, "All these things spake Jesus unto the multitude in parables, and without a parable spake he not unto them."

This text then, short in words, but full in sense, hath no less than four figurative expressions, the terms, and the other which bear any emphasis, or matter to make up the proposition have something of scheme or figure in them.

The subject here, to whom this excellent work is ascribed, *woman*, we must allow to be so far figurative as, (to say no more) by a synecdoche, under one to comprehend both sexes (or the species). For no doubt but what is asserted here of the woman her act, virtue or duty, belongs even in the first place to the other sex, man, building being more properly his, the man's, work; and it may be as truly said, "Every wise man buildeth his house."

The note or enquiries here, then might be, why, here and in other places of the holy scripture, in this book of the *Proverbs*

---

1 Figurative language is metaphorical and asks you to understand something beyond its literal meaning. Synecdoche is a figure of speech in which a part stands in for a whole; less often, a whole can stand in for a part. Allegory is story delivered through the development of parallel levels and extended comparison.

2 A parable is a comparison of two things for the purposes of teaching, usually cast as a story. It is the principal mode of teaching used by Christ in the New Testament. A proverb is a saying that is often metaphorical, and is another of the teaching methods used in the Bible. Similitudes are comparisons often contained within proverbs.

3 Ecclesiastes 12:11: "The words of the wise are as goads, and as nails fastened by the masters of assemblies, which are given from one shepherd."

more especially, so many great sayings and deeds are attributed to, or had had their instances in women, in the female, whereas the same might be exemplified or said much more of men.

It were needless to speak much of this, yet there might be some reasons given, and on this occasion I shall briefly touch upon a few, why great actions, and the procuring of great blessings, have had designedly their instances in that sex, and that the excellencies of women have been so often and in all ages recorded.

One reason might have been to put an honor on that weaker sex, lest the proud, or more exalted nature of man should undervalue, look down upon, and despise that sex, as too much inferior to men.

For that in those things wherein man's greatest excellency consists, the soul, and its faculties, we are told by scripture-philosophy, that all souls are equal, made so by God, all come out of the hand of God with equal Faculties, and when they return to God, shall in their degrees, be crowned with equal glory. All souls are of the same kind and order; souls know no sexes; when separate, are like to the angels, marry not, nor are given in marriage.[1] In Christ Jesus neither male nor female; all stand alike related to Christ, as they who hear and obey his word are his mother, and brother, and sister, stand in equality of relation in identity of sex. Souls I say in substance are alike perfect, 'tis accidental that other things come, infancy, childhood, age, infirmities; souls know nor feel such things from their own pure principles; these flow from union with the body, the crafts and temperaments of the elements, otherwise I say souls would not be *pati senium* [never decaying], souls of men and women are alike immortal.

Women have been the instruments to convey great blessings to their generations; nay, by a woman was conveyed the greatest blessing to mankind, our blessed Saviour, for whom all generations shall call her blessed.

As God made the first Adam, the father of all mankind, without the help of a woman, and by taking woman out of man's flesh peopled the world, so God took the second Adam out of woman, without the help of a man, from whence hath issued the Holy Seed, which hath replenished the Church.

Women have given as great examples of virtue in every kind (and in some kinds of learning) as men have done.

---

1 Matthew 22:30: "For in the resurrection they neither marry, nor are given in marriage, but are as the angels of God in heaven."

It were endless to instance, or compare, [all the times] we find women to have been adorned with as great eulogies in histories sacred or profane, as men have been.

Hence we find them memorable in so many addresses to them by epistles and panegyrics[1] while they were living; celebrated by elegies, funeral orations and epitaphs when they were dead; canonized, placed in the highest degrees of happiness which opinion, fame, or faith could give them after their death. I need not bring to witness the most learned of the heathen writers, Tully [Cicero], Seneca, Plutarch especially, who has written a book purposely of the virtuous deeds of women.[2] Gregory of Nazareth sets out the great praise of Gorgonia, Basil of Matrina, St. Ambrose of Marcellina, St. Jerome of Eustochium, Marcella, Asella, etc.[3] He, and St. Augustine directs many Epistles, and some of their books or treatises to Eustochium, Paulina, Proba and others; women pious and exercised in the learning which the holy scripture teaches. Nay, the beloved apostle, evangelist and divine, St. John,[4] directs his Epistle to a lady, either to a particular eminent woman as the most aver, or if to the Church catholic [universal], as some would conjecture, yet under the scheme[5] of a lady, a woman.

What honourable and frequent mention do we find in the Old and New Testament, of women eminent for prudence, constancy, courage, piety, and all graces, as if the female spirit had had the ascendant, and had been productive of the highest and most memorable achievements and effects. Most languages, and those who have set out the greatest things, have commonly shadowed

---

1 Letters written about individuals, but addressed implicitly to the public and normally circulated, either in manuscript or print. Panegyrics are poems of praise.

2 *Mulierum Virtues*, or *The Virtues of Women*, the most famous of this sort of text, and one that provided an example for the praises of exceptional women for English writers of this period.

3 These are all female saints and the male authors who wrote of them. Saints' lives provided the other main form of biographies for exceptional women. Asella is referred to again; she was a Roman girl (d. c. 406) who became a nun at the age of 10, and was later a leader of an order of ascetic, reclusive women. St. Jerome wrote a letter to her (#45 of his *Epistles*) and to her sister, Marcella, about her (#24).

4 2 *John* 1. "The elder unto the elect lady and her children, whom I love in the truth; and not I only, but also all they that have known the truth...."

5 That is, as a symbol or metaphor.

and represented them under the hieroglyphics, figure, and scheme of a woman.

The earth itself, the four parts of it, great monarchies and commonwealths, [is figured] as a great Queen or Lady. So the scripture frequently speaks of great cities, daughter of Babylon, of Tyre, Daughter of Jerusalem, of Zion.

Nay further, thus the Church, the Synagogue and Jewish, thus the Church of Christ is expressed and represented; a spotless virgin, the spouse of Christ, the King's daughter. The woman, Revelations 12.1, "The wonder in Heaven, clothed with the sun, the moon under her feet, with a crown of stars on her head;" this is a representation of the Church, Jewish by some, Christian by others.

Lastly, all the virtues intellectual, moral, prudence, justice; nay, even the theological, faith, hope and charity, in the import of their names, the properties and things ascribed to them, are represented under the schemes and figures of women. Even this wisdom itself is so set out through this whole book of the *Proverbs*. Wisdom calls, she lifts up her voice, invites by sweet, yet powerful arguments the simple, and those that lack understanding, to be her proselytes; "Say unto wisdom thou art my sister, and call understanding thy kinswoman."[1] And therefore this great action and blessing in this text figuratively expressed by *building the house* is fitly here attributed to a wise woman, as the same thing had been before, Chap. 9.1 [of *Proverbs*] of Wisdom it self, under the figure of some magnificent Queen or Lady erecting some stately fabric.[2] "Wisdom hath builded her house, she hath hewen out her seven pillars," i.e., she hath built, as all the wise do, with symmetry, with strength, beauty and order. That shows her a wise builder.

And that is the epithet or adjunct to the woman building in the text, wise, "every wise woman."

Wise. The word rendered from the original, literally is the wise of women, and so as grammarians note, admits some figure here, but we need not recede from our own translation.

Wise, the subject is so denominated from the habit, wisdom, which is demonstrated by arts suitable to it, and gives the title of wise.

But neither this, nor the habit of wisdom is to be taken in so

1   *Proverbs* 7:4.
2   I.e., construction.

strict a sense, as philosophers commonly do, making it only one of those which they call the intellectual habits, and to be only speculative, and so define it by knowledge of all things divine and human, from whence those who studied, and sought after such knowledge or wisdom, gained the title of philosophers, lovers and searchers after wisdom.

To omit what others restrain it unto, who define wisdom to be the knowledge of the highest things, and their causes.

It may suffice in this place, to take wisdom in that large sense, which this wise author of the book of the *Proverbs* doth, throughout this book, chiefly in the beginning of it; here he discovers the heavenly root of the knowledge from whence the true wisdom grows, namely the fear of the Lord. And this imports a knowledge of God, such as hath always a religious and awful fear of him joined with it, and an endeavour to know and practice all things which conduce to his worship and glory, and to man's happiness. Plainly, it is to be wise to salvation. Therefore this wisdom cannot be a single, nor only a speculative habit, nor destitute of any of the other intellectual or moral habits, but they all minister unto it as means to attain the highest end; God, and happiness: but in the first place it may intimate those habits which more immediately perfect the understanding, knowledge, prudence, discretion, sagacity, sound judgment and good understanding. These are wisdom's companions, or rather handmaids, always attending upon her, and after these all moral virtues will *vinculo sororio* [be defeated in a sisterly way], as they say, willingly follow. Whoso is wise will seek after all these, all virtue, these constitute a wise man or woman. This is the wise woman in the text.

This may answer the first question, Who?

Both why a woman is here the instance; and who is this wise woman? The subject in the proposition on which is founded this assertion in the text. She that buildeth her house.

And that brings in the second query, what is meant by building her house?

The design of King Solomon in this text, being to set out the praise of a wise woman, or rather of wisdom under the scheme and figure of a woman. He instances in that part of wisdom, or of philosophy, which is esteemed by all philosophers to be most proper to that sex, namely, the economical, or what apertains to the house, the well ordering of that: which although it be an equal duty (where the family is complete and mixed of man and wife) belonging to the man as well as to the woman, yet in regard the man's employment is commonly more abroad, and without doors, the well ordering of the house seems to be more particularly the woman's office; who therefore in our English is properly called the housewife, and if she perform that part well, good housewifery is her praise. And where even the chief government of the family is in the woman, singly, yet her part will be most within the house.

The house is the woman's province, her sphere wherein she is to act, while she is abroad she is out of her territories; she is as a ruler out of his jurisdiction.

And therefore our wise King Solomon makes it not only a brand of a bad housewife, but of an ill woman, *Proverbs* 7.11, "That her feet abide not in her house;" and St. Paul makes it a character of idle housewives, 1 *Timothy* 5.13, "That they learn to be idle, wandering from house to house." And he gives charge in the next verse. "Let the woman guide the house;" and *Titus* 2.5, "That they be as discrete and chaste," so, "keepers at home."[1] A good housewife seems wedded to her house, as well as to her husband. Thus King Solomon may intimate in the first place, the economy in general of a wise woman.

But the principal thing, and the great honour in economy is to be the founder and builder of the house. "He who hath builded the house, hath more honour than the house" (*Hebrews* 3.3), or than any belonging to the house. So that by this manner of expressing the chief thing that belongs to the house, the very building of it is here attributed to the wise woman; made her part and praise in this text.

Therefore both these terms, house and building, being, as I did premise before, figurative and metaphorical, the plain sense and meaning of them will be; that a wise (and virtuous) woman performs the principal, the greatest and most necessary thing (as building is) to the house; that is, to the family, to the children, to the servants, and to whomsoever, or whatsoever may be comprehended under this metonymy,[2] the notion of house; chiefly *viva domus*, the household, as *Proverbs* 21.27. "She looketh well to the household," or as *Joshua* 24.15, "I and my house (that is, all persons belonging to my house) will serve the Lord." And this is farther extended and comprehends all the descents, relat[iv]es,

---

1 Rainbow omits the second part of this quotation, which adds that good women are "obedient to their own husbands."
2 A figure of speech in which a name of an attribute of something stands in for the whole thing: e.g., a sceptre to stand for the power of the monarch or crown.

clienteles, as they say of families; these are belonging to the house, as the House of David, the House of Saul; all these are contained under that metonymy of the house.

So that the sum of what may thus be collected, is, that the wise woman's building her house is, doing all things which belongs to good economy; the well ordering of a family, as Aristotle in his treatise of that science tells us, that the wise matron or mother of the family is to the house, as the soul to the body, and moves all under her in their several stations, orders all things and persons within the house, and takes care for them; and all this, as by an art, as by written laws and rules of economy, or good house-wifery.

And in this text this is comprehensively the wise woman's building the house, well ordering of all within her house, belonging to her family in the largest sense.

There is, I confess, noted by some interpreters, another sense of the word house, that which they call a tropological, or some a moral sense, when the figure is carried inwardly to the soul and the manners, so that as house may signify first an artificial and material house; and then by the metonymy, the economical house, the family; so in the trope, they tell us of a moral house, whose materials are virtue, a spiritual house, which is made up of grace; but this I shall pass by here, intending to resume it briefly, when I shall come to apply the text to the present occasion.

Thus you have seen both the questions answered, *who* is the wise woman; the subject of the assertion; and *what* is asserted, in saying, she buildeth her house.

Now remains the copula, or connection of the terms, the truth of the assertion to be proved. And that, as I told you, by one great instance; waving briefly the ordinary method of logical proofs, by arguments topical or apodictical,[1] I say this shall be represented in the instance here laid before you; the remains of a great personage, in whom may be comprehended all that hath been said of a woman, a wise woman, applying her wisdom to this great end and effect (in all the senses which the letter, or figure will bear) of building her house.

So that for method's sake, the words as they stand in their natural and proper, together with their parabolical and figurative sense, shall be the clue which shall lead me through all the labyrinths, the passages and rooms of this great house, while I

---

1 Expressing necessary truth.

shall apply the letter of the text, by a figure, to the subject before us on this occasion.

At the first then, we see a woman, which might lead us to consider what is natural, either in the original from what stock she came, or the portions wherewith nature endued her.

But as to the former, I need not be her herald. Her blood flowed from the veins of three anciently enobled families, Cliffords, Viponts, and Vesseys; Lords and Barons in the north; and she added (to her escutcheons[1]) Pembroke, Dorset and Montgomery, the titles of three great earldoms in the south.

But as St. Jerome professed, when speaking upon a like Argument, the praises of Marcella, a noble Roman lady, and of high Descent: *Nihil in illa laudabo, nisi quod proprium*, he would not praise her for anything, but what was purely her own. So for me, let this deserving Lady, be praised only by her own achievements. The additions of honour wherewith her self adorned her ancestors; "The fruits of her hands, her own works, these shall praise her in the gate."[2]

You look at a woman; but, one of those whom nature had blessed with her best dowries, *mens sana, in corpore sano* [a healthy mind in a healthy body], is the sum of nature's gifts. She had a clear soul shining through a vivid body; her body durable and healthful, her soul sprightful, of great understanding and judgment, faithful memory, ready wit.

These are great advantages for wisdom and virtue; and without these, without the aids of a healthful well-constituted body, fitted to serve the commands of a great mind; seldom any great and heroic actions can be produced. Wisdom if it not be well seated, has not fit space and room, nor well disposed organs; cannot exert, or lay out it self; without tools the best artificer cannot finish any work, nor bring it to perfection, although never so well projected and begun.

Her body was a faithful servant to her mind; had served it fourscore and six years, and was useful in all the dispatches of her will. She had accustomed her body to the yoke; she had trained it up so well in all virtuous exercises, by her admirable temperance, that she had it perfectly at her command, and wholly at the discretion of her soul. A thing not very observable in this age of the world, amongst men or women. The body, the will of the

---

1 Displays of coats-of-arms.
2 *Proverbs* 31.31.

flesh, commonly governs the man. The soul in most is drudge to the body, it employs its wit, and all its faculties to serve the interests and needs of the body, to make provision for the flesh; a delicate and luxurious master.

So that, truly, if some virtuosos had not been convinced of an extraordinary and sublime spirit in man (scarce intelligible by old philosophy), and some gripes of conscience had not whispered, that it is immortal, capable of eternal bliss or pain, some of their epicurean wits would hardly have believed there is such a thing as a soul, in the vulgar notion of divines. But if they could well dress, had salt to relish, could feed and satisfy the cravings of the body; they then did, *bene sapere* [knowing well], were wise and happy enough, as happy as soul could wish. Indeed when we observe what care some of this sex, nay, of either sex, do take about their body; making it their whole day's work, first to adorn, then to glut, then to recreate their body, then to lay it asleep; not allowing one of twenty-four hours, to speak with, or pray for their soul; much less to take it to task, and employ it in religious and virtuous exercises (the meat and drink, as necessary to preserve life in the soul, as those are in the body); I say, this carnality might make the vulgar believe, that although preachers, and some women talk of souls, yet in truth, there is no such thing.

This excellent Lady then, who neglected, or spent so little time or pains about her body, except it were to make it serviceable to her soul, which she adorned with her chief care and diligence, may serve for a glass or mirror, for others of that quality, or sex, to dress themselves by her example.

So that although nature framed her but as the subject of this text, a woman, yet she having a body so well ordered, as well as built; a soul endued by nature with such acute faculties, we need not doubt to give her the adjunct, which is given to the woman here in the text, to call her wise; to say that in her the world had found, and has lost, a wise, a virtuous woman.

For that's it: virtue, which only makes and denominates a woman wise; wise and virtuous are almost terms reciprocal; every wise woman is virtuous, and all the virtuous are wise.

It was a strange question for King Solomon to ask, *Proverbs* 31.10, having had seven hundred wives, "Who can find a virtuous woman?" And it was as strange that he should answer that question, when he was become a preacher, *Ecclesiastes* 7.27, "Behold this have I found (saith the preacher), counting one by one to find out the account." And what was the sum total, when he had cast up his account? Why! it is come to one, and none;

"one man among a thousand have I found, but a woman (a virtuous woman he means) among all these have I not found;" and he had the full number of a thousand, seven hundred wives, three hundred concubines. The meaning is, that a truly virtuous woman was a rarity in his time, even while King Solomon was a preacher.

But I hope the world is better since, better for his preaching, but especially for the preaching of the gospel; and although the number of the wise and virtuous men and women be not so great as were to be desired, yet, God be thanked, we want not examples more plentiful in this looser age, of either sex; and here we have one eminent before us, a woman, who deserved the title of virtuous, and therefore of wise; a wise and virtuous woman.

Therefore to demonstrate this rarely ennobled woman to have deserved this greatest mark of honour, to have been truly wise, I will not stray from my text in the proof of it; but set forth her wisdom from the great effect of wisdom, set down in this text, under the allegory of "building her house;" taking the liberty which the scheme of the text allows, to extend it to all which so copious a figure comprehends; but still having regard to the scope, and chief intent of the text, that by building the house, we may intend the deriving of blessings, most noble, most useful, most necessary to her family, to her allies, and to the generation wherein she lived, for which that, and many other generations may call her blessed.

I did put you in mind before of several houses which the allegory comprehends, *viz.* [such as] the artificial or material house, the economical house, the family, the moral house, whose materials are virtues, and the spiritual house, built by grace. In all these she hath made it to appear that she was a great builder.

Now first, that this wise woman declared her wisdom in building her house in a literal sense, the material house, I can call you all to witness, who have seen so many houses of her famous ancestors, which time had ruined, war, or sad accidents demolished, rebuilt by her, raised out of their rubbish, or decays, to their former greatness and beauty.

To have been a great builder (if wisdom and discretion were overseers of the work) was in all ages accounted an heroic thing; sufficient to commend the fame and praise of such builders to all posterity.

To build, importing a design of a great mind, studying to be beneficial to posterity; whom builders commonly intend to accommodate and gratify. Thereby princes, and the greatest of men, have gained to themselves the greatest renown.

Certainly, none had greater fame upon earth than King Solomon, nor was his name exalted higher for any thing which his wisdom enabled him to perform, than for his building the temple, and his houses.

Thus Trajan,[1] the best of the emperors (while they were heathen), was the greatest builder, the most renowned, the best beloved. 'Tis made a signal blessing, *Isaiah* 58.12, "To be a builder of the old waste places, to raise up the foundations of many generations, to be called the repairer of the breaches, the restorer of paths to dwell in."

But, because I am recounting the praise of a woman, the first, as I take it, that is extolled for this in story, was a woman, the Babylonian Semiramis,[2] to whom, for that, and her famous acts, a prime historian[3] tells us, that no man could ever be compared.

And it was a woman also who gave the pattern to the greatest princes, how to build their monuments with most magnificence. That monument which she called after her husband, Mausolus[4] his name, had the honour to give the name to the noblest monuments of emperors, and the greatest princes in the world, the most famous of that kind since, being called mausolea.

But as in all great actions, so in this of building, the end is to be considered; which not being wisely done, many have erected buildings to their folly, and their houses (which they designed for glory) have been called by that name for want of a wise master-builder to foresee the end for which they built.

As most of the pompous builders of old, those vain persons who built their Babel, and the proud King his Babylon, to get a name, or a vain-glory, and therefore they did, as Tully terms it, *struere insanas moles*, amass together wild and confused heaps, vast bulks, things of more admiration than use.

Let us therefore see what kind of buildings this wise woman erected, and for what end they were repaired, or built. And here we shall find that piety and charity, gratitude and kindness, were

---

1   98–117 CE, Emperor of Rome, and famous for building projects, including the largest and most splendid Roman forum ever built.

2   Queen of Babylon, wife of Nimrod. During civil war, she build fortifications around the city. After that, her crown was made in the form of turreted walls.

3   Identified in the margin as Berosus, who was a Babylonian historian and priest, alive during the lifetime of Alexander the Great (356–326 BCE).

4   Mausolus (d. 353 BCE) was a Persian ruler. After his death his wife Artemesia built a tomb for him, known as the *mausoleum*.

her inciters to this work; that all her buildings were for God, or for the poor, or for the honour of her progenitors, or the benefit of her posterity: these were the ends which she propounded to herself in building.

Indeed, one of the first things (as I was informed) which she built, was (what Jacob had first done) a pillar. She built a pillar, a monument which stands in the highway, at the place where her endeared mother and she last parted, and took their final farewell. And as Jacob did, she poured oil upon this pillar, the oil of charity, pouring down then, and yearly since (and that the cruce[1] of oil may never fail, ordered to be always continued), at a set day every year a sum of money, "that oil to make glad the heart of the poor;" and withal to be used as a precious ointment to perfume her pious mother's memory, that her good name, and their mutual dearness of affection might be engraven, and remembered by their posterity and the poor to all generations.

A good omen of a happy builder, whose foundations are charity and piety, the sapphires and agates mentioned, *Isaiah* 54.11.

But her buildings for charity were larger than a pillar; such as gave shelter and maintenance to the poor. Besides the repairs and restoring of an almshouse,[2] built and endowed by her pious mother, Margaret Countess of Cumberland, she built an almshouse in this place, and made decent provision for thirteen poor women, a Mother and twelve Sisters, as she called them, to the perpetual relief of the poor and destitute; and that alms and devotion might not be separated, she gave allowance for the prayers of the church to be daily administered to them.

Indeed, she might have an eye to charity in all her buildings, by which she did set the poor on work, thus curing their idleness, as well as supplying their indigency.

Secondly, gratitude to her ancestors was another end of her building, that she might with some cost hold up, what they with such vast expense had founded and built.

Six ancient castles, ample and magnificent, which her noble ancestors had built, and sometimes held up with great honour to themselves, security to their sovereigns, and hospitality to their friends and strangers; now, by the rage of war, or time, or acci-

---

1 Cup.
2 This and the one Clifford commissioned and endowed housed and provided sustenance for poor women, usually widows. Clifford's in Appleby is still in operation.

dents, pulled or fallen down, or made uninhabitable, scarce one of those six that had showed more than the skeleton of a house; her reviving spirit put life into the work, made ("all these dry bones live")[1] these scattered stones come together; those ruins forsake their rubbish, and lift up their heads to their former height. A marvelous task it was which she undertook, to design the rebuilding so many, and such great fabrics, to rear up them, when the earthly house of her tabernacle began to stoop and decline; being about the sixtieth year of her age when she began: who then could hope to finish? But when she did consider in her great mind, did think (as *Psalms* 102.14) "upon the stones, and it pitied her to see them in the dust."[2] Her prudence (as with her hands) set on the work, raised, cemented, finished; and where others might have thought it glory enough to have been the restorer of any one, she laid the top-stone on them all. These houses, the end of her building them was, I say, gratitude to her ancestors.

Thirdly, kindness to her posterity and successors, that they might find the blessing of "Canaan, houses which they built not,"[3] accommodations ready prepared for them.

But lastly, she could not forget the main end of her building, piety to God, in rebuilding, or repairing of his houses, churches or chapels. She rebuilt, or, by repairing, restored six houses of her own, but of God's houses seven.[4] She had no dwelling for her self, where God had not a House to be worshipped publicly, besides private oratories in her houses.

If now I could set before your eyes, or before your imaginations, six castles, seven churches or chapels, besides the two almshouses, and other inferior subservient buildings, which she made, or made useful; if I could represent all these before you in one landscape or view, you would imagine you saw something greater than an Escurial:[5] an eighth wonder, or something more

---

1 *Ezekiel* 37:3–4.

2 Rainbow's marginal note here reads: "One had lain 140 years desolate, after the fire had consumed it. (Brough Castle the timber burned, 1521.) Another 320 years, after the invading Scots had wasted it. (Pendragon Castle, wasted by David, King of Scots, 1341)."

3 A reference to the book of Joshua, the leader who succeeded Moses and led Israel into the promised land.

4 Rainbow's marginal note: "Brougham, Nine-Kirks, Appleby, Bongate, Mallerstang, Barden, Skipton."

5 A monastery in Seville, Spain; one of the greatest architectural feats of the world; built in the sixteenth century.

wonderful than the seven, which the heathen world hath boasted of; at least more beneficial to the world than they. Some of those wonders were (possibly) but poetical; built but by fancy; all of them (as I take it) these great and monstrous buildings, were to no greater end than to make the name of the builders endless. But all this wise woman's buildings, as you see, were to some good end, were given either to charity towards the poor, gratitude to her ancestors, kindness to her posterity, or dedicated to the worship of God.

As that good Emperor Trajan was by his emulous successor (finding his name or motto on so many walls built by himself) called a *Parietaria*, a wallflower, a flower (which seldom dies, or easily revives) with us, a flower fragrant, and of a sweet smell; so let the name of this excellent lady live, and grow, and be a fragrancy; be a sweet favour to all those who shall possess or find hospitality, or charity, or the service of God celebrated within these walls, or any of them, which she hath thus erected or restored.

And thus much for this wise woman's building her material house.

Secondly, her family. The allegory leads me to another house worth your viewing, and that is it which seems most aimed at in the text; and the building of which is a greater instance of a wise woman than any outward building can be. This is the economical house, the building, that is to say, the well-ordering of a family.

The doing of which is a piece of so great skill and wisdom, that wise men, philosophers and moralists, Aristotle himself has given it a place, and name of a particular science (amongst those which are the prudential) economy; directing in it, by as good rules and precepts as in any other in any part of moral philosophy. And it is indeed as necessary that the world should be well instructed in this, as in any other science in the whole circle.

For mankind, which is made up of single persons, could not have been supported, if they had been to live always separate and single; and not formed themselves into society, which supposes government, made up of order, and that supposes subordination.

It is true, every particular man hath a government in himself; is a king in Plato's sense, hath a body and soul, passions and members, words, and thoughts under his power and government; ethics, moral philosophy, teaches this art of self-government.

But man being intended for society, the first rank of that is a family; 'tis the science of economy teaches to rule that well, to order the house. Now in this house the subordinate in it are chiefly the children, servants, and retainers. And to continue the allegory, the building of this house is the governing, the providing for, the nourishing and maintaining, the ordering and well-disciplining of these by certain rules, of which wise men have said much in their books; and of which we find much in the book of God; this book of the *Proverbs* most copiously. So also in the New Testament (*Ephesians* 5:6, *Colossians* 3:4, *Titus* 2, and dispersedly in several other places.)

And certainly good economy, or right ordering of a family, is a noble and profitable art, to be learned by much prudent thinking and consideration. Although the world think little of it, and few study this art, deeming themselves naturally wise enough, or inspired with the knowledge of this; if they have means and conveniencies to set up a family, they govern it by rote, not by rule; if they be rich enough to support it, they mind not to govern (morally) otherwise than by had-I-wist [known], hand over head, as things fall out contingently; I mean as to the moral, or religious part of governing, live like (Nomads or Tartars) those that live at random.

Now this neglect of government in a family, breeds the greatest mischief in the world; spreads disorder over the face of the earth. Families ill-ordered will make ill-governed cities, and these mis-governed, will fill the whole commonwealth and kingdom with disorder and confusion; families being the first principles of bodies public, the seminaries which stock cities, out of which kingdoms and commonwealths do grow.

There is no greater cause of decay to the commonwealth, nor bane to the church, than want of discipline and good order in families, especially as to one branch of them; mis-governing, and ill-educating of children who are the first elements of cities and kingdoms: undisciplined and bad children, will hardly make good men, nor honest commonwealth's-men, nor well principled subjects, of which a kingdom consists.

Train up a child then in the fear of the Lord, season a new vessel with wholesome liquor; if they at first are not seasoned with good, or if bad principles be infused into them, they will (without extraordinary Grace do renew them) carry a tang, and ill favour to old age. Mis-government in this part of the family, vicious humours in children, like a fault in the first concoction, breeds an exuberancy of habits, seldom to be corrected and purged out.

Now this part of family-government chiefly belongs to women; who, when men's occasions call them out, are commonly fixed to the house, as intelligences to their sphere; who, although the man, as the *primum mobile*,[1] directs the general motion of all; yet the particular and regular inclinations in the children are commonly formed by the woman; and if she be indeed intelligent and wise, none can do it better. Children well instituted in the *gynaeceo* [nursery], as plants well ordered in the nursery, will thrive, and prosper, and fill the world with good fruit.

Now this house, the family, and the well-governing of it in all the members (which is indeed the building of it) this wise woman did perform with greatest providence and prudence. Her children, which were but two,[2] that grew up to perfect age; she built them up in the nurture and fear of the Lord; seasoned them with sound principles of religion, as was sufficiently evident to those who have known them, and their constancy to the true religion, in which they were trained up; teaching their children the same principles which they had sucked with their mother's milk.

This excellent lady had, I say, but two to build on; but God did so bless them, even in the sight of their mother, that she saw them arrive at the pitch and praise of wise women. And by their issue they gave her pregnant hopes, that they would build up, or keep up the house of her ennobled family, like Rachel and Leah, which two did build the house of Israel. So that her children, and her children's children, and their children, did spring up, crave, and receive her blessing; and shall always call her blessed, who hath entailed such blessings upon them, by her affection, piety, and providence, *Proverbs* 13.22.

Next, as to her servants domestic, she well knew that they were *pars domus*[3] and how necessary a part of the house the servants are, and therefore to be kept tight, sustained, and carefully to be held up, if in decay, repaired; and therefore this part of her house she was always building or repairing by the hand of her bounty, as well as by good and religious order in her family. Indeed she looked on some (and possibly on some of the meaner sort of her trusty servants, whose offices might occasion their nearer attendance) to be such as Seneca allows them to be, *humiles amici*, good servants are humble friends. As friends in no ill nor insignificant complement, style themselves humble servants to their friend, true friends being willing to stoop to the meanest offices

---

1 First cause or mover.
2 Rainbow's marginal note: "Lady Margaret Countess of Thanet, and Isabella Countess of Northampton."
3 Part of the household.

of servants, when their friend's need requires it. Therefore as many great and wise governors of families have been observed to do, in certain seasons to condescend, let down themselves and their state, by taking up their discreter servants, into some degree of familiarity with them; so, I say, this heroic lady would (besides the necessary discoursing with them about her affairs) divert herself by familiar conversation with her servants; in which they were sure (besides other gains from her bountiful hands) to gain from the words of her mouth something of remark; whether pleasant or profitable, yet very memorable for some or other occasion of life. So well did she observe the wise man's caution, *Ecclesiastes* 4.30, "Be not a lion in thy house;" intimating that some are always in rage, and brawl, and fright their family from their presence; her pleasantness and affability made their very addresses a great part of their preferment.

It was indeed observable, that although she clothed herself in humble and mean attire, yet like the wise and virtuous woman, *Proverbs* 31.20, "She clothed her household with scarlet;" her allowance and gifts were so bountiful, and so frequent to them, that they might afford to clothe themselves in such garb, as best became the servants of so great and so good a mistress. And some of the wise have thought it a great error, and against the rules of economics, to be niggardly to good servants, to grow richer by such a thrift as makes the servant's back bare, or belly empty, to fill the master's purse.

But although in this she did follow the pattern given to all the wise, *Proverbs* 31.15, "Give meat to her household," and in such a plenty, that hospitality and charity might have their portion with them; while she herself was contented with any pittance, little in quantity (but enough to keep life and soul together, as we say), viands not costly or rare, nor far-fetched and dear bought, but such as were at hand, parable[1] and cheap. Yet here I may be bold to tell you something to wonder at; that she much neglected, and treated very harshly one servant, and a very ancient one, who served her from her cradle, from her birth, very faithfully, according to her mind; which ill usage therefore her menial servants, as well as her friends and children, much repined at. And who this servant was, I have named before. It was her body, who, as I said, was a servant most obsequious to her mind, and served her fourscore and six years.

---

1 Easily procured.

It will be held scarce credible to say, but it is a truth to aver, that the mistress of this family was dieted more sparingly, and I believe, many times more homely, and clad more coarsely and cheaply than most of the servants in her house; her austerity and humility was seen in nothing more, than (if I may so allude to *Colossians* 2.33) in "neglecting of the body, not in any honour to the satisfying of the flesh."

Whether it were by long custom, to prove with how little nature may be content; and that, if the appetite can be satisfied, the body may be fed with what is most common and cheap. She taught us that hunger and health seek not delicacies nor fullness.

O that those who think they cannot live, except they fare deliciously every day, would but make trial one year, how they may preserve their own health, and save their poor brethren from starving (by hunger or nakedness) out of those superfluities and surfeits, by which they destroy themselves. That those who clothe themselves in purple (beyond what their station or estate requires) would inquire into more particulars than I can yet inform them, of this great lady's abstinencies and humble attire, and how successful they were to her long life, with health and reputation.

Some texts out of this book of the *Proverbs*, the parable of Dives,[1] and even this lady's example, might supply the defective application of a sermon; reform or shame gluttony, cause vain gallantry to impose sumptuary laws to it self, sit content with home-bred fare, home-growing, and home-spun manufacture, and not run to France or Persia to fetch form or matter for their pride.

This opulent lady might, if she had pleased, have fetched from far, and at the dearest rates, provisions for the flesh, the back or belly, but her greatest appetite was after wisdom, and she knew as well as Seneca, that *corpora in sagina, anime in mane,* that in a fatted body, commonly dwells a lean, and starved soul; and had heard of St. Gregory's aphorism, wisdom is seldom found *in terra suaviter viventium,* it will not thrive so kindly in those territories, where men delight to fare deliciously every day.

We may conclude that this great matron, who had such command over her self, knew how to deny herself; had learned our Saviour's lesson of self-denial; and St. Paul's affirmation (1

---

1 The name given in the Vulgate Bible to the rich man in the parable of the rich man and Lazarus (*Luke* 16:19–31).

Corinthians 9.27); *contundo corpus meum*, "I keep under my body, and bring it unto subjection." These abridgements were in this lady a mortification, which humility and modesty concealed, but which wisdom and resolution did put in practice.

I should now have done with that part of economy which respects her servants, but that she had another way of building, as to them; namely, building them up in the most holy faith; and also giving them their meat in due season; that meat, which our Saviour told his followers would not perish, but endure to everlasting life; this he told them in the sixth chapter of St. John, when they made such haste to find him, soon after he had fed them with the loaves; and by this meat, in opposition to the perishing, some interpreters tell us, he meant his body in the holy sacrament, the meat that would nourish them to everlasting life.[1]

This spiritual meat, this lady wisely took care that it might be provided for all her household in due season; that is, at the three seasons in the year when the church requires it; and once more in the year, at the least; besides those three great festivals, she made one festival more, for all that were fit to be invited, or compelled (as in the gospel) to come to that supper.

And that all might be fitted, and well-prepared, she took care that several books of devotion and piety might be provided four times in the year; that every one might take their choice of such book as they had not before, by which means those that had lived in her house long (and she seldom turned any away) might be furnished with books of religion and devotion in every kind.

By these, and more instances, which it were easy to produce, it appeared, that this religiously wise lady had deliberately put on Joshua's holy resolution, *Joshua* 24.15, "I and my house will serve the Lord;" and might have the eulogy which that memorable Queen[2] pronounced of the best ordered family in the world, "Happy are thy men, happy are these thy servants, which stand continually before thee."

But yet house and family, in this copious allegory, may comprehend more than I have named; besides children and servants, allies, relations, and even friends, were in some sort of her family and clientele. The house of Saul and the house of David is taken for all that adhered to either house. Indeed the whole country, considering the freedom of her hospitality, was, in this sense, her

---

1   *John* 6: 27.
2   The reference here is to the Queen of Sheba.

house; nay, even all of quality that did pass through the country. It was held uncouth and almost an incivility, if they did not visit this lady, and her house, which stood conspicuous and open to all comers, and her ladyship known to be easy of access to all addresses in that kind. And seldom did any come under her roof, who did not carry some mark and memorial of her house; some badge of her friendship and kindness: she having always in store such things as she thought fit to present. She did not always consider what was great, or what might by value make the present worth acceptation, or how it suited to the condition of the person; but what (as her pleasant fancy suggested) might make her memorable to the person who was to receive it.

Now for the building, or repairing, or adorning all these kinds of houses, of which I have spoken; the material, and houses literally taken, or her household, her family of children, servants, allies, and the rest, she had a providence and forecast with herself, and also an after-cast, as you might call it, and casting up her expense, and consulting with her officers. She well understood and followed the advice of our wise king, *Proverbs* 24.27, "Prepare thy work without, and make it fit for thy self in the field, and afterward build thine house." That is, be sure you have materials in readiness for building. Now the most material thing to be prepared, and in readiness, is that which provides all materials in every kind; that is, in plain English, money; which the same wise man tells in another place, "Money answereth all things;"[1] all things useful to be prepared claim it, crave it, call for it; and, if it be present, it answers them all with satisfaction.

Before she began to build a tower (to build in any kind) she first sat down and counted the cost, as our Saviour intimates wise builders will do; she kept exact accounts weekly in books of her own method, and the totals were duly signed with her own hand.

This way of strictness, indeed hath been slighted in this looser age, as an impertinent piece of providence, in persons of great birth and estate, but yet the total neglect of it hath not only frustrated the designs of many, who had laid good foundations for building, and could get no higher; but hath let fall many well-built houses, for want of means to hold them up; and indeed hath been the occasion of ruin to many noble houses and families; while making no reckoning of what they did or might spend, have brought themselves or their successors to an easy and even reck-

---

1 Ecclesiastes 10:19.

oning; to have nothing left in remainder, or nothing proportionable to support and hold up the honour of those families and houses which their progenitors erected.

This was widely foreseen and prevented by this noble person, by which means she was able to hold up, and enlarge her houses, and so left them and her patrimony entire to her posterity, which otherwise might have been wholly wasted and dilapidated.

But yet we have not taken any view of the chief of her houses, the immaterial, inward house of her soul, so termed by Hugo,[1] so by Bede;[2] the former speaks of building the moral fabric by virtue, the other the spiritual house by Grace.

And here I must seriously profess myself to have been perplexed in my thoughts, where to begin, and how to make an end, and in what method to proceed.

If I should say she was well furnished with materials of every kind, to build up this house of her soul, that is, with all virtues belonging to her sex and condition; if I should say these virtues were perfected with divine graces, I believe I should have plenty of witnesses who now hear me.

Virtues, intellectual, moral, theological, they were conspicuous in her sayings, in her doings, in her conversation, and the manner of her life. As to her self, in great humility, modesty, temperance, and sobriety of mind; as to the world, in justice, courtesy, and benificence; and to God, in acts of piety, devotion, and religion. These have so flowed, so crowded together, into my meditations, that as they brake into my thoughts tumultuously, as it were, and without order, so I must crave your pardon and leave, if I shall take them up as they came, and speak of some few of them, without that exactness of order which might be thought requisite.

To have attained to the title in the text, to have been wise, might (as I have intimated before) comprehend all intellectual, nay indeed, all moral virtues, and divine graces. Whoso is truly wise, hath all these in some measure, or must use all diligence to have them; he must "add to faith, virtue; and to virtue, knowledge; and to knowledge, temperance; and to temperance, patience; and to patience, godliness; and to godliness, brotherly-kindness, and to brotherly-kindness, charity."[3]

---

1 Possibly Hugo Grotius (1583–1645), Dutch scholar, author of *De Satisfactione Christi* (1617).

2 The Venerable Bede (b. c. 672), English theologian and historian.

3 *2 Peter* 1:5–7.

He that will build for Heaven, or as St. Peter there speaks, be partaker of the divine nature; or as our Saviour expresseth it, would "take the Kingdom of Heaven by violence,"[1] he must accumulate, add all those virtues one to another. He that will build his hopes in heaven, must be provided of all these materials reckoned up by St. Peter; and when he hath cleared the ground from briars and thorns, purged out lust, got clear from the corruptions which is in the world through lust, he must lay the foundation of faith, and then must add virtue, knowledge, temperance, etc. all kinds of virtue and grace.

I might first tell what advantages she had for intellectual virtues, even from nature it self, which had endowed her soul with such excellent abilities, as made her ready to build up her self in the knowledge of all things decent and praise-worthy in her sex. She had great sharpness of wit, a faithful memory, and deep judgment, so that by the help of these, much reading, and conversation with persons eminent for learning, she had early gained a knowledge, as of the best things, so an ability to discourse in all commendable arts and sciences, as well as in those things which belong to persons of her birth and sex to know.

She could discourse with virtuosos, travellers, scholars, merchants, divines, statesmen, and with good housewives of any kind. Insomuch that a prime and elegant wit,[2] well seen in all human learning, and afterwards devoted to the study of divinity (by the encouragement and command of a learned King, and a rare proficient in it) is reported to have said of this lady, in her younger years, to this effect; that she knew well how to discourse of all things, from predestination to slea-silk.[3] Meaning, that although she was skillful in housewifery, and in such things in which women are conversant, yet her penetrating wit soared up to pry into the highest mysteries; looking at the highest example of female wisdom, *Proverbs* last [31]. Although she knew wool, and flax, fine linen, and silk, things appertaining to the spindle and the distaff; yet (verse 26) she could open her mouth with

---

1 *Matthew* 11:12.
2 Identified in the margin as "Dr. Donne."
3 Silk thread which could be separated into smaller filaments; for embroidery. The opposition is between something large and abstract, and something small and material; but there is also an opposition here between something traditionally masculine (philosophical and theological knowledge) and something traditionally feminine (embroidery and other stitchwork).

wisdom, knowledge of the best and highest things; and if this had not been most affected by her, solid wisdom, knowledge of the best things, such as make wise until salvation; if she had sought fame rather than wisdom, possibly she might be ranked among those wits and learned of that sex, of whom Pythagoras, or Plutarch, or any of the Ancients, have made such mention.

But she affected rather to study with those noble Bereans, *Acts* 17.11, 12[1] and those honourable women (as St. Paul there styles them) who searched the scriptures daily; with Mary, she chose the better part of learning; the doctrine of Christ.

Authors of several kinds of learning, some of controversies very abstruse, were not unknown unto her. She much commended one book, William Barklay's dispute with Bellarmine,[2] both, as she knew, of the popish persuasion, but the former less papal; and who, she said, had well stated a main point, and opposed that learned cardinal, for giving too much power, even in temporals, to the Pope, over kings and secular princes; which, she seemed to think, the main thing aimed at by followers of that court [was] to pretend a claim only to govern directly in spirituals; but to intend chiefly (though indirectly) to hook in temporals, and in them to gain power, dominion, and tribute; money and rule being the gods to which the Roman courtiers and their partisans chiefly sacrifice.

She was not ignorant of knowledge in any kind, which might make her conversation not only useful and grave, but also pleasant and delightful; which that she might better do, she would frequently bring out of the rich store-house of her memory, things new and old, sentences, or sayings of remark, which she had read or learned out of authors, and with these her walls, her bed, her hangings, and furniture must be adorned; causing her servants to write them in papers, and her maids to pin them up, that she, or they, in the time of their dressing, or as occasion served, might remember, and make their descants on them. So that, though she had not many books in her chamber, yet it was dressed up with the flowers of a library.

Go now, and tell the superfinical,[3] who disdain the meanness

---

1 People of a Macedonian city where Paul founded a church.

2 Identified by Spence as John Barclay's *Argenis*, a text that criticizes the position of Roberto Bellarmine (1542–1621), Jesuit cardinal, who defended the Catholic Church to Englishmen during the reign of King James I.

3 I.e., super-finical, meaning fussy and pretentious.

of her chamber and apartments, who cannot dress themselves, but in well-dressed and gorgeous rooms; let them come hither and see the riches of her furniture, better than silver and gold, if King Solomon (who had silver beyond weight, and gold in abundance) may be judge. The sayings of wisdom, which he determines to be more precious than rubies, these were instead of those rare trinkets so much in use, *Isaiah* 3.20. So that you may safely tell, that her furniture and chambers were adorned with many precious jewels, more eligible than all that glittering bravery which God threatened to take away from the "haughty daughters of Sion" *Isaiah* 3.18. I will not name them, but it were worth your considering the particulars set down in five or six verses of that chapter, where the pride and vanity of those "women of Sion, who sat at ease," and swam in plenty, is described, and exposed; so that the great ones of these times, of either sex, may compare, and see, with how many of those superfluities their tiring-houses abound, of which this great and noble lady had neither use nor esteem.

It was apparent that the virtue which this lady most studied and practised was humility. Those that will build high, must lay their foundation low, no fitter virtue than humility for this work, for this builder, and for that which she esteemed her greatest building, which was to build for heaven.

This virtue of humility shined through her whole conversation, her easy reception, her affability, the plainness, as I said, of her chamber and furniture, so of her apparel, her dress, her garb; she was, as the apostle advises, "clothed with humility, all over."[1] Her greatest ornaments were those of a meek and quiet spirit. She was (by the merit of her due titles) in honour three countesses, but had a stranger seen her in her chamber, he would not have thought he had seen one lady, as ladies nowadays appear. Indeed you might have sometimes seen her sitting in the almshouse (which she built) among her twelve sisters (as she called them) and, as if they had been her sisters indeed, or her children, she would sometimes eat her dinner with them, at their almshouse; but you might find them often dining with her (at her table) some of them every week, all of them once a month: and after meat, as freely and familiarly conversing with them in her chamber, as if they had been her greatest guests. And truly the greatest of her guests, her noblest children, could not please her,

---

1 1 *Peter* 5.5.

if they did not visit them, and pass their salutes at her almshouse, with those sisters, and the mother, sometimes, before they made their first address to her self, their mother; whose natural affection was known to be great, but her charity and humility greater; and she commonly admonished her children, coming from far to pay their duty to her, that before they made their address to her for her blessing, they should take the blessing of the poor, the alms-women's blessing by the way.

Nevertheless, although the nice and delicate, who look only at things after the outward appearance, might think meanly of her chamber, her accoutrements, company, and bodily presence, yet of that plainness (her choice, not necessity, compelling), the sober and wise had other thoughts. And indeed they might look at her chamber, as a temple, a court, a tribunal, an almonary;[1] a place where God was daily, nay, thrice a day, worshipped; where almost every day some addresses were made from some of the chief of these parts, and strangers of the best quality; a tribunal, where all submitted to the doom of her judgment, event to the sentence of her lips, as to an oracle; and it were not insignificant if I should call it a royal burse, or exchequer, where variety of presents and money flowed, and was issued out daily to some or other objects of her charity, kindness, or bounty.

She had known greatness, as well as any other, being bred in the courts, or in the verges of the courts, of three great princes, who (reigning in peace) had as much magnificence and glory as any that had swayed the scepter of this land.

But whether she lived in, or near it, she was one of the ornaments of it, and knew, when time and occasion served, to shine in her sphere, and to adorn her self with ornaments, such as are proper for the courts of princes. But when her outward clothing was of wrought gold, valuable in the sight of men; her inward clothing was humility, a meek and quiet spirit, which God most values, which is "in the sight of God of great price" (1 *Peter* 3.4).

It was one great sign of humility in her self, that she was not censorious of others, and of the liberty which they took, and might lawfully take, in those outward garbs, to apparel themselves according to their rank and place; which she knew they might do without affectation of pride and vanity.

When of later times, and since the happy restitution of the King[2] to his court, she sometimes beheld in visitants of several

---

1 Distributor of alms.
2 Charles II.

ranks, what others did perchance look at as affected and fantastical, she would only make such innocent and pleasant reflections, as the parties themselves were rather delighted with the freedom, than troubled with any show of censure.

She was, I say, so unwilling to be censorious, or to seem uneasy to any of those, who as she thought did necessarily pay an obedience to fashion and custom; which she knew was a kind of tyrant, and will reign over the most, while we live under the moon; that when a neighbour, a lady, whom she used (as she commonly did all) with great familiarity, expressing together with her their joy, in discourse of His Majesty's most glorious and happy return to his kingdom, and court at Whitehall, and the gallantry which at his entrance attended that place; the lady wished that she would once more go to London, and the court, and glut her eyes with the sight of such happy objects, and after that give up her self to her country retirement. She suddenly, and pleasantly replied, if I should go to those places, now so full of gallantry and glory, I ought to be used as they do ill-sighted, or unruly horses, have spectacles (or blinkers) put before mine eyes, lest I should see and censure what I cannot competently judge of, be offended my self or give offence to others. Her meaning was thought to be that she, having taken leave of worldly glory, as to her self, no unfitted for it; ought to give leave to others, to whom such things, of course, and by the places which they held, did belong, to enjoy their freedom, without her censure.

Her conversation was indeed meek, affable, and gentle, her words, according to the circumstances of persons in her presence, pleasant, or grave, always seasoned with salt, savoury, but never bitter. I had the honour to be often admitted to her discourse, but never heard (nor have been told by others) that she was invective, or censorious, or did or did use to speak ill, or censoriously of persons, or actions; but she was especially cautious in censuring public persons, or actions in matter of state. I was present when she was told of the certainty of the war with the Dutch, and of the great preparations on all hands; on which subject she only said, "If their sins be greater than ours, they would have the worst."

Constancy was so known a virtue in her, that it might vindicate the whole sex, from the contrary imputation.

She was observed to be very constant to all her determinations, and would not easily vary from what she had once declared to be her mind. She had that part of prudence which some call consultiveness, deliberating, and well-distinguishing what was fit, what indifferent, what was necessary. She used, as she said, to chew the cud, ruminating of the next day's business in her night wakings. When she had once weighted the circumstances, and resolved; she did not like to have any after considerations, or be moved by them.

This made her constant to her resolutions, even in lesser matters, as, the times of her removals from on of her houses to another.

She had six houses (as I have intimated) in each of which she used, at her prefixed times, to keep her residence.

None can call this an unsettledness, or humour of mutability; it was not only, that she might to better hold up, and keep in repair those houses, which commonly in the owner's absence (who is the soul of the house) turn to carcasses, ready to be dissolved, fall to ruin and dust; but she resolved by her presence to animate the houses which she had built, and the places where she lived; to dispense and disperse the influences of her hospitality and charity, in all the places where her patrimony lay, that many might be made partakers of her comforts and kindness.

In her frequent removals, both going and coming, she strewed her bounty all the way. And for this end it was (as may be charitably conjectured) that she so often removed; and that not only in the winter season, less fit for traveling; but also that she chose to pass those uncouth, and untrodden, those mountainous, and almost impassable ways; that she might make the poor people and labourers her pioneers, who were always well rewarded for their pains; let the season be never so bad, the places never so barren, yet we may say it, by way of allusion, *Psalms* 65.11, "She crowned the season with her goodness, and her paths dropped fatness, even upon the pasture of the wilderness; the barren mountains." If she found not mines in these mountains, I am sure the poor found money in good plenty, whensoever she passed over them.

But that which I speak of this for an instance of her constancy, is a known story in these parts.

When about three years since she had appointed to remove from Appleby to Brougham Castle (in January) the day being very cold; a frost, and misty; yet much company coming (as they usually did) to attend her removals; she would needs hold her resolution, and in her passage out of her house she diverted into the chapel (as at such times she commonly did) and there, at or near a window, sent up her private prayers and ejaculations; when immediately she fell into a swoon, and could not be recovered, until she had been laid some time upon a bed, near a great fire. The gentlemen and neighbours who came to attend her, used much persuasion, that she would return to her chamber, and not travel on so sharp and cold a day; but she having before fixed on that day, and so much company being come purposely to wait on her, she would go; and although as soon as she came to her horse-litter, she swooned again, and was carried into a chamber, as before, yet as soon as that fit was over, she went; and was no sooner come to her journey's end (nine miles), but a swooning seized on her again, from which, being soon recovered, when some of her servants, and others represented to her, with repining, her undertaking such a journey, foretold by diverse to be so extremely hazardous to her life; she replied, she knew she must die, and it was the same thing to her to die in the way, as in her house; in her litter, as in her bed; declaring a courage no less than the great Roman general, *necesse est ut eam, non ut vivam*; [it needs that I go; it is not necessary that I live] she would not acknowledge any necessity why she should live, but believed it necessary to keep firm to her resolution. She did indeed discover by this, not only a moral constancy, but a Christian courage, against the fear of death; from whence might also be well supposed, a soul ready and prepared to meet death any where, knowing what the apostle had taught her, 2 *Corinthians* 5.1, that if her earthly house of this tabernacle were dissolved, she should have a building of god, "an house not made with hands, eternal in the heavens."

That death was but a removal from one house to another, from a worse house, to a better, an earthly house to an heavenly; flitting from an house built by nature, a tabernacle earthly and dissoluble, to an house, a firm mansion, prepared by Christ, built by God, eternal in the heavens; from a tabernacle to a temple.

And having mentioned her courage, I might show, that although it be a virtue, not so often to be found, nor expected to be found in that sex; yet that she had it to an heroic degree; I will set before you but one instance, which hath been brought to me by good information.

It was in the late time of rebellion and usurpation, when they threatened to level all degrees of men and women, and had no respect to honour, either in titles or in real worth and dignity; but did studiously, and affectedly, seek to affront, and pour contempt upon those, chiefly, who by their birth and place might challenge honour, as due to them, as propriety and inheritance could entitle any to whatsoever they possessed. Having cut down honour in its great emblem, the royal oak; intending that in this our Druina,[1] no loyal oak should be left, none to give shelter to any of the royal branches (although Providence confuted them literally) but as they could, and by degrees, to extirpate all the loyal nobility; I say, when they had dried up the fountain of honour in their king, it was too great an eye-sore to behold the luster of it in his subjects; to let any noble, but especially loyal blood, run in the streams, that derived their honour from that fountain.[2]

It was even then, that this courageous lady dared to own her self loyal; then, when they had filled her castle with soldiers, and those of fierce and fanatical spirits, and none more fierce than they.

The head of those locusts, like those in the *Revelation* 9.7, "armed and crowned;" for then every fanatical head fancied himself to have, or deserve, a crown: they were the saints, and they must reign: holiness, you know, gives great pretence to govern in temporals, as well as spirituals. The head of those who at that time oppressed this noble lady, was one whom even his great master himself, looked upon as under a dispensation, more terribly fanatical than any in his host, terrible even to himself and his usurped power.[3] This dreadful man quartered himself under the roof of this noble lady; had made suspicious inquiries, or rather declared his presumptions, of her sending assistance privately [to the exiled King Charles II], where he was conscious

---

1 The name for England in James Howell's *Dendrologia: Dodona's Grove, or the Vocall Forrest*, a royalist allegory first published in 1640. Here a reference to Charles I, beheaded in 1649.

2 This convoluted analogy means that the republican forces and government, under Cromwell (the "head of those locusts" of two paragraphs below), hunted out those loyal to the Crown.

3 Major-General Thomas Harrison (1606–60), who occupied Appleby Castle in 1651. Army officer under Cromwell, regicide, and puritan, whose religious radicalism led him in the 1650s, to be ejected from the army and imprisoned several times on suspicion of involvement in seditious activities. He was hanged for treason in 1660. In her autobiography, Clifford characterizes herself as rather less aggressive than Rainbow does: "And this summer Major-General Thomas Harrison came hither with his forces, for then the war was hot in Scotland, so as then many places in Westmorland and especially my castle of Appleby was full of soldiers, who lay there a great part of that summer. But I thank God I received no harm or damage by them, for by the King and his part, who that August came into England, and within six or seven miles of Appleby Castle, though they came not to it" (*Lives*, 59).

that loyal duty required, and her affection might wish it, if there had been means with safety to convey it; but being not able to make proof of that, he would needs know her opinion, and dispute her out of her loyalty; at a time when she slept, and lived but at his mercy, giving her alarms night and day when he listed.

If she had now shrunk, and seemed to yield to his opinion, she might pretend the learned philosopher's excuse, who, disputing with a great general, and yielding up the truth of the cause, pleased (to those who upbraided him) that he had done wisely, to be confuted by him, who had so many legions, such an army to prove what he list, near, and at his command. But this undaunted lady would not so easily yield, but would be superior in the dispute, having truth and loyalty on her side; she would not betray them, at the peril of her life and fortune; but boldly asserted, that she did love the King, that she would live and die in her loyal thoughts to the King; and so with her courage dulled the edge of so sharp an adversary, that by God's merciful restraint he did her no harm at that time.

Diligence was a noted virtue in her; her active soul filling up all the gaps of time, with something useful or delightful to her self or others. But to undertake to describe this, and her other virtues, that is, her life, were endless, and not necessary; none could describe it but her self that lived it. And, indeed, by her great diligence, she did describe much of it, but if I should tell you how much, possibly you would neither credit me, nor commend so much, as admire her. But she had such a desire to know, review, and reflect, upon all the occurrences, passages, and actions of her life, as thinking it an especial mean to apply her heart to wisdom, by so numbering her days, that none of them might be wholly lost.

That (as St. Bernard advised) "her actions in passing might not pass away," she did cast up the account of them, and see "what every day had brought forth;" she did set down what was of more remark, or dictated, and caused much of it to be set down in writing, in some certain seasons, which she contrived to be vacant from addresses; judging her time to be better spent thus, than in that ordinary tattle, which custom has taught many (of her sex especially) who have no business, and know no greater duty of life, than to see and be seen, in formal visits, and insignificant parley. As if it were a game to play away time, in which all parties cheat each other, yet never feel that they are cozened of a jewel most precious and irreparable; which he that wins from another is sure to lose himself. Whatsoever kind of censure others may pass of this exactness of diary as too minute and trivial a diligence, I think we may thence charitably conclude a serenity of conscience, clear, at least, from foul and presumptuous sins, which durst bring all past actions of life, to a test, and review. Who of a thousand is there that can produce a thousand witnesses (such is conscience) of the innocency of their life? that can, or dare tell, even themselves, all that they had done or said, and open their own books to rise in judgment, for or against themselves?

Oh, that we could do so? This were *praejudicium summi illius judicii*, a forejudging of our selves, that we might not be judged, (at least) not condemned in the world.

I confess, I have been informed, that after some reviews, these were laid aside; and some parts of these diaries were summed into annals.

As she had been a most critical searcher into her own life, so she had been a diligent enquirer into the lives, fortunes, and characters of many of her ancestors for many years.

Some of them she hath left particularly described, and the exact annals of diverse passages, which were most remarkable in her own life, ever since it was wholly at her own disposal; that is, since the death of her last lord and husband, Philip Earl of Pembroke, which was for the space of six or seven and twenty years.

But this I will say, that as from this, her great diligence, her posterity may find contentment in reading these abstracts of occurrences in her own life, being added to her heroic father's, and pious mother's lives, dictated by her self; so, they may reap greater fruits of her diligence, in finding the honours, descents, pedigrees, estates, and the titles, and claims of their progenitors, to them; comprised historically and methodically in three volumes of the larged size, and each of them three (or four) times fairly written over; which although they were said to have been collected and digested in some part by one,[1] or more, learned heads, yet they were wholly directed by her self; and attested in the most parts by her own hand.

---

1   Sir Matthew Hale, lawyer, judge, and antiquary, who researched and
    helped write or wrote parts of the documentation of her family that Clif-
    ford compiled, including the works referred to here, known as *The Great
    Books of the Clifford Family* (see Appendix D). The autobiography
    included in this volume is taken from a copy of that work, and more
    information about it is included in the headnote (217-18).

★ ★ ★ ★ ★1

A little before her death, patience, and meekness, and low thoughts of herself, which had been her practice, were now her argument. Discoursing frequently, with one of her nearest attendants, and busy about her, she willed them not to take so much pains for her, who deserved less; expostulating, why any, her self especially, should at any time be angry; why any of these outward things should trouble her, who much deserved so little, and had been blessed with so much? By which it might appear that she had brought into subjection all great thoughts, she had cast down imaginations, and every high thing, bringing into captivity every high thought, and submitting the world and her soul to the obedience of Christ; her passions were mortified and dead before her: so that for three or four days of her last sickness (for she endured no more) she lay as if she endured nothing; she called for her *Psalms*, which she could not now, as she usually had done, read her self (the greatest symptom of her extremity), [and] she caused them to be read unto her. But that cordial of which I have spoken (kept, in *Romans* 8,² and in her heart), this her memory held to the last, this she soon repeated: no doubt to secure her soul against all fear of condemnation, being now wholly Christ's, having served him in the spirit of her mind, and not loved to walk after the flesh, having (as often as she affectionately pronounced the words of this chapter) called in the testimony of the spirit to bear her witness, that she desired to be delivered from this bondage of corruption; into the glorious liberty of the children of god; and so to strengthen her faith and hope by other comfortable arguments, contained in the rest of that chapter, being the last words of continuance, which this dying lady spoke.

The rest of the time, as if it had been spent in ruminating, digesting, and speaking inwardly to her soul, what she had uttered with broken words, she lay quiet, and without much sign of any perturbation; after a while in a gentle breath, scarce per-

---

1 Here I have cut about fourteen pages of the original printed version of the sermon. They contain generic praise for her continency, modesty, charity, and an account of her defence of her religion and the religious practices she supported when challenged by the representatives of the republican government.
2 Rainbow mentioned this chapter in the part of the sermon that was removed in this edition; it concerns the release from sin and suffering promised by Christ's sacrifice and resurrection.

ceptible, she breathed out that soul which God had breathed into her; rendering it even to that God which gave it. So breathed her last, and quietly slept, not to be awakened again, but by the archangel's trumpet, which it shall call her to the resurrection of the just.

Thus fell at last this goodly building; thus died this great wise woman; who while she lived was the honour of her sex and age, fitter for an history than a sermon.

Who having well considered that her last remove (how soon she knew not) must be to the House of Death; she built her own apartment there; the tomb before your eyes; against this day, on which we are all now here met to give her relics livery and seizin,[1] quiet possession.

And while her dust lies silent in that chamber of death, the monuments which she had built in the hearts of all that knew her shall speak loud in the ears of a profligate generation; and tell, that in this general corruption, lapsed times, decay, and downfall of virtue, the thrice illustrious Anne, Countess of Pembroke, Dorset, and Montgomery, stood immovable in her integrity of manners, virtue and religion; was a well built temple for wisdom, and all her train of virtues to reside in; is now removed and gone to inhabit a building of God, "an house not made with hands, eternal in the heavens."[2] To which blessed mansions let us all endeavour to follow her, by treading in the steps of her "faith, virtue and patience: that having fought the good fight, finished our course, and kept the faith, we may receive the crown of righteousness, which the Lord, the righteous judge shall give at that day to all that love his appearing."[3]

Now unto the King eternal, immortal, the only wise God, be honour and glory for ever and ever. Amen.

THE END

---

1 I.e., sizing, such as starch, that stiffens cloth and makes it ready for formal wear.
2 *2 Corinthians* 5:1.
3 *2 Timothy* 4:8.

Works Cited

Acheson, Katherine O. "The Modernity of the Early Modern: The Example of Anne Clifford." *Discontinuities: New Essays on Renaissance Literature and Criticism.* Ed. Viviana Comensoli and Paul Stevens. Toronto: U of Toronto P, 1998. 27–51.

Chew, Elizabeth V. "Si(gh)ting the Mistress of the House: Anne Clifford and Architectural Space." *Women As Sites of Culture: Women's Roles in Cultural Formation from the Renaissance to the Twentieth Century.* Ed. Susan Shifrin. Burlington, VT: Ashgate, 2001. 167–182.

Clifford, Anne. *The Diary of Anne Clifford.* Ed. V. Sackville-West. London: William Heinemann, 1923.

——. *The Diary of Anne Clifford, 1616–1619: A Critical Edition.* Ed. Katherine O. Acheson. New York: Garland, 1995.

——. *The Diaries of Lady Anne Clifford.* Ed. D.J.H. Clifford. Phoenix Mill, etc., UK; Wolfeboro Falls, NH: Alan Sutton, 1990.

——. *Lives of Lady Anne Clifford, Countess of Dorset, Pembroke and Montgomery (1590–1676) and of her Parents, Summarized by Herself.* Ed. J.P. Gilson. London: The Roxburghe Club, 1916.

Doubleday, H.A. "Ealrdoms and Baronies in History and in Law, and the Doctrine of Abeyance." *The Complete Peerage.* 2nd ed. G.E. Cokayne, original compiler. Vicary Gibbs et al, eds. London: St. Catherines Press, 1910-59. Vol. 4 (1916): 651-760.

Erickson, Amy Louise. *Women and Property in Early Modern England.* London: Routledge, 1993.

Hodgkin, Katharine. "The Diary of Anne Clifford: A Study of Class and Gender in the Seventeenth Century." *History Workshop* 19(1985): 148–61.

Lamb, Mary Ellen. "The Agency of the Split Subject: Lady Anne Clifford and the Uses of Reading." *English Literary Renaissance* 22.3(1992): 347–68. Reprinted in *Literature Criticism from 1400 to 1800, Vol. 76.* 31–41.

Lewalski, Barbara K. *Writing Women in Jacobean England.* Cambridge and London: Harvard UP, 1993.

Rainbow, Edward. "A Sermon Preached at the Funeral of the Right Honourable Anne, Countess of Pembroke, Dorset, and Montgomery." London: Printed for R. Royston and H. Broom, 1677.

Seward, William. *Anecdotes of Some Distinguished Persons, Chiefly of*

the Present and Two Preceding Centuries. 4th ed. 4 vols. Vol. I.
London: T. Cadell for W. Davies, 1804.

Spence, Richard T. *Lady Anne Clifford, Countess of Pembroke,
Dorset and Montgomery (1590–1676).* Phoenix Mill, etc., UK;
Wolfeboro Falls, NH: Alan Sutton, 1997.

Suzuki, Mihiko. "Anne Clifford and the Gendering of History."
Clio 30(2001)2: 195–229.

Stone, Lawrence. *The Crisis of the Aristocracy, 1558–1641.* Oxford:
Clarendon P, 1965.

Wilcox, Helen. "Days in the Life of a Renaissance Woman: Lady
Anne's Diary." Quarto: the Quarterly Bulletin of the Abbot
Hall Art Gallery. 28(1990)3: 11-15.

Williamson, George C. *Lady Anne Clifford, Countess of Dorest,
Pembroke and Montgomery, 1590–1676, Her life, letters and work.*
Kendal: Titus Wilson and Son, 1923.

Sources used in preparing the annotations to *The Memoir* and *The Diary*

Cokayne, G.E. *The Complete Peerage of England, Scotland, Ireland,
Great Britain and the United Kingdom.* 2nd ed. Ed. Vicary
Gibbs, et al. 14 volumes. London: St. Catherines Press,
1910–59.

Emerson, Kathy Lynn. *Wives and Daughters: The Women of Sixteenth-Century England.* Troy, NY: Whitson, 1984.

Lundy, Darryl. www.thepeerage.com. [The website includes and
cross-indexes much of the information contained in *The Complete Peerage.* The search and cross-reference facilities make
looking up names, especially women's, easier.]

Stephen, Leslie and Sidney Lee. *The Dictionary of National Biography.* 22 volumes. London: Oxford UP, 1937–38.

Index of Names in *The Memoir and* The Diary

This index includes the names of people mentioned in the *Memoir* and *Diary* who are Clifford's family members, important household members, recurring contacts, or public or historical figures. The first page reference in the index will usually lead to a footnote identifying the person. Women are indexed by their married names, with their maiden names noted in the listing. Titles are cross-referenced to the name of the person. Where a name belongs to more than one person, they are distinguished by maiden name, title, or birth and death dates.

Lady Lampwell and Countess of Warwick 107, 157, 163, 167

Rich, Lady—see Rich, Penelope; Rich, Frances (née Hatton)

Rich, Penelope (née Devereux), Lady Robert Rich and Countess of Devonshire 50, 57, 181

Rich, Robert (1559-1619), Earl of Warwick 163

Rich, Robert (1587-1658), Earl of Warwick 167, 169, 175

Rivers 73, 79, 87, 89, 93, 99, 103, 117, 119

Roos, Baron—see Cecil, William

Russell, Edward, Earl of Bedford 49, 59

Russell, Francis 58, 59, 69, 71, 73, 135, 137, 139, 149, 159

Russell, Lucy (née Harington), Countess of Bedford 49, 52, 57, 64, 91, 107, 113, 135, 167, 181

Ruthen, Barbara 109, 113, 149

Sackville, Anne (née Spencer), Dowager Countess of Dorset 121, 134

Sackville, Edward 71, 96, 101, 125, 127, 139, 140, 145, 147, 149, 151, 154, 162, 171, 178, 179

Sackville, Margaret 77, 80, 82, 84, 96, 98, 102, 120, 154, 175, 179, 181, 185, 186

Sackville, Mary (née Curzon) 63, 64, 125, 140, 149, 157, 167, 169, 182, 183, 184

Sackville, Richard, Earl of Dorset 42, 62, 63, 64, 65, 67, 71, 72, 73, 75, 77, 78, 79, 81, 82, 83, 84, 85, 86, 87, 89, 91, 92, 93, 95, 96, 97, 99, 101, 103, 105, 107, 109, 111, 113, 115, 116, 117, 118, 119, 121, 122, 123, 124, 125, 126, 127, 129, 131, 133, 134, 135, 137, 139, 141, 143, 144, 145, 147, 148, 149, 151, 153, 155, 156, 157, 159, 160, 161, 162, 163, 165, 167, 169, 171, 173, 175, 177, 178, 179, 181, 182, 183, 184, 185, 186, 187, 189

Salisbury, Earl of—see Cecil, Robert

Seymour, Anne (née Sackville), Lady Beauchamp 78, 85, 103, 107, 118, 123, 137, 140, 156, 157, 167, 169, 171, 175, 180, 184

Seymour, Edward, Earl of Hertford 118, 171, 176

Seymour, Edward, Lord Beauchamp 85, 118, 159

Seymour, Frances (née Howard), Countess of Hertford 54, 171, 177

Shrewsbury, Countess of—see Talbot, Mary

Shrewsbury, Earl of—see Talbot, Gilbert

Sidney, Barbara 145, 147

Sidney, Dorothy (née Percy) 72, 145

Sidney, Robert 72

Somerset, Countess of—see Carr, Frances